NEWBORN & INFANT INFECTIONS SIMPLIFIED

(TIPS FOR BABY FIRST-AID & CHILD EMERGENCY GUIDE!)

THE NEW MOM'S BABY CARE GUIDE TO MINIMIZING INFECTIONS AND MINOR EMERGENCIES IN THE FIRST YEAR OF LIFE AFTER PREGNANCY & CHILDBIRTH (WITH FULL-COLOR CDC IMMUNIZATION SCHEDULE!)

J. K. KARLIESE

Copyright © 2024 J.K. Karliese -All rights reserved.

The content of this book may not be reproduced, duplicated, or transmitted without direct written permission from the author or the publisher.

Legal Notice:

This book is copyright-protected and is only for personal use. You cannot amend, distribute, sell, use, quote, or paraphrase any part of this book's content without the author's or publisher's consent.

Disclaimer Notice:

Please note that the information in this document is for educational and entertainment purposes only. All efforts have been made to present accurate, up-to-date, reliable, and complete information. No warranties of any kind are declared or implied. Readers acknowledge that the author does not render legal, financial, medical, or professional advice. The content within this book has been derived from various sources. Please consult a licensed professional before attempting any techniques or recommendations outlined in this book.

By reading this document, the reader agrees that under no circumstances is the author responsible for any direct or indirect losses incurred due to the use of the information contained within this document, including, but not limited to, errors, omissions, or inaccuracies.

Under no circumstances will any blame or legal responsibility be held against the publisher or author for any damages, reparation, or monetary loss due to the information contained within this book, either directly or indirectly.

Published by **JK Kalrliese** and **JKK Books & Media**, USA
First printing edition, 2024 in the United States

A Free Gift for You

To show our appreciation, here's a FREE gift for you: a guide to help keep your family healthy by making the best nutritional choices.

To redeem your free ebook gift, **click the link below**:

https://subscribepage.io/Karliese-EatingForSuccess

Or you can **scan the QR code below** with your phone camera:

To Nicole and Jeffrey, who risked it all with me to make this dream a reality.

CONTENTS

Introduction	xiii
1. Respiratory and Eye, Ear, Nose and Throat (EENT) Infections	1
2. Gastrointestinal Conditions	55
3. Bacterial Gastroenteritis (Food-Borne & Water-Borne Infections)	76
4. Cardiovascular Infections	92
5. Neurological Infections	107
6. Immunological Infections	117
7. Urological Infections	127
8. Skin (Dermatological) Infections	136
9. Miscellaneous, Generalized, and Non-specific Infections	144
10. All You Need to Know About Fevers	162
11. Common Injuries & Acute Events in the First Year	173
12. Vaccine-Preventable Infections of Newborns and Infants	212
CDC and AAP Recommended Immunization Schedule	255
Conclusion & Recommendations	259
Resources for Parents & Caregivers	261
Bibliography	265
About the Author	277

"The amazing thing about becoming a parent is that you will never again be your own first priority."

— OLIVIA WILDE

INTRODUCTION

The stork has finally arrived! Your baby is here, and you could not be happier. Over the past nine months, you have gone through a whirlwind of emotions and new experiences. You have watched the gradual but fascinating/intriguing transformation of your body as your baby grew each day in your womb. And finally, the day came when your strength and endurance as a woman was tested to its limits. However, the memories of the intense labor pains are entirely dispelled as soon as the beautiful bawling bundle of life, an extension of you, is placed into your arms. It was then that you felt that massive surge of love and maternal protectiveness over this life that you have helped to create.

But now what? This new addition to your life and household does not come with an owner's manual. You wonder how you are supposed to know what to do with this baby. How do you take care of them, nurture them, and, most importantly, protect them from the visible and invisible dangers of this world? It is

INTRODUCTION

an entirely new chapter that you may have been unprepared for. It is a route that requires its own unique set of navigation skills.

One of the most critical responsibilities of a parent, guardian, or caregiver is keeping their children safe by ensuring their health and well-being and protecting them from harm. New moms like you are often concerned with protecting their newborns from picking up infections, especially at a vulnerable age when their immune systems are yet to mature. With this in mind, it is no surprise that every parent, guardian, or caregiver desires the correct information needed to give their babies the best and healthiest start in life. This comprehensive handbook is designed to equip the new mom and new dad with the knowledge, tools, and resources necessary to recognize, prevent, and effectively manage or treat common illnesses, ailments, and disease conditions that can affect newborns and infants in the first year of life. The book will focus on acute-type infections (infections that come and go) rather than chronic-type infections (infections that persist over a prolonged period). Chapters 1 to 10 cover the most common newborn and infant infections and ailments, which will be discussed across several categories and following the various body systems. These chapters will address the following aspects of each infection: causative organism, mode of transmission, signs and symptoms, diagnosis, treatment, prevention, caregiver tips, and any available vaccine for the condition. The discussions will provide tips on recognizing and managing these symptoms and when professional medical attention is necessary. Chapter 11 covers common injuries and acute events in the first year of life, including life-saving interventions for emergencies. Chapter 12 is the book's last chapter, which covers vaccine-preventable childhood infections and provides the most recent CDC schedules for ensuring on-time immunizations for the prevention of deadly childhood

INTRODUCTION

diseases. Most importantly, this book empowers new parents to confidently care for the most precious and vulnerable members of their household: their babies.

1

RESPIRATORY AND EYE, EAR, NOSE AND THROAT (EENT) INFECTIONS

"Even when freshly washed and relieved of all obvious confections, children tend to be sticky."

— FRAN LEBOWITZ

*I*f you are like most parents, especially first-time parents, you worry about your newborn or infant getting sick and what you should do. You are alarmed whenever the baby sniffles, sneezes, refuses the breast or bottle, or feels warm. You wonder when you should be concerned about a fever, a cough, or a cold. You may ask yourself when the right time is to call the doctor or even head to the emergency room (ER). Sometimes, the parental anxiety surrounding these concerns can become more overwhelming than the actual cause of the worries. Be reassured that you are not alone in feeling this way and that these feelings and concerns are quite valid and normal. Fortunately, most newborn and infant illnesses are mild, requiring a few hugs, cuddles, and tender loving care (TLC), and the baby is back to its regular routine. However, there are those few instances when an illness requiring more targeted care arises. Those instances are the reason for this book. This book aims to allay most of the above parental concerns by helping you understand what signs to watch for in your baby and which symptoms could be managed at home versus those needing immediate escalation. The author hopes that by the end of these chapters, you will feel more confident in your decisions as a parent or guardian of a precious little one. We will begin by discussing and understanding the common infections affecting the babies' airways (respiratory tract), eyes, ears, nose, and throat. Are you ready? Let's go!

THE COMMON COLD

Although most common cold infections are considered to be mild, they can cause severe illness in people with compromised immune systems, asthma, other chronic respiratory conditions, or other severe underlying medical conditions.

Cause: The most frequent cause of the common cold is rhinoviruses, which belong to the same virus group as enteroviruses (CDC, 2023 March 9).

Method of transmission: Rhinoviruses are transmitted from one person to another through respiratory droplets, dispersed into the atmosphere when an infected person coughs or sneezes without covering the nose and mouth (CDC, 2023 March 9). An individual acquires these infectious droplets by breathing them in or by touching their face (eyes, nose, or mouth) after touching a surface or an object contaminated with the respiratory droplets. Close personal contact, such as kissing, hugging, or shaking hands and then eating or touching the face with unwashed hands, are other ways that the rhinoviruses are transmitted between people.

Signs and symptoms: Some people (including children) will show no symptoms or mild symptoms after exposure to rhinoviruses. This depends on their immune response to the viral antigens, especially whether their immune system has been exposed to that same rhinovirus or another virus with similar antigenic properties (CDC, 2023 March 9). The most frequently seen symptoms associated with rhinovirus infections are runny nose (rhinorrhea), sneezing, nasal congestion, sore and/or itchy throat, cough, body aches, headaches, fatigue, crankiness, loss of appetite, and mild fever (Murkoff & Widome, 2018; CDC, 2023 March 9). Common colds usually last 7-10 days, with the 3rd day being the worst symptomatically.

Treatment: Common cold infections are considered to be self-resolving. This means they would typically go away over a specific period (usually days or weeks) and do not necessarily require a particular treatment. There is no specific treatment medication for common cold infections in newborns and infants. The "treatment" guidelines provided by the American Academy of Pediatrics (AAP) and the Centers for Disease Control and Prevention (CDC) for these infections are focused on the management and control of the symptoms.

Management Tips for Parents/Caregivers: The AAP thinks home remedies may sometimes work better than traditionally recognized medications for managing the common cold (AAP's HealthyChildren.org, 2024). Prevention and management tips for the common cold include the following:

- **For runny nose**: Use a bulb syringe to suction out as much liquid discharge or mucus as possible from the baby's nose since newborns and infants cannot blow their nose. (Older children would usually be asked to blow their nose). It is reassuring to know that a watery, runny nose is the body's attempt to eliminate the viruses (AAP's HealthyChildren.org). Never give over-the-counter (OTC) cold and cough medicines to a baby under 4 years old (aap.org, 2024).

- **For a blocked or stuffy nose**: Use saline nasal drops or sprays to loosen the mucus by instilling drops or by spraying into one nostril at a time, and then followed by suctioning out the loosened mucus plugs with a bulb suction syringe. Two (2) to three (3) drops or one (1) to two (2) sprays into the opening of each nose (nostril) at a time is sufficient for infants. Saline nasal drops and nasal sprays are considered over-the-counter (OTC) and can be purchased from any pharmacy in the United States without a prescription. It is suggested that caregivers perform nasal washes/rinses with saline drops whenever the infant has a blocked nostril and is observed to be breathing through the mouth (AAP's HealthyChildren.org). Never give over-the-counter (OTC) cold and cough medicines to a baby under 4 years old.
- **For sticky and stubborn mucus (mucus plugs)**: A moistened cotton swab may be used to dislodge and extract mucus plugs from the nostrils and around the nose.
- **For loss of appetite/poor feeding**: Mothers are still encouraged to continue breastfeeding their infants during common cold infections. If the baby refuses to feed or feeds less, try nasal suctioning with saline drops and a bulb suction syringe before attempting to feed. It is okay for a baby to refuse direct breastfeeding

(nursing) during a common cold infection because of the interference of the stuffy nose with proper latching onto the breast. If the baby is still unable to nurse even after nasal suctioning, try expressing out (or pumping) breast milk into a bottle and then try bottle-feeding.
- **For coughing**: Keep the baby fed to maintain body fluid balance and use a humidifier to keep the air in the home moist. These interventions will keep the airway moist and prevent mucus from drying up along the airways, causing cough and nasal blockage.
- **Additional tips for comfort**: (1) Prevent possible dehydration by keeping the baby well-fed with breast milk or formula and by giving Pedialyte. Please DO NOT GIVE WATER to babies. Having sufficient fluid (positive fluid balance) in the body allows the tissues and organs of the body to function optimally. It also makes the mucus produced by the mucous membranes thinner in consistency, which makes it easier for the mucus to be swept outward by the ciliary hairs lining the airways, and this, in turn, makes it easier for the baby to cough out or sneeze out the mucus containing viral particles. (2) Use a humidifier to moisten the home's air. Keeping the air moist will keep the mucus in the nose from drying up, thereby making the airway less dry and less likely to form the crusts and mucus plugs that cause airway irritation and coughing. (3) For older children, having the child sit in the bathroom and breathe in the warm mist from the shower can be helpful. However, this home remedy is not advised for babies and infants.

Caution:

- Do NOT give oral OTC cough and cold medicines to newborns, infants, and children younger than four years. They can cause serious harm to young children.
- Do NOT give honey to newborns and infants less than one-year-old for cough relief. This home remedy is not helpful for babies and can actually result in a deadly infection called *infant botulism*.
- Do NOT give free water to babies less than 6 months old or dilute prepared formula with water for these babies. To hydrate a baby, give Pedialyte.
- Do NOT give aspirin to a baby or a child
- Do NOT elevate the head of the crib of a newborn baby or infant. This is a temptation all mothers must resist. Recommendations based on various research studies state that babies and infants should sleep on their back on a firm, flat mattress or sleeping surface with a fitted sheet and no loose objects or soft items in the crib to avoid the possibility of sudden infant death syndrome (SIDS), which is the leading cause of injury death in infancy (AAP, 2023).

Prevention

How to protect yourself and your baby

- **Strict hand hygiene:** Handwashing is the most effective way to prevent infections (CDC, 2023). Effective handwashing for at least 20 seconds after you touch surfaces or objects with germs is the best prevention method for protecting yourself and your baby. If soap and water are unavailable, you can use an alcohol-based

hand rub. Refer to the CDC-recommended handwashing protocol.
- **Avoid touching your face (eyes, nose, and mouth) with unwashed hands.**
- **Regularly clean and disinfect** toys, objects, and surfaces that come in contact with the baby.
- **Avoid close contact with sick persons.**
- **Consider wearing a high-quality, well-fitting face mask for certain situations:** Consider masking up around sick people; in public places; in crowded indoor settings such as church, school, grocery store, and public transportation; and during fall and winter seasons when respiratory disease activity is high in your community (CDC, 2023 March 9).

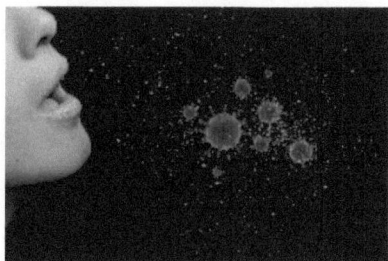

Spread of infectious germs by respiratory droplets

How to protect others

You may take the following steps to protect others when you or your baby are sick with the rhinovirus common cold:

- Stay home when sick and keep your children home from daycare and school if they are ill.
- While sick, avoid close contact with others (this

includes kissing, hugging, sharing eating utensils, or shaking hands).
- Cover your nose when you sneeze or cough. Make it a habit not to sneeze or cough randomly into the air. Instead, you should cough and sneeze into a tissue and then throw it away, OR cough and sneeze into your upper shirt sleeve(s), OR cover your mouth and nose completely with your hands while you cough or sneeze and then wash your hands with soap and water immediately.
- Make handwashing a habit - Wash your hands often, especially after coughing, sneezing, or blowing your nose. If soap and water are unavailable, you may use an alcohol-based hand sanitizer (See CDC's Clean Hands Save Lives).
- Frequently disinfect high-touch areas, surfaces, and objects such as toys, doorknobs, and mobile devices.

When to call the doctor: There is usually no need to call the doctor about the common cold

COUGH

A cough that interferes with feeding, sleep, and playing is one symptom most parents would rather ignore. It is certainly no fun hearing your baby hacking through a cough in the middle of the night or struggling to eat in between coughing episodes.

Cause: Cough in a newborn or infant is usually a symptom rather than a disease. As a symptom, cough may be associated with multiple upper airway illnesses and conditions such as the common cold, seasonal allergies, pneumonia, airway obstruction, and so on.

Method of transmission: This depends on the causative illness associated with the cough.

Signs and symptoms: Cough is a symptom. In situations such as whooping cough, where the cough is the disease, the quality, timing, and features of the cough will then be considered part of its signs and symptoms. Whooping cough (Pertussis) will be discussed in Chapter 10 with other vaccine-preventable diseases.

Treatment: Keeping the baby hydrated with Pedialyte and well-fed with breastmilk or formula is a good strategy for managing wet, productive cough. The takeaway knowledge pearl is for the caregiver to understand that OTC cough medicines and honey should NEVER be given to a baby under any circumstances. If the cough is accompanied by a fever, children's acetaminophen (Tylenol) or ibuprofen (Motrin) may be given to the infant strictly based on the pediatrician's dosing recommendations. Another crucial key takeaway here is that aspirin should NEVER be given to babies.

Prevention: Following the standard infection prevention protocols (handwashing and respiratory protocols) described under the "Common Cold" section above should be sufficient to protect your baby and yourself.

Tips for Parents/Caregivers & When to call the doctor:

- Any cough lasting over 10-14 days is a cause for concern and should warrant a visit to the pediatric primary care provider.
- Any sudden coughing episode accompanied by reddening of the face, gasping for breath, and/or breathing difficulty should be considered an emergency because it may be a sign of choking. In this instance, it is

recommended to begin applying basic rescue skills for a choking infant as taught by the American Heart Association (AHA).
- A harsh, barking cough that sounds like a seal's call (high-pitched whistling sound at the end of the cough), which is accompanied by labored or noisy breathing, possible fever, and upper respiratory symptoms, is very suggestive of croup (an infection and inflammation of the voice box, vocal cords, and windpipe). Croup is seen more in toddlers and children than in infants and newborns, but it is still possible in this young age group. This type of cough requires an emergency room visit right away due to the potential for rapid deterioration due to respiratory compromise.

RSV AND RSV BRONCHIOLITIS

RSV...this has recently become the medical buzzword and "the word on the street"! According to the CDC, RSV is the most common cause of hospitalization in children under the age of one year. The American Academy of Pediatrics reports that two to three out of every 100 infants diagnosed with RSV infection may require hospital admission. Furthermore, they may need supplemental oxygen to help them with breathing and/or intravenous (IV) fluids to help with hydration if they are not eating or drinking. Almost every child gets RSV infection at least once before the age of two. RSV infections are mostly seen during the winter and early spring seasons.

Cause: RSV and RSV bronchiolitis are caused by the Respiratory Syncytial Virus (RSV). RSV infection affects the upper respiratory tract and is mostly associated with cold symptoms. In contrast, RSV bronchiolitis is associated with lower respiratory tract symptoms and is associated with cold symptoms *plus* bronchiolitis, which is an inflammation of the bronchioles and bronchial tree (*RSV: When It's More than Just a Cold*, n.d.).

Method of transmission: Similar to the common cold, RSV is transmitted via respiratory droplets, nasal mucus, and saliva from infected persons when they are inhaled or come in contact with the face (eyes, nose, or mouth) of the uninfected person. The peak period of virulence (infectiousness) occurs in the first 2 to 4 days of the infection.

Signs and symptoms: For most children, RSV presents like a common cold with similar symptoms of runny nose, nasal congestion, sneezing, cough, poor feeding, irritability/fussiness, and mild fever. But for some other infants (especially premature babies), the RSV infection may progress into a more severe version (bronchiolitis) to include lower respiratory symptoms such as rapid breathing, wheezing, hacking cough, and increased breathing effort which includes nasal flaring, belly breathing with tugging between the ribs (retractions), and grunting during breathing (*RSV: When It's More than Just a Cold*, n.d.). Lethargy, sleepiness, and dehydration are other complications that are seen in babies with RSV infection (Murkoff & Widome, 2018).

Duration of illness: Mild cases of RSV infection typically last between 3 to 5 days. But for premature infants, infants with other medical complications, and infants experiencing the more severe RSV bronchiolitis, the infection lasts much longer.

Treatment: For mild cases of RSV infection, you would treat the infant using the same methods and interventions as the common cold (see the Common Cold section). The most important treatment strategy for mild, uncomplicated RSV infections in infants is nasal suctioning. But for the more severe cases (RSV bronchiolitis), the infant may likely require hospitalization, during which additional treatments are given, depending on the severity of the disease and the symptoms presented by the baby. Some of the additional treatments that are typically used for RSV bronchiolitis in hospitalized infants include:

- Supplemental oxygen (either by simple nasal cannula or by heated high-flow nasal cannula, also known as Optiflow)
- Nebulizer treatments to help open up the airways
- Intravenous corticosteroids to help reduce inflammation of the respiratory tract
- Oral rehydration therapy using fluids such as Pedialyte (if the infant is able to eat and drink by mouth) to prevent or reverse dehydration
- Intravenous fluids administration to prevent or reverse dehydration

According to the CDC, there is no clinical research evidence supporting the use of deep suctioning (suctioning of the lower pharynx or larynx), antiviral medications (such as ribavirin), or chest physiotherapy in the management of RSV bronchiolitis (CDC, 2021 May 3).

Prevention & Tips for Parents/Caregivers: Implementing the following strategies will help prevent RSV infection in newborns and infants:

- Prioritization of effective handwashing by caregivers
- Keep the baby away from other siblings as much as possible, especially if they have runny nose, cough, or fever symptoms.

- Keep the baby away from visitors and others who do not live in the household and from public and crowded places such as grocery stores and daycare during the winter and spring.
- Avoid smoking in the house and keep the baby from friends and visitors who smoke.

RSV Immunization: This is the most effective prevention method for RSV infection. Two methods/options are available:

(a) **RSV immunization for the pregnant mom**: This is achieved by giving the maternal RSV vaccine at 32 to 36 weeks of the pregnancy if the baby will be born during the RSV season (winter or spring).

(b) **RSV immunization for the baby**: For high-risk infants and toddlers, giving an intramuscular shot of one of the two FDA-approved human recombinant monoclonal antibodies with activity against respiratory syncytial virus - palivizumab (Synagis) or nirsevimab (Beyfortus) - has been shown to reduce the risk of both RSV-related hospitalizations and health care visits in infants by about 80 percent (*RSV: When It's More than Just a Cold*, n.d.). These shots work differently than a vaccine because they provide ready-made antibodies that start working to protect babies right away, and this protection lasts throughout a typical RSV season.

When to call the doctor: Caregivers should call the doctor in the following situations:

- **Respiratory distress**: The baby shows apparent signs of breathing difficulties, such as pulling hard on abdominal and chest muscles to breathe; skin between the ribs is getting sucked in with each breath; bluish or darkening

change of skin color, especially around the mouth, increased wheezing, grunting, or other sounds during breathing; gasping for air while breathing; and unresponsiveness.
- **Persistent fever**: In addition to the respiratory symptoms, if the baby is having a fever of **100.4oF (38oC)** or higher that isn't lowered by acetaminophen (Tylenol) or ibuprofen (Motrin) or that lasts more than 4 or 5 days, you should contact your pediatrician or take the baby to the emergency room right away.

INFLUENZA (FLU)

It's that dreaded time of the year, the fall and winter seasons, when it seems like no matter what you do, the kids get sick every week. You dread taking them to daycare and kindergarten each day because you know that the daily exchange of germs occurs there, but at the same time, you are unprepared and unwilling to keep them home, either. It's the dreaded "flu season", which is inevitable yearly. The above scenario is every parent's nightmare.

Influenza infection (often referred to as "the flu" or "the seasonal 'flu), is described by the CDC as a highly contagious respiratory illness that causes millions of illnesses, hundreds of thousands of hospitalizations, and tens of thousands of deaths across the United States (Flu Information, *Flu: A Guide for Parents*. (n.d.)). Among all children, the burden of influenza is most severe on the youngest ones, with the rates of influenza-associated deaths and hospitalizations being highest among infants during the first 6 months of life (Mattila et al, 2021).

Cause: Influenza infection is caused by influenza viruses, which infect the nose, throat, and lungs and typically occurs more (prevalent) between October and April, a period popularly known as "the flu season" (Murkoff & Widome, 2018).

Method of transmission: Flu viruses are spread mainly by respiratory droplets that are generated when an infected person (someone with the flu) talks, sneezes, or coughs or when they touch objects and surfaces that have been contaminated with the virus and then touch their mouth, nose, or eyes. Like other respiratory illnesses, the flu's transmission and spread can be significantly mitigated by following basic standard precautions, especially handwashing.

Signs and symptoms: The signs and symptoms of the flu usually begin suddenly. Following are common signs and symptoms that are often experienced during illness with the flu:

- Fever and/or chills (It is important to note that not everyone with the flu will have a fever).
- Cough
- Sore throat
- Runny nose (rhinorrhea) or stuffy nose (congestion)
- Muscle or body aches
- Headaches
- Fatigue (tiredness)
- Vomiting and/or Diarrhea (both tend to be more common in children than adults).

Treatment: Oseltamivir (Tamiflu) is currently the only antiviral drug that is FDA-licensed and recommended for use in young infants from age 6 months (Mattila et al, 2021). A 2021 research study conducted by Mattila et al provided data to support the conclusion that infants treated with oseltamivir showed a rapid decrease in the viral load present in nasopharyngeal secretions and also a shortened duration and severity of their symptoms.

Complications of the flu: Sinus infections, ear infections, worsened asthma and other preexisting airway disorders, and pneumonia are common flu complications in infants and children. Other possible severe but rare complications that could be triggered by the flu are inflammation of the heart (myocarditis), brain (encephalitis), muscle tissues (myositis, rhabdomyolysis), sepsis, and multi-organ failure.

Prevention: Other than proactive lifestyle modifications such as handwashing and mechanical preventive devices such as facemasks and gloves, annual vaccination is a significant means of influenza prevention. Prevention of influenza in infants is challenging because influenza vaccines are not FDA-licensed for use in children younger than 6 months of age, and even in older infants, the immune response to influenza vaccination may be suboptimal compared with that later in childhood (Mattila et al, 2021). There are 2 versions of the available flu vaccine: Trivalent flu vaccines and Quadrivalent flu vaccines.

1. Trivalent flu vaccine: The trivalent flu vaccine is a type of inactivated influenza virus vaccine designed to offer protection against three strains of the flu virus - two strains of influenza A and one of influenza B. The selected strains are based on what researchers expect to be the most widespread strains for each year. The trivalent inactivated vaccine (TIV) is considered to be the most widely used seasonal influenza vaccine. It is made up of the three currently circulating seasonal influenza virus strains at the time: two influenza A virus types (H3N2 and H1N1) and a B type. Popular TIV brand names are Fluvirin, Agriflu, and Flucelvax by Novartis; FluLaval by ID Biomedical Corporation Canada; Fluvax and Afluria by CSL Australia. All of them are egg-based inactivated (non-live) trivalent flu vaccines. All inactivated flu vaccines (trivalent TIVs and quadrivalent QIVs) are approved for use for children six months and older, including pregnant women and persons with chronic medical conditions. The CDC and the AAP recommend one dose injected intramuscularly into the vastus lateralis (thigh muscle) for infants or the deltoid (upper arm muscle) for older children and adults. However, children aged six months to 8 years who did not receive the seasonal flu vaccine during the previous influenza season should receive two doses administered at least four weeks apart.

2. Quadrivalent flu vaccine: The quadrivalent version of the flu vaccine is designed to protect recipients against four strains of the influenza virus and includes two strains of influenza A and two strains of influenza B. Thus, it offers the same benefits as the trivalent with the additional protection against an extra strain of influenza B virus. There are two significant sub-types of quadrivalent influenza vaccines:

- **Quadrivalent Inactivated Vaccines (QIVs)**: For the 2023-24 flu season, three different types of the quadrivalent inactivated flu vaccine are available - QIVe, QIVc, and QIVr. Brand name examples of QIVs are Flucelvax Quadrivalent by Novartis, Afluria Quadrivalent, Fluarix Quadrivalent, FluLaval Quadrivalent, and Fluzone Quadrivalent.
- **Live Attenuated Influenza Virus (LAIV)**: The LAIV is a quadrivalent influenza vaccine made from attenuated (weakened) forms of the influenza viruses. Although the LAIV does not cause influenza infection, it is capable of causing mild and transient flu symptoms, including rhinorrhoea, nasal congestion, muscle pain (myalgia), malaise, fever or sore throat. The LAIV is a nasal spray (Nasal Spray Flu Vaccine, FluMist Quadrivalent). It is a one-dose-only vaccine. However, children aged 2–8

years who have not received any seasonal flu vaccine during the prior influenza season should receive two doses of the LAIV at least four weeks apart. Note that the LAIV is approved for use only in persons aged 2–49 years who do not have underlying medical conditions. The LAIV/Nasal Spray Flu Vaccine should not be administered to pregnant women or children under two years old.

Some important takeaway notes:

(1) FluMist Quadrivalent (Nasal Spray Flu Vaccine) should never be given to babies under two years and pregnant women.

(2) There are two FDA-approved versions of Flucelvax: trivalent and quadrivalent.

(3) The three flu vaccines that are preferentially recommended for people 65 years and older: Fluzone High-Dose Quadrivalent, Flublok Quadrivalent recombinant flu Vaccine, and Fluad Quadrivalent Adjuvanted Flu Vaccine.

Tips for Parents/Caregivers:

- The American Academy of Pediatrics (AAP) and the CDC recommend that children get the flu vaccine every year in the fall, beginning at age six months. They further suggest that some children aged six months through 8 years of age may need two doses of the flu vaccine for best protection. Per CDC recommendation, the best time for kids to get the flu shot is *by the end of October* before the flu begins spreading.
- The nasal spray version of the flu vaccine is approved for ages 2 through 49 years. However, the CDC advises that individuals (including children) with certain

underlying medical conditions should not get the nasal spray vaccine. Why? Because it is composed of live attenuated (weakened) influenza virus (LAIV) particles, it may pose a risk for immunocompromised individuals or those with other underlying medical conditions. Children under two years old cannot get the nasal spray flu vaccine.

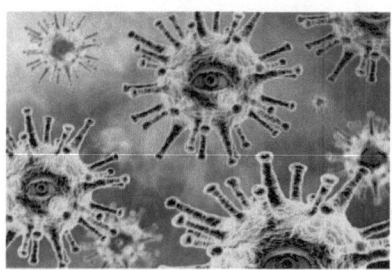

Electron micrograph of viral particles

CROUP

Croup is a childhood illness that causes swelling of the voice box (larynx) and windpipe (trachea), which causes the airway below the vocal cords to become narrowed, thereby making breathing difficult and noisy for the affected child (*Croup In Young Children*, n.d.). The narrowing of the bronchial tree associated with croup is significant in very young children (infants and newborns) because of their already small and immature airways. Croup infection is characterized by a harsh barking cough and a raspy breathing sound called **stridor**. According to the CDC, children between 3 months and five years of age are most likely to get croup infection. It is believed that the disease is not as common in older children because their windpipe is more developed. Therefore, the swelling associated with croup is less likely to interfere with their breathing.

Croup occurs most commonly during the fall and winter months.

Cause: Although the most significant and common cause of croup is viruses, there are two primary sources of croup infection:

Viral Croup: Viral croup is an infectious form of croup. It is the most common type of croup, caused by a viral infection of the voice box and windpipe. It usually begins with similar symptoms as the common cold but then quickly progresses into a barky cough, hoarse, raspy voice, and a noisy musical breathing sound (stridor). Viral croup is often associated with a fever.

Spasmodic croup: Spasmodic croup is a non-infectious croup. It is less common than viral croup and is thought to be caused by stomach acid reflux or allergens. It is characterized by sudden-onset raspy, gasping breathing with inspiratory stridor (a high-pitched whistling sound when breathing in) and a barky cough. There is usually no fever with spasmodic croup. This type of croup closely resembles asthma or allergic bronchitis and often responds to allergy or reflux medications.

For the scope and purposes of this book, we will be focusing on viral croup.

Method of transmission: The infectious type of croup (Viral Croup) is transmitted via airborne respiratory droplets, similar to the common cold and flu.

Signs and symptoms: As previously described above, the signs and symptoms of croup are: barky cough, raspy, hoarse voice, breathing difficulty, noisy high-pitched (whistling) breathing sound known as stridor, and possible low-grade to rare high-grade fever. Parents and caregivers need to note that stridor in an active or crying child is considered to be minor in most cases. However, when a stridor is present in a child at rest, it is regarded as a sign of possible severe croup, and the child should be taken to the ER for respiratory evaluation and support. The danger in this instance is that with severe croup with apparent airway narrowing due to swelling, there is impaired oxygen inhalation and circulation, resulting in the child not getting sufficient oxygen delivery to tissues and organs.

Treatment: **For mild viral croup**: (1) keep the child calm and un-agitated with distractions, toys, hugs, singing, and patting. (2) Keep the air cool and humidified to improve breathing. (3) Keep the child hydrated by nursing, feeding, using Pedialytes, and administering oral fluids (older babies). (4) Treat fever with antipyretic as needed – acetaminophen (weight-dosed for all ages) or ibuprofen (for children older than six months). **For severe viral croup** (with stridor at rest): Take the child to the ER, where they will be given breathing treatments with racemic epinephrine and respiratory corticosteroids to reduce airway inflammation. The child may occasionally require oxygen support via a plain nasal cannula or humidified high-flow nasal cannula (Optiflow).

Tips for Parents/Caregivers: Watch for the following signs and symptoms as evidence of increasing severity of the infection and as a guide to know when to take the child to the ER:

- The child has stridor (makes a whistling sound that gets louder with each breath) even while at rest.
- The child seems to be struggling to catch their breath, or they are pulling on belly muscles and bobbing their head up and down while breathing. You may also notice a flaring of the nostrils as they breathe or note that the skin between their ribs and above their collar bones is being sucked in with each breath.

- The toddler or an older child cannot make normal verbal sounds or speak due to lack of breath.
- You notice the child has a bluish tinge (or darkening) around their lips or fingernails.
- The newborn or toddler is drooling more than usual, or the older child has difficulty swallowing saliva.

One or more of the above observations should be a reason to escalate care by taking the child to the emergency room. Various YouTube websites for medical institutions have some excellent audio vocalizations of how stridor sounds.

Note:

Antibiotics treat bacteria and are not effective for treating viral croup. Cough syrups are also not helpful in this instance and may harm the child. Remember: Never give over-the-counter cough syrup to a baby.

- Epiglottitis (also known as acute supraglottitis) is another infection that causes stridor and mimics viral croup, but this one is caused by the bacteria Hemophilus influenza type b. It is a hazardous infection that can resemble croup, but fortunately, this infection is much less common now because of the Hemophilus influenza type b (Hib) vaccine. In this case, the affected child is typically aged 2 to 5 years and presents with sudden-onset high fever, muffled voice, lots of drooling, and a peculiar sitting position whereby the child preferentially sits upright with their neck extended and face tilted upward to make their breathing easier. This is called the "sniffing" position. If you call your pediatric provider and they suspect epiglottitis, you must rush the child immediately to the ER. Keep the child comfortable in any position they desire, and do NOT offer them anything to eat or drink. This infection requires treatment with intravenous antibiotics, and the child may also need a tube placed in their windpipe to help them breathe (intubation). If not treated promptly, this disease could rapidly lead to complete blockage of the child's airway. The best protection against epiglottitis (acute supraglottitis) is for the child to get their first dose of the Hib vaccine at age two months. This vaccine will also protect them against meningitis, an infection that causes swelling of the brain's lining.

CONJUNCTIVITIS (PINK EYE)

The conjunctiva is the eyes' white part, including the eyelids' inner part (Boyd, 2023). Conjunctivitis is commonly referred to as "pink eye." It is defined as an inflammation of the white part of the eye and the inner lining of the eyelid (conjunctiva), usually caused by infection or allergies. In a typical case of conjunctivitis, the white part of the child's eyes appears red and swollen (inflamed), often with a sticky white or yellow discharge. (Boyd, 2023). Light sensitivity is a common feature across all types of conjunctivitis. Conjunctivitis may occur in one eye (unilateral conjunctivitis) or both (bilateral conjunctivitis). There are different types of pink eye; most are very contagious and easily spread from one person to another.

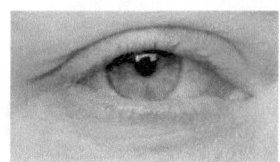

Inflamed and reddened conjunctiva as seen in "pink eye"

Types and Causes: There are three leading causes of conjunctivitis, and therefore, there are three main types of conjunctivitis based on the causative agent: viral conjunctivitis, bacterial conjunctivitis, and allergic conjunctivitis. Bacterial and viral conjunctivitis are contagious because they are easily spread from person to person. Contrastingly, allergic conjunctivitis is not contagious and is associated with a susceptible individual's allergic response to antigenic substances. A fourth type of conjunctivitis (neonatal conjunctivitis) is seen only in newborns and will also be discussed.

(a) Viral conjunctivitis: It is usually caused by the common cold virus that causes runny nose and sore throat (rhinoviruses). It has also been associated with the flu virus and other upper respiratory infections. Infection typically occurs when snot or other fluid/droplets are accidentally transferred by the infant or child from the nose to the eyes, for example, by rubbing the eyes with unwashed hands after sneezing or wiping the nose, by using the same tissue for blowing the nose and then wiping the eyes, and so on. Viral conjunctivitis is the most common type of conjunctivitis, often presenting as red eyes with a watery discharge and a burning, gritty sensation. It usually begins in one eye and may spread to the other eye within days. It is also important to note that the eye discharge associated with viral conjunctivitis is usually watery rather than thick.

(b) Bacterial conjunctivitis: Bacterial conjunctivitis is the second most common type of pink eye and is also very contagious. It is caused by infection by certain bacteria, and the affected child presents with the following signs and symptoms: sore, painful, reddened eyes with profuse amounts of yellow, sticky discharge (pus) and crusting of the eyelids or lashes, especially in the morning. Occasionally, some bacterial conjunctivitis presents with little or no discharge. Some common causes of bacterial conjunctivitis are *Staphylococcus aureus*, *Streptococcus pneumoniae*, *Hemophilus influenzae*, and *Moraxella catarrhalis*. Other less common causes are *Chlamydia trachomatis* and *Neisseria gonorrhoeae*. Most cases of bacterial conjunctivitis are caused by the Streptococcus species of bacteria, particularly *Streptococcus pyogenes* (the sore throat strep). It sometimes occurs together with ear infections in infants.

(c) Allergic conjunctivitis: A child with allergic conjunctivitis presents with itchy, swollen (inflamed), red, and watery eyes with puffy eyelids. Symptoms usually occur in both eyes and may include allergy symptoms such as an itchy nose, sneezing, a scratchy throat, or asthma. It is a non-contagious type of pink eye that is associated with an allergic reaction to irritating or antigenic substances in the environment, such as pollen, dander, hay, animals, cigarette smoke, car exhaust fumes, swimming pool chlorine, chemicals, or other substances in the atmosphere.

(d) Newborn conjunctivitis: Conjunctivitis in a newborn is pretty standard and may be caused by a blocked tear duct, irritation produced by the topical antimicrobials given at birth, or infection with a virus or bacterium passed from the mother to her baby during childbirth.

Method of transmission: Viral and bacterial conjunctivitis are transmitted by direct contact with or transfer of the offending agent, as described in the sections above. Transmission may occur by contact with another infected person's body fluids or aerosolized droplets or from autologous infection (self-infection) whereby one inadvertently infects one's own self by transferring the germs from a part of the body (nose, throat, etc.) to another part of the body (eyes). Daycare centers and schools are the two most common places where children get exposed to and infected with pink eye germs. Allergic conjunctivitis is not transmitted from one person to another but results from an individual response to a triggering agent.

Signs and symptoms: The signs and symptoms for each type of pink eye have been described above under the subtitle "Types and Causes."

Treatment: Treating a pink eye infection usually depends on the conjunctivitis you are dealing with. *Allergic conjunctivitis* is treated with allergy medications (eye drops and oral medications) prescribed by a pediatrician. These allergy medications are usually antihistamines that help reduce the body's exaggerated response to the triggering antigens. They work by reducing inflammation and itchiness. *Bacterial conjunctivitis* infection may be treated with an antibiotic eye drop prescription by your pediatric provider or eye doctor (ophthalmologist), depending on the severity of the symptoms. Antibiotics are ineffective for treating viral and allergic pink eye. Viral conjunctivitis does not require a specific treatment because it is self-resolving; the body fights the virus independently. Supportive strategies such as placing a cool, wet washcloth over the child's eyes can help relieve the eye discomfort and make them feel more comfortable.

Prevention: The most effective preventive method for allergic conjunctivitis is by avoiding exposure to the triggering agent. Hand hygiene (hand washing or using alcohol-based hand sanitizer) and other universal standard precautions are the most effective methods for preventing bacterial and viral conjunctivitis. For all infectious conjunctivitis, parents and caregivers should avoid sharing personal items such as washcloths, towels, and pillows between infants and infected siblings or between infants and other infected family members.

SORE THROAT

A sore throat is described as itchy, scratchy, or painful-to-swallow sensations or symptoms in the throat. A sore throat infection is medically and diagnostically different from strep throat. Most sore throats (except for strep throat) do not need antibiotics. Microorganisms or specific environmental triggers may cause sore throats. By contrast, strep throat is specifically caused by Group A Streptococci (GAS), which will be discussed in detail in the next segment.

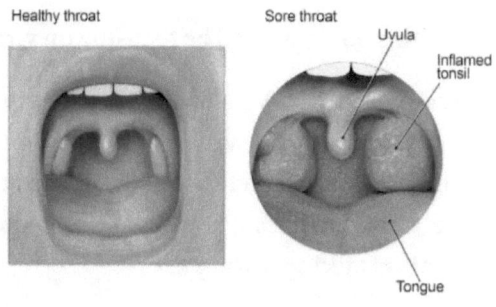

Healthy throat vs. "Sore throat."

Cause: The various causes of sore throat can be grouped into four:

1. **Viral causes**: Viruses are the most common cause of non-GAS sore throat. According to the CDC, rhinoviruses (which cause the common cold) and influenza viruses are the most implicated viral causes.
2. **Bacterial causes**: Streptococci bacteria (specifically group A streptococci) cause a more severe type of sore

throat called Strep Throat, which will be discussed in the next segment of this chapter.
3. **Allergic-related**: This type of sore throat is caused by exposure to environmental allergic triggers. The symptoms presented here are more allergic-type itching, inflammation, and soreness rather than pain.
4. **Smoking/Exposure to secondhand smoke**: Tobacco smoke and exposure to tobacco smoke or other chemical irritants have been associated with sore throat. This type of sore throat is often accompanied by coughing and hoarseness of the voice.

For the scope of this book, we will be focusing on viral sore throat.

Method of transmission: Viral sore throat (often associated with common cold and flu viruses) is transmitted through respiratory droplets or direct contact. Respiratory droplets containing the viral particles are expelled into the air through coughing, sneezing, talking, eating, etc.

Signs and symptoms: The symptoms frequently seen with viral sore throat are voice hoarseness with or without throat pain, which may or may not be accompanied by cough, runny nose, or "pink eye" (conjunctivitis). Any combination of these symptoms indicates that viruses rather than strep throat bacteria cause the sore throat.

- **Treatment**: Most viral sore throat infections will resolve on their own. Some cases present with minimal symptoms, whereas others may be more problematic for the infant and require a doctor visit. During the visit, the doctor or other pediatric provider will ask questions about the symptoms, perform a physical exam, and perhaps order a throat swab to rule in/rule out bacterial causes before deciding on the appropriate treatment. Using a clean humidifier or cool mist vaporizer in the child's room will help ease symptoms. Also, ensure that the child is well-hydrated.

Prevention Tips for Parents/Caregivers: The following tips will help keep the sore throat germs away:

- *Proper hand hygiene*: Clean hands are the best protection against many infectious diseases of newborns and infants, including sore throat.
- *Avoid sick contacts*: Avoid (or minimize at the very least) exposing the child to close contact with anyone who has sore throat, common cold, flu, or other upper respiratory infections.
- *Avoid smoke exposure*: Avoid smoking in the home or exposing your newborn infant to secondhand smoke.

A general guide for using over-the-counter (OTC) medications in infants:

Product Labels/Inserts/Instruction: Parents and caregivers should always carefully read and follow the instructions provided on OTC medicine product labels or inserts before giving medicines to infants and children. It is essential to remember that some OTC medications are not recommended for children of certain ages.

Dosages: Parents and caregivers should remember to ask their pharmacist or pediatric provider about the correct dosage of OTC medications for their infant's age and size/weight. Most infant medications require weight-based dosing.

Updated medication information: It is important always to provide updated information about all prescription and OTC medications that your child is taking to the pediatric provider during each office visit.

Lozenges and Honey: Do not give honey to any child younger than one year. Do not give lozenges to any child younger than four years.

Pain relievers: As a general rule, follow these guidelines for treating pain/fever at home:

- Children younger than 6 months: Only give acetaminophen (Tylenol).
- Children 6 months or older: It is generally okay to give acetaminophen (Tylenol) or ibuprofen (Motrin).
- **Never give aspirin to infants and children.** Why? Because it can cause Reye's syndrome which is a very serious but rare illness that affects all organs of the body, but can especially cause harm to the liver and brain of children. This guideline is so important that it is issued and published by the government as the "Surgeon General's Advisory on the Use of Salicylates and Reye Syndrome in Children" (see the References section to get the exact web page for the Surgeon General's Advisory).

Cough and cold medicines:

- Children younger than 4 years old: For any child less than 4 years of age, do not administer OTC cough and cold medicines unless specifically instructed by a doctor or pediatric provider. Why? These group of medications are capable of causing serious and

occasionally life-threatening side effects in young children.
- Children 4 years or older: You will need to discuss with your pediatric provider to determine if OTC cough and cold medicines are safe to give to your child.

GROUP A STREP (GAS) INFECTION (ALSO KNOWN AS GROUP A STREP PHARYNGITIS OR GROUP A STREP PYOGENES OR "STREP THROAT")

Group A Strep (GAS) infection, also known as "Strep throat" is defined as an infection and inflammation of the throat and tonsils caused by a group of bacteria called Group A Streptococci, specifically *Streptococci pyogenes*.

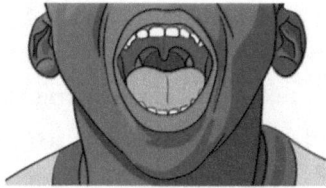 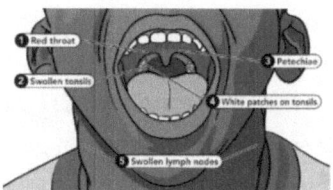

Cause: GAS pharyngitis is caused by Group A *Streptococcus pyogenes*, a group of round bacteria arranged in chains when viewed under a microscope.

Method of transmission: Group A strep bacteria are very contagious bacteria and easily spread through direct contact and respiratory droplets (details of this transmission route have been previously discussed under the sections for common cold, flu, and sore throat). The *incubation period* after successful transmission is 2 to 5 days (the period between exposure to the germs and becoming ill with the strep throat infection).

Signs and symptoms: Overall, strep throat is considered a mild disease, but it can also be quite painful. Symptoms that are commonly associated with the infection include the following: quick-onset sore throat that looks angry-red with red and swollen tonsils; white patches or streaks of exudative pus on the tonsils; painful swallowing; petechiae (tiny red spots) on the roof of the mouth; swollen cervical lymph nodes (cervical lymph nodes are located in the front of the neck); and fever.

Diagnosis: Your pediatric provider will swab the infant's throat to test for strep throat. Two types of tests are available for strep throat: (a) **the rapid strep test** involves swabbing the throat with a long cotton-tipped stick and testing the material collected on the swab for the presence of GAS antigens using a serological kit. It is a quick (rapid) test that results in minutes but is less accurate than the throat culture. (b) **throat culture**: this method also involves swabbing the throat, but this time, the material collected on the swab is placed on a special bacteria-growing medium in Petri dishes in the lab and allowed to grow, after which the growth pattern and characteristics are used to determine if the bacteria are beta-hemolytic group A *Streptococcus pyogenes*. This culture method is more accurate but takes a longer time. It also has the advantage of determining the best antibiotic for treating the specific infection caused by the organism isolated from the culture.

Treatment: Once a strep throat diagnosis has been made by the pediatric provider after assessment of the child, antibiotics will be prescribed to eliminate the infection and prevent progression to rheumatic fever and other possible cardiac-related complications. ß-lactam antibiotics are currently the treatment of choice for streptococcal infections. Amoxicillin and penicillin oral therapy for ten days remains the first-line therapy for strep pharyngitis for children who aren't allergic to penicillin (PCN).

For PCN-allergic infants, clindamycin, clarithromycin, or azithromycin are recommended, but it is worth noting that GAS antibiotic resistance to azithromycin and clindamycin is becoming increasingly common.

Important Tips for Parents/Caregivers: The following are helpful tips for managing strep throat infections:

- Strep throat infections must be completely treated with the full course of antibiotics to prevent complications in the future. Untreated or partially treated strep throat infections have been associated with rheumatic fever and acute myocarditis, whereby the organism is transported through the blood circulation to the heart, where it attacks the heart valves.
- An infant or child with strep throat infection should be kept home and away from daycare and school until they no longer have fever **AND** they have taken the prescribed antibiotics for at least 12-24 hours. (You should ask your pediatric healthcare provider how long your baby or infant should stay home away from daycare or school after starting antibiotics.).
- Any of the following symptoms occurring together with your strep throat symptoms would require you to take the child to see the pediatric provider: difficulty breathing, difficulty swallowing, blood in saliva or phlegm, excessive drooling (in very young children), physical evidence of dehydration which includes dry lips and mouth or sunken eye sockets, joint swelling and pain, and rash.

Nuggets of knowledge

Did you know that the two bacteria, Group A Strep (GAS), also known as Streptococcus pyogenes, and Group B Strep (GBS), also known as Streptococcus agalactiae, are both part of the normal flora of humans? Both organisms are considered opportunistic pathogens because they cause disease in immunocompromised persons (such as babies born with immunodeficiencies, infants who have received organ transplants and are on immunosuppressive medications, infants undergoing cancer treatments, and so on) or in certain conditions whereby the target individuals are at higher susceptibility.

Group A Streptococcus (GAS), Streptococcus pyogenes, is spread by direct contact between human hosts. It is responsible for common, frequent, benign, and non-invasive infections such as strep throat (acute strep pharyngitis) and impetigo. It is also responsible for certain invasive diseases such as bacteremia, necrotizing skin infections, streptococcal toxic shock syndrome, puerperal fever/infections, meningitis, and pleuropneumonia.

Group B Streptococcus (GBS), Streptococcus agalactiae mainly resides in the digestive tract of humans and from there may be transferred from time to time to the female genital tract (especially the vagina), where they can colonize without causing an overt infection (carrier state), or they can cause UTI and occasionally lead to bacteremia. From the female genital tract, GBS can readily be passed on to an unborn baby during pregnancy. This maternal-fetal transmission occurs when the fetus comes in contact with vaginal secretions, amniotic fluid, or the birth canal of a colonized mother.

NEWBORN GROUP B STREP (NGBS) INFECTION

Newborn babies acquire newborn (or Neonatal) Group B Strep (NGBS) infection from the mother during pregnancy, labor, or childbirth. Approximately 5 to 40 percent of women are estimated to carry GBS in their vagina during pregnancy (Institut Pasteur, 2021). These women are "silent carriers" because they show no signs of the infection and are described as "GBS-colonized." It is for this reason that pregnant women are screened for GBS between 34 and 38 weeks of pregnancy. Pregnant women who show clinical signs of GBS infection typically present with symptoms ranging from urinary tract infections (UTI) to sepsis (generalized blood and tissue infection). The most severe and invasive GBS infections in pregnant women present as bacteremia (bacterial infection in the bloodstream) and are also sometimes associated with intrauterine infections (infection of the placental tissue of the uterus – the placenta carries and nourishes the fetus/baby until birth).

Cause: Group B *Streptococcus* (GBS), also known as ***Streptococcus agalactiae*** is the causative agent of NGBS infection.

Method of transmission: The mode of transmission of GBS is mother-to-child (maternal-fetal) transmission, which occurs if the fetus (unborn baby) inhales or ingests infected amniotic fluid from an infected mother, or when the fetal membranes rupture during labor, or during the delivery process when the baby passes through a GBS-colonized birth canal of an infected mother.

Signs and symptoms: There are two types of GBS infections in newborns: early-onset and late-onset infections. Most **early-onset NGBS infections** (approximately 80 percent of early-onset infections) occur during the first 24 hours of the birth of the baby and would typically present with respiratory distress and bacteremia. Neonatal meningitis (inflammation of the covering of the brain) is a less common to rare clinical presentation in early-onset NGBS (seen in about 10-20 percent of cases). **Late-onset NGBS infection** usually occurs between the first week of birth and the third month after birth and, in most cases, is typically associated with serious medical conditions such as bacteremia and meningitis.

Statistics show that infant death associated with NGBS infections has decreased notably since the introduction of the GBS screening test for pregnant women and the follow-up prophylactic antibiotic treatment that is given during childbirth for GBS-positive mothers.

Prevalence/Occurrence: It is estimated that the transmission rate of GBS from infected mothers with GBS to newborns is 50 percent on average. Furthermore, approximately 1 to 2 percent of these exposed newborns will subsequently develop an infection if antibiotic prophylaxis is not administered to the GBS-colonized mothers during childbirth (Institut Pasteur, 2021).

What the parent/caregiver sees: Unexplained fevers and fussiness that do not respond to multiple administrations of acetaminophen (Tylenol), especially in a newborn or infant less than 3 months old, are reasons to take the baby to the emergency room immediately. Once the preliminary diagnosis of sepsis or meningitis is determined at the hospital, the baby will be admitted and treatment initiated, pending blood culture and/or cerebrospinal fluid culture results. At this point, the hospital personnel take over care.

Treatment:

(a) **For the pregnant woman**: Pregnant women who do not have penicillin (PCN) allergy are treated prophylactically with a ß-lactam antibiotic (examples: penicillin or amoxicillin). Pregnant women allergic to penicillin are treated with a macrolide antibiotic. Examples of macrolide antibiotics are azithromycin, clarithromycin, erythromycin, spiramycin, and telithromycin. The most commonly prescribed macrolide for PCN-allergic pregnant women is erythromycin.

(b) **For the newborn**: For the infected newborn, the treatment mainly involves the intravenous administration of a ß-lactam antibiotic (usually amoxicillin), which is possibly given in conjunction with another antibiotic (such as gentamicin) for the first 48 hours over a period of 10 days up to 3 weeks depending on the site of infection.

Prevention: The digestive tract of humans is the main reservoir of Group B Strep (*Streptococcus agalactiae*). From there, the bacteria may get transferred to and colonize the female genital tract, often on a sporadic basis. Therefore, good personal hygiene, especially front-to-back wiping of the genital area, is essential for women, especially during pregnancy. Currently, no vaccine is available for group B strep infections, although there are ongoing Phase III trials for vaccine production to prevent this disease (Institut Pasteur, 2021). For pregnant women, screening for *Streptococcus agalactiae* is recommended between 34 and 38 weeks of pregnancy, and prophylaxis is given for positive screening.

SINUS INFECTION (ACUTE SINUSITIS)

The American Academy of Family Physicians (AAFP) estimates that about 6 to 7 percent of children presenting with respiratory symptoms have a sinus infection, better known medically as acute sinusitis (Hauk, 2014). Sinuses are the air-filled pockets in the facial part of the skull bone (cranium). Sinus infections occur when fluid builds up in these sinuses, thereby allowing germs to grow (CDC, 2021 April 26). These germs may be viruses or bacteria.

Cause(s): Viruses cause most sinus infections, but bacteria may also be responsible. In most cases, the infection is a mixture whereby viruses initiate the infection, and bacteria come in and further complicate it. The typical sinus infection in an infant or child begins as a common cold with a stuffy nose that does not improve after one week.

Risk factors: Here are some factors that can increase the risk of an infant getting a sinus infection: recent or previous common cold infection, history of seasonal allergies, exposure to secondhand tobacco smoke, presence of nasal polyps (abnormal growths on the lining of the nose or sinuses) or some other structural anomaly of the nose or sinuses, and a weakened immune system either due to disease or due to taking immunosuppressive drugs such as cancer (anti-neoplastic) drugs and transplant (anti-rejection) drugs.

Method of transmission: The method of transmission for the common cold and other upper respiratory infections discussed in the prior sections is the same.

Signs and symptoms: Common signs and symptoms include runny nose, stuffy nose, facial pain or pressure, headache, postnasal drip (fluid/mucus/phlegm constantly drips down the back of the throat, often causing irritation and coughing), sore throat, cough, and bad breath (CDC, 2021 April 26).

Diagnosis & Treatment: The American Academy of Pediatrics (AAP) specifies strict guidelines for diagnosing acute bacterial sinusitis in children, including infants. A diagnosis of acute bacterial sinusitis can be made when a child presents with an acute upper respiratory infection (nasal discharge or daytime cough) that persists for more than ten days with no improvement or that gets worse (described as worsening or new nasal discharge, daytime cough, or fever after improving at first), or that is severe (defined as concomitant fever of at least 102.2°F [39°C] with purulent (pus-containing) nasal discharge lasting for at least three consecutive days). Wald et al. (2013).

Once the pediatric provider diagnoses acute bacterial sinusitis, antibiotic therapy will be prescribed for children with severe, worsening, or persistent acute bacterial sinusitis. Usually, amoxicillin alone or a combination of amoxicillin/clavulanate is the first-line antibiotic of choice for treating acute bacterial sinusitis. However, the AAP also recommends outpatient observation (watchful waiting or delayed prescribing) for two to three days as an option for children with persistent illness, the goal being to wait for 2-3 days to give the immune system time to fight off the infection before initiating antibiotics.

Prevention and Tips for Parents/Caregivers:

Relief of sinus pain and pressure: Below are some tips for relieving sinus pain and pressure:

- Place a warm compress over the nose and forehead to help relieve sinus pressure.
- Use saline nasal spray to help with decongestion.
- Breathe in steam from a hot shower (for older infants).

OTC medications: Parents and caregivers should refer to the discussion on using OTC medications for infants and children under Section 1.7 Sore throat.

Strict hand hygiene practices: Following the CDC hand hygiene guidelines, clean your hands before handling your baby and your baby's food.

Keep current on recommended vaccinations: Receive recommended vaccines, such as the flu vaccine and pneumococcal vaccines.

Avoid sick contacts: Avoid close contact with people with colds or other upper respiratory infections.

Avoid tobacco smoke exposure: Don't expose your child to secondhand smoke.

Keep home air clean and humidified: Use a clean humidifier to moisten the air at home.

EAR INFECTION (ACUTE OTITIS MEDIA, AOM)

Two main types of middle ear conditions affect infants: acute otitis media (infection and inflammation of the middle ear) and otitis media with effusion (a condition of fluid build-up in the middle ear that is not due to an infection). The difference between the two conditions is that otitis media with effusion does not cause fever, ear pain, or pus build-up in the middle ear. In contrast, acute otitis media causes all the above-listed symptoms. For the purposes of this book, we will focus on acute otitis media, which is an actual/ true infection of the middle ear and a common condition of infanthood.

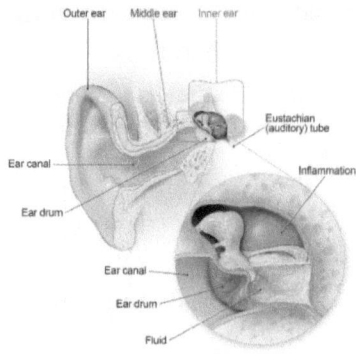

Cause: Middle ear infection (acute otitis media, AOM) may be caused by bacteria or viruses. The two most common bacteria associated with middle ear infections are *Streptococcus pneumoniae* and *Hemophilus influenzae*. Upper respiratory viruses, such as those that cause the common cold, are also capable of causing and have often been implicated in middle ear infections (CDC, 2021 July 1).

Method of transmission: There are various ways by which germs are transmitted to the middle ear to cause infections: transfer of germs (primarily viruses) from the upper airway to the middle ear through the interconnecting cranial passages (sinuses); post-nasal drainage of mucus and fluid from the nasal sinuses to the throat and ear passages where the accumulated fluid breeds bacteria; direct transfer of bacteria into the ear by inserting dirty fingers and objects into the ear; and by traumatic events to the middle ear that breaks the skin barrier (such as a perforated ear drum) which then permit opportunistic pathogens to establish an infection in the middle ear.

Signs and symptoms: Acute AOM signs and symptoms in an infant include: ear pain, rubbing and/or tugging on the affected ear(s), fever, inconsolable crying/fussiness/irritability, difficulty falling asleep and staying asleep, and difficulty feeding. The above-listed symptoms are considered mild and the child can still be managed at home with anti-pyretics, pain relievers, and comfort measures without the necessity of a doctor visit. However, in the event of the following symptoms it is highly recommended that the infant be taken to see the pediatric provider:

- Any discharge, fluid, or pus draining out of the affected ear(s)
- A fever of 102.2°F (39°C) or higher
- Evidence or signs of hearing loss
- Worsening of the mild symptoms described earlier
- Any middle ear infection symptoms lasting more than 2 to 3 days

Diagnosis: The pediatric provider can diagnose a middle ear infection by asking the parent or primary caregiver about the infant's symptoms and by performing a physical examination of the child. This usually involves looking inside the baby's ear(s) using a lighted otoscope to examine the eardrum and look for swelling (inflammation) and/or pus in the middle ear.

Treatment: According to the CDC, AOM is the most common childhood infection for which antibiotics are prescribed. Severe cases of actual middle ear infections, such as AOM infections lasting more than 2 to 3 days, will need antibiotic treatment right away., However, many other middle ear conditions, such as mild AOM, otitis media with effusion, and otitis media caused by respiratory viruses, can improve without antibiotics. In mild cases of AOM, it is postulated that the body's immune system can overcome the infection on its own without using antibiotics. For such cases of mild AOM, the pediatric provider may recommend watchful waiting (whereby the provider suggests waiting for 2 to 3 days to allow time for the body's immune system to fight off the infection on its own) or delayed antibiotic prescribing (whereby the provider prescribes an antibiotic but suggests that the parent/caregiver wait 2 to 3 days before filling the prescription to see if the child may recover on their own without needing the antibiotic).

For severe acute AOM requiring antibiotic therapy:

1. **Amoxicillin** remains the first-line drug of choice for children who have not received amoxicillin within the past 30 days.
2. **Augmentin (Amoxicillin/clavulanate)** is preferentially recommended in the following situations: (a) if amoxicillin has been prescribed and taken by the child within the past 30 days, (b) if purulent conjunctivitis (pus-producing eye infection) is also present with the AOM at the same time, or (c) if the child has a history of recurrent AOM that has shown to be unresponsive to amoxicillin therapy.
3. **Cephalosporins,** such as ceftriaxone, cefdinir, cefuroxime, or cefpodoxime, may be appropriate for children who do not have type 1 hypersensitivity to penicillin.

Prevention and Management Tips for Parents/Caregivers:

The following tips will keep the child more comfortable and help them feel better:

- Give provider-approved pain relievers and fever reducers

- Give plenty of fluids (Pedialyte, water, breast milk, formula)
- Allow as much rest/nap time as the child desires
- Implement preventive measures: (a) Avoid exposing infants to second-hand tobacco smoke; wash or sanitize hands before caring for or feeding your baby; breastfeed your baby exclusively until six months of age and if possible, continue to breastfeed for at least 12 months; and ensure that your infant is up to date on their recommended immunizations such as the flu vaccine and the pneumococcal vaccine. Notably, the pneumococcal vaccine protects against a common cause of middle ear infections, *Streptococcus pneumoniae*.

Common Respiratory Infections	Common Cause			Are Antibiotics Needed?*
	Virus	Virus or Bacteria	Bacteria	
Common cold/runny nose	✓			No
Sore throat (except strep)	✓			No
COVID-19	✓			No
Flu	✓			No
Bronchitis/chest cold (in otherwise healthy children and adults)		✓		No**
Middle ear infection		✓		Maybe
Sinus infection		✓		Maybe
Strep throat			✓	Yes
Whooping cough			✓	Yes

*Antiviral drugs are available for some viral infections, such as COVID-19 or flu.
**Studies show that in otherwise healthy children and adults, antibiotics for bronchitis won't help patients feel better.

PNEUMONIA

Pneumonia is an airway infection of the lower respiratory tract (lungs) that can cause mild to severe illness across all ages. It is usually a complication of a primary respiratory illness. The three major types of pneumonia based on causative agents are: (a) bacterial pneumonia, (b) viral pneumonia, and (c) fungal pneumonia. Immunizations can prevent certain types of pneumonia. Following good hygiene practices can also prevent pneumonia and other respiratory infections.

Pneumonia can also be defined or classified based on the source or setting of transmission of the organism: (a) community-acquired pneumonia (b) healthcare-associated pneumonia, and (c) ventilator-associated pneumonia.

Cause: As stated earlier, pneumonia can be caused by viruses, bacteria, and fungi.

Viral pneumonia: The most common causes of viral pneumonia in the United States are (a) Influenza viruses (b) Respiratory syncytial virus (RSV), and (c) SARS-CoV-2 (COVID-19) virus. Other viruses often implicated in pneumonia are human metapneumovirus (HMPV), parainfluenza virus (HPIV), adenoviruses, and rhinoviruses.

Bacterial pneumonia: The two most common causes of bacterial pneumonia are: (a) *Streptococcus pneumoniae* (also known as pneumococcus): It is the most common cause of pneumonia in the adult population. (b) *Mycoplasma pneumoniae*, which is the most common cause of pneumonia in the pediatric population (infants and children). Other bacterial causes of pneumonia are *Hemophilus influenzae*, *Legionella* species (causes Legionnaire's disease and Pontiac fever), *Chlamydia pneumoniae*, and *Chlamydia psittaci* (a type of bacteria found in bird droppings and which can infect humans through inhalation and cause a rare and mild pneumonia (lung infection) illness called psittacosis. **Note**: Families with pet birds should take special precautions when cleaning out bird cages by avoiding vigorous shaking or other actions that would disperse particles from the bird droppings into the air. Also, strict hand hygiene protocols should be followed when handling birds and cleaning bird cages.

Fungal pneumonia: Certain fungi release spores into the air, and when these spores are breathed in, they typically infect the lungs and cause pneumonia. The three most common community-acquired pneumonia in the United States associated with fungi are coccidioidomycosis (Valley fever), histoplasmosis, and blastomycosis. *Pneumocystis* pneumonia (PCP) is another severe pneumonia caused by the fungus *Pneumocystis jirovecii*. Fungal pneumoniae are rare, and when they occur, they are usually seen in immunocompromised individuals such as HIV/AIDs patients, patients on prolonged corticosteroid therapy, and patients on immunosuppressive medications such as transplant patients and cancer patients.

Atypical pneumonia: The term "atypical pneumonia" is used to label certain pneumonia infections that present with clinical symptoms that are different from typical pneumonia. Atypical pneumonias have the following characteristics:

- They cause symptoms that are slightly different from the typical pneumonia symptoms.
- The appearance on chest x-ray is different
- They do not respond to or respond differently to antibiotics used to treat the bacteria that cause typical pneumonia.

The "atypical bacteria" that cause atypical pneumonia are:

- *Chlamydia pneumoniae*: common among school-aged children
- *Chlamydia psittaci*: caused by *Chlamydia psittaci*, from infected pet birds (cockatoos, macaws, parrots, parakeets, pigeons, and doves) and poultry (turkeys, ducks). The organism is very rarely found in chickens.
- *Legionella pneumophila*: *Legionella* species (especially *Legionella pneumophila*) cause severe pneumonia.
- -*Mycoplasma pneumoniae*: It causes a milder form of pneumonia commonly called "walking pneumonia."

Method of transmission: The transmission route for pneumonia is through aerosolized respiratory droplets released when an infected person coughs, sneezes, talks, and so on. *Community-acquired pneumonia* is an infection that develops outside of the hospital environment (within the community). *Healthcare-associated pneumonia* is an infection that develops within the hospital setting, usually during or after residing in a healthcare or group residential facility such as a hospital, nursing home, renal dialysis center, or long-term care facility. *Ventilator-associated pneumonia* is an infection acquired during or immediately after using a ventilator machine for respiratory support.

Signs and symptoms: Pneumonia symptoms are variable but usually include fever, diaphoresis (sweating), chills; cough with purulent (yellowish or greenish) or bloody sputum; mild chest discomfort or sharp, stabbing, pleuritic pains, particularly when breathing deeply or coughing. The pain may be localized to one chest area or more widespread. Other symptoms seen include shortness of breath with rapid and shallow breathing (increased respiratory rate), loss of appetite, fatigue, and nausea/vomiting in infants and small children. Note that newborns and infants may not show any signs of a pneumonia infection. Occasionally, they may vomit, have a fever and cough, or appear restless, sick, tired, and without energy.

Diagnosis: Diagnosing pneumonia involves a multi-dimensional approach, which includes the patient's medical history, physical examination findings, and diagnostic testing results (including chest X-ray, blood tests, and sputum culture). A CT scan, bronchoscopy, or pleural fluid culture may be necessary for severe cases of the disease.

Treatment: There are various treatment options for pneumonia depending on the type of pneumonia and the causative organism. Antibiotics will usually be prescribed for acute bacterial pneumonia to treat the suspected bacteria causing the pneumonia (antibiotics are ineffective against viral pneumonia). Anti-pyretics and analgesics (acetaminophen and ibuprofen) are recommended for fever and pain control based on the pediatric provider's prescribed dosages. Severe cases of pneumonia will likely require a hospital stay for the child, where they would be treated with intravenous fluids and antibiotics, as well as supplemental oxygen therapy.

Tips for Parents/Caregivers:

- Increasing the child's fluid intake is recommended to help loosen secretions and mobilize phlegm.
- Giving the child warm fluids to drink, giving the infant warm steamy baths, and using a humidifier in the child's room will assist with opening the airways to make breathing easier.

- Keep the infant away from second-hand smoke inhalation.
- Encourage lots of bed rest for the child to promote healing of the lungs and recovery of strength.
- Do NOT give aspirin to an infant or child.
- Do NOT administer over-the-counter cough and cold medicine to an infant.

ASTHMA VS REACTIVE AIRWAY DISEASE (RAD)

Asthma is a chronic lung disease with acute exacerbations (flare-ups) that could potentially be deadly. Asthma may be defined scientifically as a heterogeneous chronic airway disease prevalent in childhood, usually characterized by respiratory symptoms including wheezing, breathlessness, chest tightness, and cough, together with variable expiratory airflow obstruction (Tesse, Borrelli, Mongelli, Mastrorilli, & Cardinale, 2018). Asthma affects over 25 million Americans, including 5,5 million children (American Lung Association, n.d.). Although there is no cure for asthma, it can be managed so that the affected child continues to live an everyday, healthy life. Reactive Airway Disease (RAD) is a general term used for asthma and other chronic airway conditions, such as allergies, in a child under five years old until the child is old enough to undergo lung function testing to confirm or rule out an asthma diagnosis. Another reason for the delayed formal diagnosis of asthma in children younger than five years is that sometimes young children have asthma and allergy symptoms when they are very young. Still, as their lungs develop, the symptoms go away (American Lung Association, n.d.).

Cause: The specific cause of asthma is undetermined, but researchers postulate that genetic, environmental, and occupational factors have been linked to the likelihood of a child developing asthma (CDC, 2019, September 6). The genetic predisposition to an allergic disease is called "atopy," and it is thought to be capable of playing a significant role in the development of allergic asthma developing allergic asthma. However, not all asthma is allergic asthma.

Method of transmission: Asthma is not a contagious disease. It is not passed from one person to another.

Signs and symptoms: Asthma is characterized by repeated episodes of wheezing (usually expiratory), shortness of breath (dyspnea), chest congestion (often described as chest tightness), and nighttime or early morning coughing. **(a) Signs of a mild asthma attack**: These signs can also be considered as "warning signs" of an impending severe asthma attack, and they include – itchy or watery eyes, itchy throat, sore throat, increased frequency of sneezing; nasal congestion (stuffy nose); rhinorrhea (runny nose); and tiredness. **(b) Signs of a severe asthma attack**: increased breathing rate (fast breathing); noisy breathing; chest tightening; wheezing (usually expiratory, but can be both inspiratory and expiratory); coughing; runny nose with intermittent nasal and sinus congestion; watery eyes; evidence of increased work of breathing in infants, especially during activity (example: grunting while feeding, retractions in various locations such as between ribs, above the sternum, and the collar bone); subdued activity (baby shows less energy than usual and appears tired); and increased fussiness (which will usually be accompanied by increased work of breathing).

Asthma flare-ups: A child with asthma has susceptible airways that would likely react to many things in the air and environment (asthma triggers). When exposed to these asthma triggers, the child's sensitive airways may constrict (shrink and get smaller), thus making breathing more difficult and laborious with resultant wheezing sounds. This is called an "asthma flare-up." Some of the most common asthma triggers are exhaust smoke from automobile vehicles, tobacco smoke, dust mites, environmental smog (also known as outdoor air pollution), cockroach allergens, pets, mold, smoke from burning wood or grass, chemicals such as household cleaning products, and infections like the flu. During an asthma flare-up, the insides of the child's bronchial airways swell even more and can produce extra mucus. The presence of copious amounts of mucus narrows the space available in the airways of the bronchial tree for the air to move in and out of the lungs. The muscles that wrap around these airways may also tighten (bronchospasms and bronchoconstriction), thus making breathing even harder. When all of this happens, it is called an "asthma flare-up", also known as an "asthma episode" or "asthma attack."

Diagnosis: No single 'gold-standard' test can be used to diagnose asthma accurately. However, Lung Function tests {Peak Expiratory Flow (PEF) and spirometry} can assist the pediatric provider in diagnosing asthma in children older than five years. For children less than two years of age, the term "Reactive Airway Disease" is often tentatively used in place of the term "asthma" until the child is old enough to undergo a confirmation of the asthma diagnosis with either of the lung function tests mentioned above – PEF and spirometry. Your pediatric provider will follow strict guidelines established by the American Academy of Pediatrics to make a diagnosis of asthma (for children) or Reactive Airway Disease (for infants).

Treatment: There is no treatment/cure for asthma, but asthma can be controlled by taking medicines (rescue medicines and controller medicines) and avoiding the triggers that can cause an attack. Parents and caregivers need to have a basic knowledge and understanding of the drugs used to control and manage asthma. There are two main groups/categories of medications used for asthma management:

- **Rescue Medicines**: Every asthma patient needs a rescue medication to be used at the first signs of an asthma attack/flare-up. They usually come in the form of an inhaler or a nebulizer (aerosol). They begin to work very quickly but last for a short time. They act by making it easier for the child to breathe right away by rapidly opening up (widening) the airways and reducing spasms. Rescue asthma medications should not be needed or used more than two times per week, and they may not work for a flare-up in patients who use them more than two times per week. Rescue medications may be administered to a child between 15 to 20 minutes before intense activities such as exercising or playing (Nationwide Children, 2024).
- **Controller Medicines**: These regular maintenance medicines help prevent asthma symptoms and flare-ups. They reduce swelling and mucus in the airways and may be given to the child daily even if they are feeling well. Controller medicines are not helpful during an asthma flare-up and, therefore, should not be given once an asthma attack/flare-up has started.

Prevention & Management: Every child diagnosed with asthma must have an Asthma Action Plan (AAP), which is an individualized plan that the child's pediatrician develops and provides to the child's parents/caregivers detailing the step-by-step actions to take in managing the different phases or presentations of asthma, especially specifying what to do during flare-ups.

Tips for Parents/Caregivers: The parent or caregiver should contact the pediatric provider or take the baby to the ER if the rescue medication has been given, but the child continues to have the following symptoms:

- Fast breathing, wheezing, and/or coughing worsen.
- Gasping (hard and fast breathing, usually with the mouth open)
- Retractions (that is, the skin is sucked in between the ribs or around the collar bone or breast bone with each breath such that the ribs and neck muscles show when the child is breathing).
- Nasal flaring (the nose opens wide or fans out with each breath).
- Shortness of breath - the infant has to catch their breath and finds it hard to eat, drink, walk, or talk (babble) due to panting or catching their breath.
- Continued coughing with possible vomiting after coughing (post-tussive emesis)
- Signs of hypoxia (reduced oxygen delivery to body tissues): The baby's lips and fingernails turn dark, grey, or blue.

Some additional tips:

- Always use your asthma rescue medication as directed by your child's medical provider.
- Your child's asthma rescue medication, rescue inhaler, and spacer should be with them at all times, including at the daycare or pre-school, if they attend one.
- Controller medications should be refilled every 1 or 2 months as directed by the pediatric primary care provider (pediatric PCP) on the prescription. If you are

unsure about the frequency of refills, the pharmacist can provide this medication refill information.
- Every child diagnosed with asthma or reactive airway disease should have an Asthma Action Plan created by the provider and the parent/caregiver. The plan tells the parent/caregiver when and how to give each medicine.
- It is very helpful to keep an asthma diary because it helps you track symptoms and how often your child uses his or her rescue medicine. Be sure to take the asthma diary with you for every doctor visit because it provides valuable information to assist the provider with creating an individualized treatment plan for your infant.
- Extended family members (grandparents, aunts, uncles, etc.), paid caregivers (nannies), close family friends, and daycare or school personnel who care for your child at any time should know that the child has asthma or RAD. They should also know where the rescue medications are kept and how to give them if needed.

2

GASTROINTESTINAL CONDITIONS

"Handwashing is like a 'do-it-yourself' vaccine—it involves five simple and effective steps (Wet, Lather, Scrub, Rinse, Dry) you can take to reduce the spread of diarrheal and respiratory illness so you can stay healthy."

— CDC

GER (SPIT-UP) VS GERD

*G*astroesophageal reflux (GER), often described as acid reflux or infant spit-ups, is a common diagnosis in newborns, infants, and young children. GER occurs when liquids or solids back-track from the stomach back into the esophagus (the food pipe that leads up to the throat and mouth), with or without vomiting. In most cases, GER occurs without causing any symptoms, although occasionally, it may cause acid indigestion/acid regurgitation (heartburn), especially in older kids and adults. GER is usually a mild episode and can occur multiple times daily in healthy infants and children (spit-ups). It is one of the most common reasons for pediatric primary care visits and referrals to the pediatric gastroenterology specialty. Most infants with GER are happy and healthy despite spitting up or vomiting.

Gastroesophageal reflux disease (GERD), on the other hand, is a more severe and long-lasting (chronic) version of GER that occurs when GER is associated with repeated bothersome/troublesome symptoms, such as irritability, weight loss or poor weight gain, or other symptoms related to coughing and/or wheezing (*Could my child have acid reflux?* n.d.), and may lead to complications over time. Researchers propose that about 20 percent of the United States population (both adults and children) have GERD (El-Serag, Sweet, Winchester, & Dent, 2014).

Cause: What causes acid reflux (GER) in infants? In infants, structural immaturity of the gastrointestinal (GI) tract plays a role in creating the conditions for GER. Furthermore, research has shown that occasionally, the natural barriers against reflux in the human GI tract are not entirely developed in infanthood, which increases the possibility of liquid or food back-flushing from the stomach into the esophagus. What about older children? In older children, other factors come into play and may contribute to GER in addition to the factors present in infanthood. These additional factors that can contribute to the development of acid reflux include being overweight or obese, certain medications (non-steroidal anti-inflammatory drugs, NSAIDS, such as Ibuprofen), certain trigger foods, and regular exposure to secondhand tobacco smoke. In rare instances, anatomic (structural) issues with the GI tract or systemic disease conditions can increase the risk of reflux. These must be ruled out before a pediatric PCP can diagnose GER/GERD.

Method of transmission: GERD is a non-communicable/non-infectious disease that cannot be transmitted from one person to another.

Signs and symptoms: The most common symptoms of GER/GERD are regurgitation (infants and young children) and heartburn (adults and older children). Other symptoms experienced by infants are coughing, irritability, poor feeding, and feeding discomfort (Hitchcock & Romantic, 2023).

Diagnosis: Clinical diagnoses of GER and GERD are made when a pediatric PCP or GI specialist obtains a good history of the infant or child's symptoms. During the physical exam to indicate the more severe GERD, they will ask the child's parent(s) or primary caregiver questions. In the absence of any concerning symptoms or clinical history, a diagnosis of GER can be made without additional testing or invasive procedures. However, if there is a concerning symptomatic or historical finding, the pediatric PCP or GI specialist may perform more invasive procedures such as upper GI endoscopy or esophageal pH monitoring.

Treatment: GER in infants is managed with simple strategies such as keeping the baby upright during and for 20 to 30 minutes after feeding before laying them down and burping the baby after each feed. GERD treatment for infants and young children follows a very conservative approach. After the 2018 joint committee meeting between the pediatric GI societies in North America and Europe, the recommended *initial treatment* for GERD in infants is to do a trial of hypoallergenic formula (or maternal elimination diet for breastfed infants) before considering prescribing medications for acid suppression.

Additional beneficial non-pharmacological treatment strategies recommended for GERD in infants are reducing the volume of breastmilk or formula feedings, thickening the breastmilk or formula feeding, changing the feeding positions of the infant, and avoiding any trigger foods. The overall treatment guidelines for infants and children are to limit acid-suppression treatment with medications. However, if it becomes necessary to give medications, **H2 blockers** {famotidine (Pepcid) and cimetidine (Tagamet)} and **proton pump inhibitors, PPIs** {lansoprazole (Prevacid); omeprazole (Prilosec); and esomeprazole (Nexium)} are the drugs of choice for both infants and children. In this instance, the general recommendation is to have the infant/child undergo a fair monitored trial of the medications for 4 to 8 weeks before assessing efficacy in controlling the symptoms. Note that H2 blockers work more quickly than PPIs, usually providing relief within 15 to 30 minutes. On the other hand, PPIs provide longer-lasting relief when they finally kick in, thus making them the better option for frequent, severe cases of GERD.

Tips for Parents/Caregivers: Note that ranitidine (Zantac), a once popular H2 blocker used for treating GER/GERD has been removed from the United States market due to concerns about safety in relation to cancer.

VOMITING VS PROJECTILE VOMITING

Vomiting (emesis), more commonly known as "throwing up," is the expulsion of stomach contents by forceful regurgitation through the mouth. It is a symptom of other diseases or conditions rather than a disease in itself.

Projectile vomiting is a more intense type of vomiting whereby the stomach expels its contents with more force than usual, such that the vomit is forcefully propelled a distance away from the person vomiting. The majority of the cases of projectile vomiting seen in babies between birth and age 6 months are associated with a physiologic condition called pyloric stenosis.

Cause: Vomiting is most often caused by a virus or stomach bug, but it is also associated with multiple infections and disease conditions: food poisoning, bacterial GI infections such as salmonella infection, GERD, pyloric stenosis, and so on. Vomiting caused by a virus typically lasts only a few days and can often be treated at home with rest and fluid-electrolyte replacement. Projectile vomiting due to pyloric stenosis is caused by an enlargement of the muscles in the lower part of the stomach, which then causes a narrowing of the opening of the pylorus (the connecting aperture leading from the stomach into the small intestine) and, thus, eventually prevents food from moving from the stomach to the intestine. The backed-up food in the stomach gets forcefully expelled by the baby.

Symptoms of pyloric stenosis, a cause of projectile vomiting: The classic scenario of the baby suffering from this disorder is that of a hungry, ravenous baby who eats voraciously and then vomits the entire feed shortly after eating. This baby has a good appetite and has no problem sucking the nipple but continues to lose weight because they cannot keep the food down. The infant is typically hungry right after vomiting and wants to feed again (constant hunger). The vomiting is forceful (projectile vomiting) and a wave-like motion of the baby's abdomen can be observed shortly after feeding and just before vomiting occurs. Other symptoms noted are frequent belching, abdominal pain (baby writhes in pain between feeds), and dehydration from loss of fluids and electrolytes. The signs of dehydration in a baby are as follows: the baby has sunken eyes, dry mucous membranes in the mouth, reduced or absence of tears when crying, reduced number of wet diapers, depressed fontanels on the head, and loss of skin elasticity.

Method of transmission: The source of vomiting usually determines the transmission mode. Vomiting associated with viral and bacterial infections are frequently transmitted through the oral or fecal-oral routes. Projectile vomiting associated with pyloric stenosis is a structural anomaly and therefore is non-communicable (cannot be transmitted from one person to another).

Diagnosis: In most cases, a thorough history and review of symptoms are sufficient to diagnose the cause of the vomiting for cases of viral and bacterial infections. For cases of pyloric stenosis, the diagnosis can be made with a combination of reported **history and symptoms**, a **physical exam** by the pediatric PCP {which will reveal an abnormal pylorus, which feels like an olive within the abdomen when pressing (palpating) over the stomach, and physical signs of dehydration}, and **radiologic imaging** (either an abdominal ultrasound or a barium X-ray).

Treatment: Vomiting caused by viral agents usually self-resolves after a few days and, therefore, will only require support, oral hydration, and possibly electrolyte replacement as needed. Vomiting caused by certain bacterial infections, such as salmonellosis, would require antibiotic therapy in addition to oral or IV hydration and possible electrolyte replacement as needed. Pyloric stenosis is treated with either a minimally invasive **laparoscopy** or by an abdominal surgery called a **pyloromyotomy**, whereby the thickened outer muscle of the pylorus is divided while leaving the internal layers of the pylorus intact. This corrective surgical maneuver opens a broader channel, allowing the stomach's contents to pass more easily into the intestines (John Hopkins Medicine, 2019). Depending on severity, additional supportive measures such as intravenous hydration and electrolyte replacement are often needed.

Tips for Parents/Caregivers: For all cases of vomiting, keep the child as comfortable as possible and have Pedialyte handy for oral fluid replacement. If the patient stops drinking completely at any time, it is an indication to contact the pediatric PCP or go to the ER.

DIARRHEA

Like vomiting, diarrhea is a symptom of a disease rather than a disease by itself. Diarrhea is defined as loose, watery stools occurring three or more times per day (National Institute of Diabetes and Digestive and Kidney Diseases 2019, October 23). Diarrhea may be classified into three types, based on how long it lasts (duration): acute, persistent, or chronic. **Acute diarrhea** is the most common type, typically lasting 1 or 2 days, and is self-resolving. **Persistent diarrhea** is diarrhea that lasts longer than 2 weeks and less than 4 weeks (that is, 15 days – 27 days). **Chronic diarrhea** is described as diarrhea occurring over at least 4 weeks (28 days or more), with symptoms that may be **continual** (symptoms are continuous with no breaks) or **sporadic** (symptoms that come and go). Acute diarrhea occurs more frequently than persistent or chronic diarrhea across all populations, including children. Researchers estimate that about 179 million cases of acute diarrhea occur annually in the United States (NIDDK, 2019 October 23). Diarrhea can become dangerous if it progresses to severe dehydration. The two important complications of severe diarrhea are dehydration and malabsorption.

Causes of diarrhea: Most diarrheas resolve themselves within 2 to 4 days, so formally diagnosing the cause becomes unnecessary.

Causes of Acute and Persistent Diarrheas: The most conventional causes of acute and persistent diarrhea are viral infections, bacterial infections, parasitic infections, and traveler's diarrhea.

- **Viral gastroenteritis**: Diarrhea caused by viruses is called viral gastroenteritis and is considered one of the most common causes of acute diarrhea. Transmission is typically through the fecal-oral route by drinking or eating fecal-contaminated water or food. The viruses often implicated are Rotavirus and Norovirus
- **Bacterial gastroenteritis**: When bacteria cause acute GI symptoms, including diarrhea, it is called bacterial gastroenteritis. Transmission occurs through the fecal-oral route (ingesting fecal-contaminated water or food). Salmonella, Shigella, Campylobacter, and Escherichia coli are often the implicated bacteria. Chapter 3 will provide more detailed discussions on bacterial gastroenteritis.
- **Parasitic gastroenteritis**: In this condition, parasites ingested through food or water travel to various parts of the GI tract and cause irritation or release toxins that trigger diarrhea. *Entamoeba histolytica, Giardia lamblia,* and *Cryptosporidium enteritis* are the most common parasites associated with diarrhea.
- **Traveler's diarrhea**: Traveler's diarrhea is caused when food or water is eaten in a foreign country. It causes diarrhea in the visitors but typically not in the indigenous citizens. This is often attributed to bacteria,

viruses, or parasites that do not typically cause diarrhea in the locals because their immune system recognizes these indigenous micro-organisms and has already developed antibodies that quickly remove them from the body system before they can establish an infection. By contrast, a visitor/foreigner has not been exposed to these native microorganisms. So it takes more time for their immune system to build antibodies to fight these microbes after the initial exposure. Typically, by then, the microbes would have already established an infection. However, this infection only lasts a few days because the foreigner's body soon makes sufficient antibodies to get rid of the infection within 2 to 4 days of establishing a diarrheal infection.

Causes of chronic diarrheas: Chronic diarrheas last four (4) or more weeks (diarrhea ≥ 4 weeks = chronic diarrhea) and are usually caused by any of the following factors: food allergies such as shellfish allergy or soy allergy; food intolerances such as lactose intolerance; certain infections; diseases of the digestive tract such as Crohn's' Disease and Inflammatory Bowel Disease; abdominal surgery; and long-term use of certain medicines that can cause chronic diarrhea such as methylphenidate (Cellcept).

Methods of transmission: Acute and persistent diarrheas are usually transmitted through the oral or fecal-oral route. Most chronic diarrheas are due to non-infectious causes and, thus, are not transmissible from person to person. However, a few chronic diarrheas associated with infectious agents can also be passed to another person through the fecal-oral route.

Signs and symptoms: Diarrhea in an infant, toddler, or young child manifests as follows:

- frequent dirty diapers (infant or toddler) or urgent need to have a bowel movement (young child)
- nausea
- abdominal pain
- abdominal cramping
- In addition to the above, diarrhea caused by infectious agents such as bacteria and parasites may have the following additional symptoms: (a) fever, (b) chills, (c) bloody stools, (d) nausea, (e) vomiting, (f) light-headedness, and dizziness.

Diagnosis: Diagnosing diarrhea relies on thorough history taking and symptom review.

Treatment: Most viral acute diarrheas are self-resolving. Bacterial and parasitic diarrheas require a prescription from the pediatric PCP. Chronic diarrheas are treated and managed based on the cause. For example, a child who suffers from diarrhea due to Crohn's disease would be under the specialized care of a pediatric GI doctor. In contrast, a child with diarrhea due to lactose intolerance would only be given a non-lactose formula. Generally, keeping an infant with diarrhea adequately hydrated and constantly monitored for signs of dehydration is essential.

Tips for Parents/Caregivers: It is imperative that every parent or caretaker of an infant, toddler, or young child with diarrhea monitor the child for the following symptoms and, if present, should seek a doctor's care immediately:

- Any watery stools (diarrhea) lasting more than 24 hours
- A fever of 102 degrees or higher
- Severe pain in the abdomen or rectum
- Stools containing blood or pus

- Stools that appear black and tarry
- **Evidence of dehydration in an infant, toddler, or child** – few or no wet diapers for three or more hours; constant thirst; dry mouth, absence of tears when crying; decreased skin turgor (elasticity); sunken eyes, cheeks, or soft spot on top of the head; and a general lack of energy.

Travel Tip for Parents/Caregivers: Parents and caregivers should carefully monitor the food and water used to prepare a baby's formula or water given to a child to drink while traveling in another country. Authentic, sealed bottled water is recommended for preparing baby food and drinking during travels to foreign countries, especially developing countries.

DEHYDRATION

Dehydration is a symptom of a disease and not a disease by itself. It is a consequence of any disease process that involves the loss of body fluids in one form or another, such as through vomiting, diarrhea, bleeding, and so on. Most mild and moderate cases of dehydration in infants, toddlers, and young children can be corrected by oral rehydration using electrolyte fluids such as Pedialyte. Severe cases of dehydration would require an ER visit or a hospital admission where intravenous fluid rehydration and electrolytes would be given and the source of the dehydration treated before the baby is sent back home.

Note: The earlier sections of this chapter extensively discuss dehydration. For in-depth discussions, please refer to sections 2.2 and 2.3.

CONSTIPATION

Your ordinarily happy baby suddenly seems more restless and fussier than usual. You also notice that he/she is not eating as much and seems to be spitting up more than is typical for him/her. A quick mental calculation and you also note that the baby has not had a "poop" in a couple of days, and the last one they had was a small thick smear and took much effort to come out. The above scenario is an all-too-familiar one for experienced moms.

It is quite common for new moms to worry that their baby is either "pooping too much" or "isn't pooping enough". **Breastfed babies typically stool one or more times a day during the first month of life**. Most breastfed newborns will stool after each feed, and this is normal. The stool is typically loose and seedy. As newborns grow and get older, they may go several days without stooling as their digestive system matures and efficiently extracts as much nutrients and energy as possible to fuel rapid growth—the newborn who stools less than once a day is usually considered under-fed rather than constipated. **Formula-fed babies** usually have a bowel movement (BM) at least once most days but may go for 1 to 2 days without having a bowel movement.

So, what is the definition of constipation in an infant? Constipation in infants may be loosely defined as a condition whereby an infant has fewer than 1 to 2 bowel movements in a week, and/or passing stools that are dry, hard or lumpy, and having difficulty (straining) or pain passing the stool (NIDDKD, 2020 February 6). Remember that an infant's BM pattern can and does easily change if their diet changes, such as switching from breastmilk to formula, starting solid foods, or drinking less formula than usual. As a general guide, if your baby's stool (poop) is not soft or easily passed, then it may be constipated (Nationwide Childrens, 2019). For the most part, constipation in infants and children lasts a short time and is not considered dangerous unless there is a bright red bleed from the rectum (lowest part of the large intestine just after the anus); there is dark red blood in the stool; the constipation is accompanied by vomiting and/or weight loss; or there is evidence of impaired innervation or other neurological compromise. Constipation is not a disease but is usually a symptom of another medical problem (NIDDKD, 2020 February 6).

Cause: Constipation in infants may be caused by any of the following:

- Food allergies such as milk-protein allergy,
- Dietary transition (for example, transitioning from exclusive breast milk to formula),
- Use of very high-calorie formula,
- Incorrect recipe for preparing powdered formula
- Symptoms of an underlying disease condition or health issues (examples are Crohn's Disease, Inflammatory Bowel Disease, Hirschsprung disease, Celiac disease, Spina bifida, spinal cord or brain injuries, metabolic disorders, hormonal disorders, and any tumors that can block or narrow the colon and rectum.).
- Use of certain medicines that cause constipation as a side effect – examples are iron supplements; antacids containing aluminum and calcium; narcotic pain medicines such as oxycodone or Hycet (contains hydrocodone); anticholinergics and antispasmodics; anticonvulsants for treating seizure disorders; and certain antidepressants (NIDDKD, 2020 February 6).

Constipation in older children often occurs from delay in having a bowel movement or from holding in their stool to avoid having a BM at school due to an unfamiliar environment. This is typically the case for new preschoolers and elementary school children. The physiological explanation for this is that when stool stays too long in the large intestine (colon), too much fluid is absorbed from the stool by the colon, making the stool hard, dry, and difficult to pass. Fecal impaction and rectal prolapse are two unpleasant and painful complications of constipation in older children.

Method of transmission: Constipation is not infectious and, therefore, is not transmissible from person to person.

Signs and symptoms: Here is a list of general symptoms of constipation in a newborn, infant or toddler:

- Constantly passing foul-smelling gas
- Passing stools that are hard, dry, or lumpy
- Having stools that are difficult or painful to pass
- Having a swollen abdomen (abdominal bloating)
- Increased effort to pass stool (straining) lasting more than 10 minutes, with or without passing stool.
- Having thick smears of stool in the diaper after prolonged periods of straining
- Abdominal pain or cramping, as evidenced by writhing by an infant or crying by the baby when he/she is moved or the abdomen is touched
- Unusually fussy
- Restlessness/irritability (changing positions frequently)
- Unusually frequent spit-ups
- Having fewer than 1-2 BMs in 2 weeks (newborn/infant) or having fewer than 1-2 BMs in a week (preschoolers and older children).

Diagnosis: Your pediatric PCP will usually diagnose constipation based on symptom review, bowel history and habits, and physical exam. Lab testing and imaging are rarely utilized for diagnosing constipation unless it has become complicated and developed into a fecal impaction.

Treatment: For babies at least one month old, you may offer them a little apple or pear juice. Rationale: The sugars in these fruit juices are not digested very well by the baby's GI system, so these juices tend to draw fluid into the intestines and help loosen the stool. Note that although fruit juice is typically not recommended for babies under one year of age, it is generally acceptable to give them one (1) ounce a day for every month of life up to about 4 months (based on this rule, a 3-month-old baby would get 3 ounces). **For babies that have started taking solid/baby food**: Once your infant has started transitioning to solid foods, you can try giving them purees made from vegetables and fruits, especially good-old reliable prunes. If these dietary adjustments do not help, it may be time to contact your pediatric PCP. At this point, the PCP may prescribe a stool softener or gentle laxative. So many options are available, including Miralax, docusate sodium (Dulcolax), and glycerin suppositories. Do not give your infant an OTC enema or laxative without your pediatric PCP's approval.

Prevention & Tips for Parents/Caregivers: Parents and caregivers must remember that most of the time, a newborn or infant who has not had a bowel movement in several days may not be constipated. This is largely because they may not have developed a bowel routine yet. Some babies take a while to develop a regular bowel movement (BM) pattern. Some helpful preventive tips for infant constipation are:

- keep your baby active to keep the gut moving

- keep your older infants well-hydrated
- if your baby is prescribed narcotic pain relievers or other medications that cause constipation for any reason, be sure to increase your intake of fruits, vegetables, and fiber-rich baby food; also, talk to your pediatric PCP about prescribing a stool softener.
- Help your baby establish a routine schedule for bowel movements

HAND, FOOT, AND MOUTH DISEASE (HFMD)

Hand, foot, and mouth disease (HFMD) is a ubiquitous and highly contagious childhood infection primarily caused by coxsackievirus types A16 and A6 but has also been associated with enterovirus type 71. It is an infection that affects mainly the skin and the mouth and typically targets infants and children younger than 5 years of age. The disease gets its name based on the fact that the characteristic rash manifests as painful papules and blisters over the extremities (hands and feet) and genitalia (diaper area) and also involves ulcers in the mouth, palate, and pharynx (Ventarola, Bordone & Silverberg, 2015). The presence of the rash in the diaper area has led to the disease sometimes being referred to as "hand, foot, mouth, and butt disease".

Cause: HFMD is caused by coxsackievirus types A16 and A6. **Coxsackieviruses** are one of the four groups of viruses collectively known as "enteroviruses." The other three members of the enteroviruses group are polioviruses, echoviruses, and enteroviruses (which are named by numbers). These viruses cause various illnesses, usually during the summer and early fall seasons, especially in young children (Klatte, 2024).

Method of transmission: HFMD and other diseases caused by coxsackieviruses are transmitted through human respiratory droplets, which become suspended in the air when an infected person talks, sneezes, and coughs. Children may also become infected by touching contaminated surfaces or objects to their faces, mouths, nostrils, or hands, thus transferring the virus from those surfaces or objects to their faces, mouths, or nostrils.

Signs and symptoms: HFMD manifests with the following clinical signs and symptoms:

- Rash: The archetypical rash associated with HFMD occurs over the palms of the hands, soles of the feet, and within the oral cavity (mouth). However, rashes are also known to occur over the face, arms, legs, and within the diaper area (groin).
- Fever
- Headaches
- Poor appetite
- Oral ulcers or sores (herpangina): These are painful ulcers or sores that occur on the roof of the mouth and the tonsils. Herpangina is typically seen in infected children between the ages of 3 and 10. It often develops suddenly and may include symptoms such as high fevers and headaches. (Note: Herpangina is not related to herpes infections.)

Most cases of HFMD resolve spontaneously within 3-6 days.

Diagnosis: In most cases, the diagnosis of HFMD is based on clinical findings, including detailed history, symptom review, and physical assessment, usually without any need for lab work.

Treatment: Due to its self-limiting and spontaneously resolving nature, HFMD is best managed using a combination of (a) supportive care aimed at symptom management to keep the child as comfortable as possible as the disease runs its course, (b) maintaining hydration, and (c) pain control. Secondary infection rarely occurs with HFMD.

Tips for Parents/Caregivers: Adopting good hand-washing habits is one way to reduce the chances of spreading the coxsackieviruses that cause HFMD. As stated earlier in this discussion, the disease spreads very quickly, and it is pretty common for an entire daycare full of toddlers or an entire classroom of children to quickly contract the disease within one day of exposure to an infected child. Therefore, it is no surprise that based on the data from a 2011 research study conducted by Ruan et al (2011), the American Academy of Pediatrics recommends good hand hygiene and social distancing as the most reliable control measures for HFMD and herpangina.

FIFTH DISEASE (PARVOVIRUS B19 DISEASE) – "SLAPPED CHEEK SYNDROME"

Fifth Disease (erythema infectiosum), commonly called "Slapped Cheek Syndrome" (SCS), is a common childhood disease caused by the virus Parvovirus B19 (now re-named as Erythrovirus B19). This disease typically presents as an acute, self-limiting, spontaneously-resolving, biphasic (occurs in two phases) illness that typically begins with non-specific flu-like symptoms after exposure to the virus and subsequent multiplication of the virus in the bloodstream (viremia). This initial phase is followed by a second phase with more specific signs and symptoms, including rash and/or joint disease and degeneration (arthropathy). The disease is called Slapped Cheek

Syndrome because of the distinctive facial rash that develops in the affected child. The term "Fifth Disease" came from the fact that the Parvovirus infection was historically ranked fifth on the list of common childhood illnesses characterized by a rash (Mayo Clinic, 2018). Most Fifth Disease infections are mild and subclinical (clinically asymptomatic).

Cause: Fifth Disease (Slapped Cheek Syndrome) is caused by human Erythrovirus B19 (previously called Parvovirus B-19).

Mode of transmission/spread: The infection is spread/acquired through the respiratory route or via contaminated surfaces and fomites. When Parvovirus B19 infection occurs in pregnancy. It may often be asymptomatic or less severe for the pregnant mother, but there is a 30 percent risk of transplacental transmission to the unborn baby which may result in possible miscarriage or hydrops fetalis (Botgros & MacMahon, 2021).

Signs and symptoms: As stated earlier, most individuals with parvovirus B19 infections show no symptoms. Even when symptoms do occur, the presentation varies greatly depending on the age of the person infected. In general, the disease is less severe in young children than it is in adults. More serious presentations of the illness occur in individuals with certain anemias or those who have a compromised immune system. Below are early signs and symptoms of Parvovirus B19 infection in children:

- Fever
- Runny nose
- Headaches
- Stomach upset (GI discomfort)
- Facial rash: a distinctive facial rash appears a few days after early symptoms (malaise, fever, flu-like illness).

The rash is described as pink-red, lacy, with a slightly raised appearance, and occurs on both cheeks of the child, giving the impression of a "slapped" cheek. It may be itchy, especially when it occurs on the soles of the feet (Mayo Clinic, 2018). The rash typically occurs near the illness's end and mostly in very young patients (infants and toddlers). Adults (such as pregnant women) who may develop Fifth Disease do not typically present with the slapped cheek rash. Instead, they often complain of joint aches and soreness (especially the wrists, hands, ankles, and knees) that may last days to weeks.

Diagnosis: The clinical diagnosis of the disease in newborns, infants, and toddlers relies on symptom review, physical exam, and a thorough clinical history (chart review).

Treatment: Although seeing a pediatric PCP is not usually necessary for the Parvovirus B-19 infection, the presence of the following underlying health conditions will necessitate a visit to the pediatric PCP because these conditions may increase the risk of complications:

- Sickle cell anemia
- Impaired immune system (Immunocompromised)
- Pregnancy

Prevention: There is no vaccine available to prevent human parvovirus infection. However, once a person (child) is infected, they acquire lifelong immunity from the disease.

Tips for Parents/Caregivers: (1) Parents and caregivers may reduce the chances of getting an infection by maintaining good hand-washing habits for the infant/toddler and the caregiver.

(2) Also, avoid touching the face with unwashed hands. (3) Avoid sick contacts. (4) Avoid sharing food and drinks, especially the utensils.

3

BACTERIAL GASTROENTERITIS (FOOD-BORNE & WATER-BORNE INFECTIONS)

"Clean hands save lives. Make handwashing a habit to protect yourself and others."

— CENTERS FOR DISEASE CONTROL AND PREVENTION (CDC)

These infections arise from oral ingestion of contaminated food and/or water. Discussion on this topic was introduced under section 2.3 Diarrhea. The pathogens that cause bacterial gastroenteritis can cause either of 2 types of diarrheas:

Secretory diarrhea

Secretory diarrhea is caused by noninvasive bacteria that cause little or no inflammation in the intestinal mucous membrane. There are no leukocytes in the feces of the infected person. This type of diarrhea involves the loss of large volumes of fluid through the feces because the stool is completely watery. The bacterial pathogens associated with secretory diarrhea are:

- *Vibrio cholerae*,
- Entero-Toxigenic *Escherichia coli (ETEC)*,
- Entero-Pathogenic *E. coli (EPEC)*, or
- Entero-Hemorrhagic *E. coli (EHEC)*

These pathogens generally share the commonality of being noninvasive and causing little or no inflammation in the intestinal mucous membranes. Passing of large volumes of watery stool is also a characteristic feature of this type of diarrhea.

Inflammatory diarrhea

Inflammatory diarrhea is caused by invasive bacteria that attack the intestinal mucosa, triggering a massive influx of neutrophils into the intestine. For this type of diarrhea, neutrophils or lactoferrin are present in the patient's stool samples. The stool volume is usually less than that of the secretory type but contains blood and/or mucus. The following bacterial organisms cause inflammatory diarrhea.

- *Shigella* species
- *Campylobacter* species
- *Entero-Invasive E. coli (EIEC)*
- *Non-typhoidal Salmonella* serotypes such as *Salmonella typhimurium* and *Salmonella* enteritidis.
- *Clostridium difficile colitis*

When should a parent or caregiver sound the alarm for an infant with diarrhea?

It is recommended that caregivers call their children's PCP right away if the baby has diarrhea and/or any of the following:

- Baby is **3 months or younger**
- Baby records a **rectal temperature of 100.4°F (38°C)** or higher
- Baby is **vomiting**
- Baby **lacks energy** (lethargy) or is irritable (fussy) and does not want to feed or does not feed as usual.
- Baby shows evidence of **dehydration**, such as absence of saliva/drooling (dry mouth) or dry diaper for 3 or more hours (or less than 6 wet diapers per 24 hours.

ESCHERICHIA COLI (E. COLI) GASTROENTERITIS

Escherichia coli (E. coli) is a group of rod-shaped, gram-negative bacteria that occur in a wide variety of natural habitats, including the environment (soil, water), various foods and plants, and the intestines of humans and animals. Most *E. coli* strains are harmless, but some strains can cause human illness. Some illnesses associated with *E. coli* infection are urinary tract infections, diarrhea, respiratory diseases, pneumonia, abdominal infections, pelvic infections, some wound infections, and so on (CDC, 2019). Some E. coli infections can breach the blood-brain barrier to cause systemic infections such as neonatal meningitis and neonatal or infant bacterial sepsis (bacteremia). For the scope and purposes of this book, we will limit our discussion to those species of *E. coli* that cause gastroenteritis, including diarrhea.

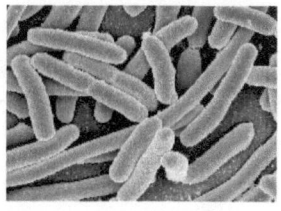

Electron micrograph of gut bacteria

Causative Agent(s): Gastrointestinal infections by *Escherichia coli* are classified based on their pathogenicity (disease-causing) mechanisms (Collier, 2023). Based on these molecularly-differentiated pathogenicity mechanisms, *E. coli* enteric infections involve six different subtypes of the bacteria:

- Enterotoxigenic *E coli* (**ETEC**) causes diarrhea in travelers (traveler's diarrhea).
- Enterohemorrhagic E coli (**EHEC**) causes hemorrhagic colitis, which may lead to a diffuse systemic disease called hemolytic uremic syndrome (HUS).
- Enteropathogenic *E coli* (**EPEC**) causes childhood diarrhea.
- Entero-invasive *E coli* (**EIEC**) causes Shigella-like dysentery associated with bloody and non-bloody diarrhea by producing a Shiga toxin; hence, it is also designated with the name Shiga toxin-producing *E. coli*, STEC.
- Enteroaggregative *E coli* (**EaggEC**) is often implicated in persistent diarrhea in children in developing countries.
- Entero-adherent *E coli* (**EAEC**) causes childhood and traveler's diarrhea, specifically in Mexico and North Africa.

It is important to note that despite the different names assigned to these E. coli subtypes, there are no differences in the antimicrobial susceptibilities of these different *E coli* bacteria. They are all equally susceptible to the same antibiotics, and therefore, antibiotics that target *E coli* would treat all these organisms equally, regardless of the pathogenicity designation (Collier, 2023). It is also essential to be cognizant of the fact that ETEC, EPEC, EAggEC, and EAEC attach to and invade the small intestines. In contrast, EIEC and EHEC preferentially colonize the large intestines before causing diarrhea (Collier, 2023).

For this book's scope, target audience, and purpose, the discussion will be limited to EPEC, EIEC, ETEC, and EHEC.

Associated Illnesses: Childhood diarrhea (EPEC); Shigella-like dysentery characterized by bloody or non-bloody diarrheal illness (EIEC); traveler's diarrhea (ETEC); and hemorrhagic colitis and hemolytic uremic syndrome (EHEC).

Transmission: Gastrointestinal infections by *E. coli* are transmitted through the oral and fecal-oral routes.

Signs and symptoms: The causative *E. coli* serotype involved typically determines the presenting signs and symptoms of the enteric infections.

a. *E coli* traveler's diarrhea: Patients with *E coli* traveler's diarrhea present with watery, non-bloody diarrhea that does not contain white blood cells (polymorphonuclear leukocytes, PMNs) when viewed under the microscope in the laboratory. The affected individual (usually adults and rarely children) loses much water very quickly through large volumes of watery diarrhea and may appear dehydrated, depending on the severity of the infection. Your pediatric PCP may seek to rule out the following similarly-presenting infections: rotavirus infection, Norwalk virus infection, Salmonella infection, and Campylobacter diarrheal infection (Colier, 2023).

b. *E coli* childhood diarrhea: This infection produces a noninflammatory watery, non-bloody diarrhea that is devoid of PMNs (similar to traveler's diarrhea of adults) but this time observed especially in children. The affected infant or child also appears dehydrated, with the classic signs of sticky or dry mucous membranes, skin tenting, sunken eye sockets, depressed fontanels (in newborns and infants), reduced urine output, and reduced or absent tears. The differential diagnoses for *E. coli* childhood diarrhea include *Vibrio cholerae* infection and rotavirus infection, and the pediatric PCP will need to rule out these two diseases to make a definitive diagnosis of *E. coli* childhood diarrhea (Collier, 2023).

c. Shiga–toxin-producing E. coli infection: Contaminated foods, especially fruits, and vegetables, are the most common source of infection for this type of *E. coli* enteric infection. This infection usually occurs in outbreaks, such as the May to July 2011 outbreak of gastroenteritis caused by Shiga–toxin-producing E. *coli* in Germany.

d. *E coli* dysentery: Patients with *E coli* dysentery (usually caused by EIEC or occasionally by EHEC) present with symptoms of fever, bloody diarrhea, dehydration, and clinical evidence of significant inflammation of the intestinal mucous membranes as shown by the presence of large amounts of white blood cells (polymorphonuclear leukocytes, PMNs) in the stool samples from the laboratory stool microscopy report. The three clinical findings of fever, bloody stools, and PMN leukocytes in the stool are diagnostic. The pediatric PCP must distinguish *E coli* dysentery from these three similarly-presenting illnesses:

shigella dysentery (shigellosis), typhoid fever, and amebic dysentery.

e. *E coli* hemolytic uremic syndrome (HUS): Patients with *E coli* hemolytic uremic syndrome (HUS) (caused by EHEC) have symptoms of fever, bloody or non-bloody diarrhea, dehydration, hemolysis, thrombocytopenia, and uremia {defined as a clinical syndrome characterized by high concentrations of urea in the blood and associated with a combination of fluid, electrolyte, and hormonal imbalances and metabolic abnormalities, which develop alongside deterioration of kidney function that may subsequently result in complete loss of kidney function requiring dialysis (Alper, 2019)}. The pediatric PCP may need to clinically differentiate E. coli HUS from the following similarly-presenting illnesses: *Shigella* infections, Clostridium difficile enterocolitis, ulcerative colitis (UC), Crohn's disease, diverticulosis, and possibly appendicitis (Collier, 2023).

Diagnosis: Depending on the type of E. coli infection and the presenting diarrheal illness, the pediatric provider may differentially diagnose similarly presenting diarrheal illnesses, as discussed above under the segment "Signs and symptoms."

Treatment: Treatment for E. coli enteric infections involves a combination of intravenous or oral antibiotic therapy (depending on the type, severity, and dissemination of infection); supportive care such as hydration, adequate oxygenation, and blood pressure support if indicated. Some important treatment tips include: (a) Antimicrobials that are known to be useful in treating cases of traveler's diarrhea include azithromycin, fluoroquinolones, and rifaximin. (b) Antibiotics should not be used for treating enterohemorrhagic *E coli* (EHEC) or STEC (Shiga toxin-producing *E coli*) infections because the antibiotics may lyse (break apart) the bacteria, resulting in the release of the bacterial toxin into the bloodstream, which then increases the chances of developing hemolytic uremic syndrome, HUS as a complication. (c) **Antimotility (anti-diarrheal) agents such as loperamide (Imodium) should not be given to children** and should not be used to treat persons with entero-invasive *E coli* (EIEC) infections (Collier, 2023).

Prevention/Tips for Parents/Caregivers: To reduce the chances of exposure to and infection by E. coli infections, teach children to avoid swallowing water from lakes and public pools; adhere to strict, consistent and proper hand-washing techniques and habits; be careful with handling and preparing risky foods such as soil-harvested fruits and vegetables (roots, legumes, leafy greens like spinach, broccoli, and sprouts); and watch out for cross-contamination by fecal matter. Cook hamburger meat until it is well done. Only give children pasteurized milk and juice. Wash raw produce (especially leafy greens) very thoroughly with several rinses before using it for salads or cooking. Keep raw foods and meats separate from washed and ready-to-cook foods and meats. Wash cooking utensils, countertops, and cutting boards with hot, soapy water before and after they come into contact with fresh produce or raw meat (Mayo Clinic, 2022).

There are currently no vaccines or preventive medications to protect against E. coli infections although there are ongoing research efforts focused on investigating potential vaccines.

SALMONELLA

According to the American Academy of Pediatrics' Healthy Children online magazine publication, *Salmonella* bacteria cause more than a million infections yearly in the United States

(Frenck, 2023). Sometimes, the resulting illness could be severe enough to require a hospital admission.

Associated Illness: Salmonella gastroenteritis; Typhoid fever; Paratyphoid fever

- **Salmonella gastroenteritis** is caused by zoonotic nontyphoidal *Salmonella enterica* serotypes that can infect any animal species without a particular adaptation to humans. The most common *S. enterica* serotypes isolated from Salmonella gastroenteritis are *Salmonella enterica* serotype *typhimurium* and *Salmonella enterica* serotype *enteritidis*.
- **Typhoid fever**, by contrast, is a severe Salmonella infection caused by Salmonella enterica serotype typhi (aka Salmonella typhi). This strictly human-adapted pathogen infects only humans but not other animals. This human adaptation of the S. typhi pathogen implies that the transmission route for typhoid fever is strictly fecal-oral because humans are the only hosts for the organism. This means that whenever there is an outbreak of typhoid fever, it is an indication that there is fecal contamination of the food and/or water supply in the area by human feces, which is a huge public health concern (Raffatellu et al, 2006). Fortunately, typhoid fever is a rare occurrence in developed countries such as the United States.

Transmission Route: Oral route. Infants may get exposed to *Salmonella* if they are given contaminated food to eat or if they come into contact with contaminated surfaces or sick family members. Exposed older children get sick after eating food and/or drinking water contaminated by Salmonella. Some of the foods that have been implicated in Salmonella outbreaks are poultry, dairy products, eggs, beef, and fish. The following animals have been linked with Salmonella outbreaks: infected pets (home-grown backyard chickens, ducks, and other poultry), reptiles (lizards, snakes, turtles, and other reptiles), and infected pet food. The incubation fever for Salmonella gastroenteritis is 6 hours to 48 hours. This time period reflects when the child is infected but has not yet started to show symptoms. The incubation period for Salmonella gastroenteritis is much shorter than that of Typhoid fever (3 to 60 days).

Vulnerable Population(s): Salmonella gastroenteritis infections occur most often in infants and children younger than 4 years. Why? Because their immune systems are still developing for that age group. Furthermore, non-breastfed babies (formula-fed babies) are more likely to develop an infection after exposure to Salmonella because they do not have maternal antibodies to help fight the organism.

Signs/symptoms/Complications: **Symptoms**: Symptoms include diarrhea, abdominal cramps, vomiting, loss of appetite, fever, headaches, and lethargy. **Complications**: Some disease complications associated with invasive untreated or poorly-treated Salmonella infections are bacteremia, meningitis, and osteomyelitis. Recent data from a research effort by Cremon et al. (2013) has shown that Salmonella-induced gastroenteritis during childhood (but not during adulthood) may be a risk factor for Inflammatory Bowel Disease, IBS (Cremon et al., 2013).

Diagnosis: The pediatric PCP has several tools for diagnosing and confirming Salmonella gastroenteritis. These include serological testing for Salmonella antigens in either stool or urine samples or in blood samples (if typhoid fever is suspected);

laboratory culture and isolation using special bacteria growth medium (agar);

Treatment: For *Salmonella*-associated diarrhea (Salmonella gastroenteritis), the treatment is supportive (fluids and rest). Antibiotics are not typically prescribed because they do not improve the child's recovery. The only exception is for infants under 3 months of age – the recommendation is to treat them with antibiotics because they have an increased risk of the infection spreading from the intestine to the blood and other organs in the body (systemic spread of the infection). Another exception for using antibiotics to treat Salmonella gastroenteritis is when the infection has disseminated (spread) to the blood, brain, bone, or other organs of the body. Most *Salmonella* gastroenteritis infections last for 4 to 7 days and may be self-limiting and spontaneously resolving (capable of clearing up independently without treatment).

For the child with severe Salmonella-associated diarrhea, there is a high likelihood of dehydration, and the child may also be treated with either oral rehydration therapy (if they can eat/drink by mouth) or intravenous (IV) fluids (Frenck, 2023).

For a child with typhoid fever, antibiotic therapy is usually required in addition to supportive care and managing possible dehydration.

Prevention & Tips for Parents/Caregivers: Caregivers can protect their little ones by reducing the chances of infection using the techniques below:

- Good hygiene techniques for food preparation
- Avoid storing food items or preparing food near waste disposal items such as wet or dirty diapers. Separate

food and drink items from waste disposal areas or items.
- High-risk food sources such as poultry, eggs, and ground or minced meat should be cooked thoroughly.
- Avoid giving your child water or milk from questionable sources in endemic areas.

If possible, avoid high-risk pets such as chickens, lizards, turtles, and snakes. If your family must have them, adhere to strict hand hygiene practices.

If a family member plans to travel to typhoid-endemic areas or a developing country, consult with your PCP about getting the necessary vaccination(s) before making the trip.

SHIGELLA GASTROENTERITIS (SHIGELLA DYSENTERY) INFECTION

Shigella gastroenteritis, also known as "dysentery" or "Shigella dysentery," is a severe bloody diarrheal infection associated with high morbidity and mortality, especially among children in developing and under-developed countries of the world. It is caused by various species of the genus *Shigella*, a highly transmissible human enteric pathogen, Libby et al (2023). According to the WHO, Shigella infections are a leading cause of diarrheal death among children in low-income and middle-income countries (Tickell et al, 2017). Shigella gastroenteritis is not a common infant disease in the United States.

Causes: Shigella dysentery infection is caused by the *Shigella* genus comprising four entero-invasive species—*S dysenteriae, S sonnei, S flexneri,* and *S boydii*. A unique subtype of the *Shigella dysenteriae* species called *Shigella dysenteriae* type 1 has also been implicated. These species vary in the tendency and degree to which they cause dysentery, with *S dysenteriae* type 1 and *S flexneri* being the most involved in causing dysentery (bloody diarrheal stools) (Tickell et al, 2017).

Associated Illness(es): Dysentery (also known as Shigella dysentery) is a disease characterized by bloody mucoid diarrhea stools.

Transmission: Transmission is by **fecal-oral route** via ingestion of contaminated food or water. Shigella organisms are highly contagious because they have a very low infectious dose (as low as 10^2 colony-forming units, CFUs), which has been attributed to the acid-resistance properties of the organism. In lay terms, this means that the number of *Shigella* organisms required to cause the disease is usually only 10 to 100 organisms! *Shigella* species, similar to *Salmonella* species, have no known animal reservoir except humans. Therefore, any outbreak of shigellosis or dysentery is a reliable indicator of human fecal contamination of food and water sources, which is a huge public health concern.

Signs and symptoms: The affected child has the following symptoms: characteristic watery, bloody, and sometimes mucoid diarrhea, abdominal pain, painful stooling, fever, loss of appetite, and nausea/vomiting. Dehydration is often an unavoidable consequence of the rapid loss of body fluid and electrolytes through diarrhea (Durani, 2023).

Diagnosis: Your pediatric PCP will diagnose the disease using a combination of the following clinical tools: detailed history, presenting signs and symptoms, physical exam, and laboratory testing (usually either stool culture to isolate the Shigella organism or rapid diagnostic test to detect the presence of antigens that are specific to the bacteria).

Treatment: The WHO guidelines stipulate using a full course of antibiotics (e.g., Ciprofloxacin, pivmecillinam, and gaitifloxacin) to treat children with dysentery. A 2023 clinical research study conducted by Libby et al. (2023) reveals that due to the clinical severity, massive disease burden, longer-term complications, and the emergence of antimicrobial resistance, *Shigella* is a priority for vaccine development in the target population of young children who are living in low- and medium-income countries. The study also reassures that vaccines targeting the most common *Shigella flexneri* serotypes and *Shigella sonnei* are currently being developed. It may often be necessary to treat the child for dehydration simultaneously. Infant or Children's acetaminophen (Tylenol) is effective in managing the high fevers associated with the disease.

Prevention Tips for Parents/Caregivers: Parents and caregivers can prevent shigellosis and dysentery by adhering to the following guidelines:

- Proper hand-washing protocol and techniques, especially after using the toilet or changing a diaper, during food preparation, and before eating.
- Other essential preventative measures include proper food handling, storage, and preparation. Appropriate food storage temperatures should be maintained to prevent the growth of bacteria.
- Any child with shigellosis or other forms of diarrhea should not be dropped off at daycare or school until they are totally recovered.
- Any parent or caregiver caring for a child with diarrhea must wash their hands before touching other people or handling food.

- Properly clean and disinfect any toilet used by someone with shigellosis or other forms of diarrhea.

Children with diarrhea should not be allowed to swim in a public pool until one week after the diarrhea has stopped. A very small number of Shigella organisms can cause dysentery, and swimming with an actively infected person can easily transmit the disease.

LISTERIOSIS (LISTERIA MONOCYTOGENES)

The CDC describes listeriosis as a significant infection usually caused by eating food contaminated with the bacterium *Listeria monocytogenes*. Pregnant women and their fetuses <u>and</u> newborns are among the 4 groups of individuals that are most likely to be sick from exposure to the bacteria. The other two members of the susceptible groups are older adults and individuals with weakened immune systems. Most infections by Listeria are sporadic, but outbreaks do occur. Neonatal listeriosis is acquired through infected pregnant mothers and could be quite severe Taillefer, Boucher, Laferrière, & Morin, L. (2010).

Cause: *Listeria monocytogenes*.

Associated Illness: **Intestinal Listeriosis** and **Invasive Listeriosis**. Intestinal listeriosis is an infection with Listeria monocytogenes limited to the intestinal tract. By contrast, invasive listeriosis occurs when the bacteria have spread beyond the intestines to other tissues and organs. For the purposes of this book, we will focus on intestinal listeriosis.

Transmission: Oral route via ingestion of contaminated foods (milk, cheese, chicken, eggs, dairy products generally, sliced deli meats, ice cream, mushrooms, packaged salads, and leafy green vegetables).

Signs and symptoms: Intestinal listeriosis is characterized by two crucial symptoms: diarrhea and vomiting.

Diagnosis: The intestinal illness usually does not require laboratory testing and is diagnosed solely based on history and clinical findings. This invasive illness may be diagnosed using a combination of clinical findings and laboratory testing (positive isolation of Listeria from a culture of body fluid or tissue).

Treatment: Most Listeria gastroenteritis infections resolve on their own without antibiotic treatment. However, complicated and invasive forms of the disease do occur and are treated with antibiotics.

Tips for Parents/Caregivers: Avoid giving these to your infants and toddlers to prevent Listeria infection:

- Raw (unpasteurized) milk, yogurt, and ice cream
- Unpasteurized soft cheeses, including queso fresco and brie
- Unheated cheeses sliced at a deli
- Purchase and use only pasteurized milk, yogurt, ice cream, and other dairy products.
- Deli meat, cold cuts, hot dogs, and fermented or dry sausages should be reheated to 165°F or until steaming hot before eating.

4

CARDIOVASCULAR INFECTIONS

"Every child deserves a healthy start in life. Preventing childhood diseases is essential for their well-being and our collective future."

— MICHELLE OBAMA

Most cardiovascular issues of the newborn and infant are related to congenital abnormalities and cardiac defects and anomalies. Rarely are newborns and infants found to have primary infections of the cardiovascular system. When infections of the heart and its vessels occur in the newborn and infant, it is usually a result of a secondary infection elsewhere that becomes seeded to the heart and blood vessels (sequelae) through blood circulation. We will discuss the most commonly seen clinical situations in infants and toddlers where these secondary infections occur – myocarditis, cardiomyopathy and Kawasaki disease.

PEDIATRIC CARDIOMYOPATHY

In 2021, when I first met her at the pediatric outpatient clinic where I worked as a primary care provider, Rosaline was a bright and energetic pre-teen who initially flashed a shy smile at me and then later, when she felt more comfortable, would not stop talking as she rattled on about her school, friends, volleyball tournaments, and so on. She was one of those kids who did not need your response to carry on a conversation. In fact, she would ask the question and answer it before you could consider if you knew the answer or not. It was, therefore, shocking to see her at the cardiac intensive care unit in a coma and on life support, fighting to stay alive. It was even more shocking to find out later, after she was able to make it out of the cardiac ICU, that she was paralyzed and neurologically devastated, having suffered multiple strokes during her admission. Her mom had explained that it all started after Rosaline had a mild bout of viral upper airway infection and recovered from it. However, a couple of weeks later, she still felt weak and complained of head pain, dizziness, and low-grade fever. Subsequently, she was found unresponsive on the couch in their family's living room later that day. Her mom had called 911 and began CPR before the paramedics arrived and quickly transported her to the nearest hospital emergency. Thus began a totally unexpected journey that changed everything for this family.

Perhaps you have come across a similar scenario recently. Unfortunately, cardiomyopathy, which is considered to be mainly a disease of adults, has recently seen an increase in the number of children and infants affected. The North American Pediatric Cardiomyopathy Registry reports that 1 to 1.5 out of every 100,000 children in the United States are diagnosed with cardiomyopathy yearly (Amdani & Makhoul, 2023). However, this statistical number is considered conservative because it does not include all the types of cardiomyopathies.

So, what is cardiomyopathy? Cardiomyopathy is a chronic heart condition characterized by deterioration of the heart muscle (myocardium) such that it becomes abnormally shaped, thickened, and/or stiffened (Amdani & Makhoul, 2023). The physiologic result of these abnormal changes is that the heart cannot pump blood effectively and, therefore, cannot supply the body's organs and tissues with enough oxygen-rich blood to function. Severe cases of cardiomyopathy can lead to heart failure or sudden death. It is important to emphasize that cardiomyopathy can occur in any child of any age, gender, race, or economic background.

Cause: In children, cardiomyopathy has many causes, although some of the causative mechanisms are not fully understood. The mechanism by which cardiomyopathy develops in infants and children is poorly understood. Below are some of the common causes of cardiomyopathy in infants and children:

- A viral infection
- Congenital and acquired cardiac anomalies
- Metabolic, mitochondrial, or systemic diseases in body parts other than the heart.
- Persistent cardiac arrhythmia/ectopy (abnormal heart rhythm).
- Genetic inheritance of the condition from one or both parents.

Mode of transmission: Cardiomyopathy is non-contagious. It cannot be passed from one person to another.

Signs and symptoms of pediatric cardiomyopathy: The signs and symptoms of pediatric cardiomyopathy vary greatly. Some affected children show no symptoms, while others (mainly older toddlers and children) may show any combination of the following symptoms: chest pain, extreme fatigue (e.g., a very sleepy infant who tires very easily while trying to feed), rapid or irregular heart beat (tachycardia), dizziness, and/or fainting.

Infants with cardiomyopathy may experience the following symptoms: poor weight gain, extreme sleepiness, difficulty feeding, or excessive sweating.

Diagnosis: Clinical diagnosis of cardiomyopathy depends on the type and clinical presentation of the condition. The diagnostic process can be roughly summarized as follows:

- The general pediatric primary care practitioner who suspects cardiomyopathy would refer the child to see a pediatric cardiologist (usually in a hospital);
- The pediatric cardiologist confirms the diagnosis using a combination of the following diagnostic tools: an echocardiogram (echo) and an electrocardiogram (EKG, or ECG). In addition, a chest x-ray, cardiac catheterization, and genetic testing may be necessary.

It is important to note that early diagnosis and treatment of this disease are critical to preventing further complications and progression to heart failure.

Types of Cardiomyopathies: There are five (5) clinical presentations of cardiomyopathy:

- Dilated Cardiomyopathy (DM)
- Hypertrophic cardiomyopathy (HCM)

- Restrictive cardiomyopathy (RCM)
- Arrhythmogenic right ventricular cardiomyopathy (ARCM), and
- Left ventricular non-compaction cardiomyopathy (LVNC)

Treatment: Currently, there is no cure for cardiomyopathy, but several treatment options are available. The treatment plan implemented depends on the type of cardiomyopathy and its severity. Below are some options that would be considered (depending on the type of cardiomyopathy diagnosed):

- **Medications**: This is usually the first treatment option for improving heart function. Different classes of medications may be prescribed depending on which heart function needs to be optimized or regulated.
- **Implantable Cardioverter Defibrillator (ICD)**: An ICD controls heart rhythm and rate and may need to be implanted in children with retractable irregular heart rhythms (arrhythmia).
- **Myectomy**: This is a surgical procedure that offers relief of symptoms in children with hypertrophic cardiomyopathy (HCM).
- **Ventricular Assist Device (VAD)**: This option is good for patients who are already in heart failure with severely impaired cardiac function of their own heart and whose heart failure has not been effectively controlled with only medications. The VAD is an external machine implanted in the failing heart and does the work of pumping and distributing blood in a way similar to the heart. Most patients with a VAD use it as a bridge to getting a heart transplant eventually. Occasionally, there are patients with a VAD who are not

candidates for heart transplant, and in such patients, the VAD serves as the heart until they pass away.
- **Heart Transplant**: For children with advanced heart failure that cannot be managed with medications or palliated with surgery, the next option would be to get a heart transplant. The heart transplant evaluation and workup is a rigorous process that will be extensively discussed in a separate book by the same author.

Tips for Parents/Caregivers: Regular medical checkups are very important for children because they allow for the monitoring of heart function, blood pressure, cholesterol levels, and other cardiovascular risk factors.

Nuggets of knowledge
Warning signs of sudden cardiac arrest

If your child experiences any of the following symptoms, you should take them to see a pediatric cardiologist for an extensive cardiac evaluation because they are considered high-risk factors/warning signs of an impending cardiac arrest:
- Chest pain or discomfort during physical activity
- Fainting or near fainting without warning or during physical activity
- Seizure activity without warning or during physical activity
- Excessive fatigue associated with exercise
- Unusually fast heart rate or rhythm while at rest and with an unknown cause

PEDIATRIC MYOCARDITIS

Myocarditis is an inflammatory condition of the heart whereby the muscular walls of the heart (myocardium) become inflamed due to an infection, typically resulting in poor cardiac (heart) function. For most affected children, myocarditis is triggered by a viral infection that involves the heart.

Cause: Myocarditis in children has been linked to several possible causes, including infection, medications, chemicals, radiation, and certain diseases that cause inflammation in many different organs of the body (for example, lupus). There are no specific known risk factors for developing myocarditis. However, age, sex, and genetic composition may all play a role in determining how severe the disease becomes once you have it. It is worth mentioning that the population group with the highest risk for serious disease resulting from myocarditis is newborns, with the mortality rate for this group as high as 50 to 70 percent (Cincinnati Childrens, 2022). In children, viral infections are the most common causes of myocarditis, and the most commonly implicated viruses are:

- Parvoviruses
- Influenza viruses
- Adenoviruses and coxsackie viruses
- Viruses such as rubella, rubeola, and HIV

Mode of transmission: Myocarditis is a non-communicable (non-contagious) disease that cannot be transmitted (passed) from person to person.

Signs and symptoms: Infants may have cool, pale hands and feet, and their kidneys may not work correctly, resulting in reduced urine output (fewer wet diapers). This is due to impaired blood circulation and distribution to organs and tissues resulting from the heart's impaired contractility and cardiac output. Other possible symptoms that could be seen are fever, flu-like illness, fatigue, malaise, chest pain, cough, and palpitations. For severe cases of myocarditis that are progressing towards congestive heart failure, the child may experience swelling in the face, feet, or legs, and they may have belly pain and nausea resulting from liver inflammation.

Diagnosis: The diagnosis of myocarditis is similar to that of cardiomyopathy. The most precise way to make a diagnosis of myocarditis is by obtaining a heart biopsy during a cardiac catheterization. Other available diagnostic options (chest x-ray, electrocardiogram, echocardiogram, heart ultrasound, and blood tests such as liver function assay, kidney function test, complete blood count, and complete metabolic panel) are similar to those used for cardiomyopathy. See Section 4.1, subtitle "Diagnosis" for more details.

Treatment: There is no cure for myocarditis, but the inflammation of the myocardium will usually go away on its own even if not treated. In general, the goal of medical therapy for myocarditis is to support heart function so that adequate blood circulation is maintained. It is usual for most children diagnosed with myocarditis to spend time in an intensive care unit for initial management and careful monitoring. If untreated, about 10 to 20 percent of affected children will recover on their own, and this recovery usually occurs within two to three months from the onset of the disease. By contrast, the remaining 80 percent of affected children will develop a residual chronic heart disease called dilated cardiomyopathy (DCM), which is a sequela of myocarditis. Children with DCM may develop progressive heart failure and eventually require a heart transplant (Cincinnati Childrens, 2022). See Section 4.1, subtitle "Treatment," for additional information regarding treatment options for these pediatric heart diseases.

Prevention: Parents must ensure that children complete the course of any antibiotics prescribed for infections, especially strep throat and other respiratory infections. Improperly treated strep infections have been implicated in many cases of pediatric myocarditis and other cardiomyopathies.

Treatment Tips for Parents/Caregivers: (1) Bed rest is essential and highly recommended for the child diagnosed with myocarditis. (2) Physical activity is typically restricted for a period ranging from weeks to months. After recovery, the child's physical activity should slowly increase over time.

KAWASAKI DISEASE

Kawasaki disease (KD), previously known as Kawasaki syndrome (KS), is an acute febrile illness of unknown etiology that primarily affects children who are younger than 5 years of age (CDC, 2020 June 4). The disease is characterized by swelling and inflammation of medium-sized blood vessels (vasculitis), especially of the coronary arteries, a common target of the disease (Sosa, 2022). The proclivity of the disease to attack the coronary arteries increases the chances of developing coronary artery aneurysms and, therefore, sudden death (Sosa, 2022), but this is not a common scenario. The incidence of KD in the continental United States is approximately 25 out of every 100,000 children under the age of 5 years.

Brief History and Description: The disease incidence of KD was first identified and documented in Japan by Tomisaku Kawasaki (after whom the disease was named) in 1967, and the first cases outside of Japan were reported in Hawaii in 1976

(CDC, 2020 June 4). Kawasaki disease is the most prominent cause of acquired heart disease in infants and young children in the United States, with over 4,200 children being diagnosed with the disease each year (Healthy Children, 2024). Research shows that the disease more commonly affects children younger than 5 years old, with the majority of susceptible children being less than 2 years old. However, the disease can also affect older children. The disease more often affects boys than girls (Hoerst, 2023). It is also more commonly seen in the winter and spring months (winter-spring seasonality following the seasonal flu pattern) than the rest of the year. Kawasaki disease affects more children of Asian or Pacific Island ancestry than other racial ethnicities. However, it is capable of affecting children in all racial and ethnic groups.

Cause: The exact cause (etiology) of KD is unknown, but because it has been associated with a high fever and swelling of the lymph nodes, Kawasaki disease appears to be somehow related to an infection. It has also been proposed that the disease may be a reaction by the body's immune system. Furthermore, it appears to occur in children with a genetic predisposition to the disease.

Mode of transmission: Kawasaki disease is not contagious, so it is not transmitted from person to person. It does not spread among family members or children in childcare centers.

Signs and symptoms: The following are the principal signs and symptoms of KD - (fever lasting ≥ 5 days + ≥ 5 classic signs/symptoms below):

- High and prolonged fevers [usually **38-40 degrees Celsius or higher** (i.e. **100.4^{0}F – 104^{0}F or higher**), lasting more than 5 days).

- A nonspecific red rash that usually affects the groin area and may peel
- Eye redness without any drainage (that is, non-exudative conjunctivitis)
- Ruby-red lips and tongue (also known as "Strawberry tongue")
- Lymph nodes that appear enlarged on one side of the neck (Unilateral lymph node enlargement).

Secondary signs and symptoms of KD include the following:

- Swelling, redness, and peeling of the palms of the hands and soles of the feet (occasionally followed by peeling of the skin in these specific areas).
- Painful joints (joint pain – arthritis)
- Increased fussiness and irritability in younger children (newborns, infants, and young toddlers)
- General loss of appetite and feeling of malaise, especially in younger children (due to irritation and inflammation of the mouth, lips, and throat)
- In some children, enlargement of the gall bladder may cause belly pain and vomiting
- Abdominal pain
- Diarrhea

Note: Skin peeling on the hands and feet, joint pains, abdominal pain, vomiting, and diarrhea are considered second-phase (secondary) symptoms of KD.

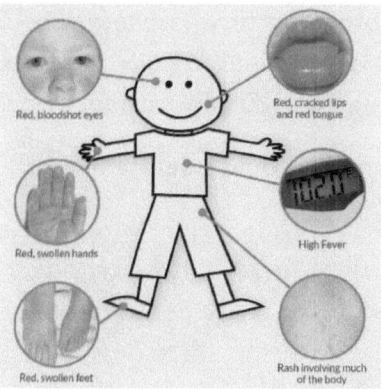

Kawasaki Disease symptoms summary - courtesy Kawasaki Kids Foundation

Diagnosis, Clinical Features, and Types of KD:

KD is the most prominent cause of acquired heart disease in the United States. The disease is associated with severe complications that include coronary artery dilatations and aneurysms (CDC, 2020 June 4). There are two diagnostic forms of Kawasaki Disease: **Complete KD** and **Incomplete KD**.

Complete KD diagnosis: The typical diagnostic criteria for classic (or complete) Kawasaki disease are:

- Presence of ≥5 days of fever (38-40°C or higher), and
- Presence of ≥4 of the 5 primary clinical features described above in the section for signs and symptoms.

Incomplete KD diagnosis: Incomplete KD is diagnosed when a patient presents with a fever lasting 5 days or longer, with two or three major clinical features and laboratory findings characteristic of the disease or echocardiographic irregularities. These correlating laboratory findings include increased erythrocyte sedimentation rate (ESR), high level of C-reactive protein (CRP), hypoalbuminemia, anemia, elevated alanine aminotransferase (ALT), thrombocytosis, leukocytosis, and pyuria. The American Heart Association (AHA) endorses using an algorithm to diagnose incomplete KD in its current guidelines.

Significant complications/sequelae of KD: How does KD affect the heart?

KD affects the heart by causing the following complications/sequelae:

- Coronary artery aneurysms (described as widening/bulging/ballooning/dilation of the coronary arteries)
- Leakage of the heart valves, especially the mitral valves (mitral valve regurgitation)
- Fluid build-up around the heart (pericardial effusion)

The coronary arteries convey oxygen-rich and nutrient-rich blood to the heart itself. By causing bulging or ballooning of the coronary arteries (aneurysms), KD hinders oxygen and nutrient supply to the heart. This makes coronary artery aneurysms the most significant sequela of Kawasaki Disease (KD). However, when KD is treated appropriately, completely, and promptly, the risk of developing complications involving the coronary arteries decreases to about 5 percent. Regardless of whether there is coronary artery involvement or not, your child with KD will need to be monitored by a pediatric cardiologist through childhood and often into adulthood.

Treatment: The principal goal of treatment is to prevent coronary artery disease. The recommended standard treatment for KD is intravenous immunoglobulin (IVIg) and high-dose aspirin. This combined treatment substantially decreases the development of coronary artery abnormalities after a KD infection (CDC, 2019). IVIg is an intravenous infusion treatment administered in the hospital, which means that the child will be admitted as an inpatient to receive it. Children are usually admitted to the hospital to receive this treatment for two to five days. The IVIg infusion is most effective if given within the first 10 days of the illness, and it decreases the risk of coronary artery involvement from 25 percent to less than 5 percent. The high-dose aspirin is given every 6 hours. It helps reduce swelling and inflammation in the affected blood vessels. It is essential to note that KD treatment is one of the few exceptions where children less than 2 years of age are recommended to be given aspirin therapy.

Other medications that may be used as adjunctive treatments or for IVIG-resistant KD include corticosteroids, infliximab, cyclophosphamide, methotrexate, and ulinastatin. In addition to aspirin, other anticoagulants that may be used are clopidogrel, dipyridamole, warfarin, and heparin.

Tips for Parents/Caregivers:

- **When to call the doctor**: If your child has had a fever for 4 to 5 days with any of the key signs and symptoms described above, ask your doctor whether he or she could have Kawasaki disease.
- There is no specific, single test to diagnose Kawasaki disease. However, if Kawasaki disease is suspected, your pediatric primary care provider may order tests to monitor heart function (such as an echocardiogram) and may take blood and urine samples. In addition, your doctor may refer you to a pediatric specialist in infectious disease, rheumatology or cardiology for more guidance in diagnosis and treatment.

- **Bed rest is key to recovery**: Children treated for Kawasaki Disease are discharged from the hospital on a low dose of aspirin to take by mouth every day for 6 to 8 weeks. As these children recover, they may seem extra tired or appear "off" for several weeks. Rest is very important for their recovery.
- Parents and caregivers should understand that peeling of skin on the hands and feet is expected and should not cause alarm.
- It is very important to closely monitor children who are recovering from Kawasaki Disease to make sure they are improving and to check for the development of coronary aneurysms. Aneurysms most often form after the first couple of weeks of illness, so children should be scheduled for an echocardiogram and a check-up at two weeks and again at 6 to 8 weeks after their fever first started.
- **Avoid live vaccines after KD treatment**: Live viral vaccines should be postponed at least 11 months after IVIG therapy because IVIG can cause the vaccines to be ineffective. Live vaccines include the **MMR** (measles, mumps, rubella) and **Varicella (chicken pox)**. Children over six months should receive the inactivated influenza (flu) vaccine injection rather than the live intranasal flu vaccine.

5

NEUROLOGICAL INFECTIONS

"It's a good thing babies don't give you a lot of time to think.

— ANITA DIAMANT

Similar to the cardiovascular system, infections of the neurological system are not common in newborns and infants. The following are infection-related neurologic illnesses of newborns and infants:

MENINGITIS OF NEWBORNS, INFANTS, AND YOUNG CHILDREN

Meningitis is the enlargement (inflammation) of the three-layer membranes (meninges) that encapsulate the brain and spinal cord. Sometimes, the swelling associated with meningitis affects the brain itself. Meningitis is linked to various factors, including medications, injuries, and chronic diseases like cancer and lupus, but the most significant cause is infection (AAP, July 2023).

Types of meningitis

There are five types of meningitis infections, which are briefly described below.

Bacterial meningitis

Bacterial meningitis is a severe illness resulting from bacteria invading, colonizing, and infecting the meninges that shield the two major central nervous system organs, the brain and spinal cord. Meticulous attention must be paid to prompt recognition, timely treatment, and close monitoring of children with bacterial meningitis because it is associated with high morbidity and mortality, and survivors usually experience debilitating neurologic sequelae such as hearing loss and possibly paralysis.

Several types of bacteria may be involved in bacterial meningitis. This type of meningitis is infectious and, therefore, can be and is usually spread from person to person. The causative bacteria may be native/normal flora (that is, can be found in or on the bodies of healthy children and adults), or they may be non-native or foreign. Sometimes, a person may be a carrier of these causative agents so that they do not become sick even though they have been infected with the organism. Nevertheless, they can continue to spread the infectious causative agent to others around them. Bacterial meningitis can potentially be deadly. Hence, getting help right away for the infected child cannot be over-emphasized. The most implicated bacteria associated with meningitis in newborns, infants, and young children (toddlers) are Streptococcus pneumoniae, Neisseria meningitis, and Hemophilus influenza). Other possible agents are Streptococcus agalactiae,

Staphylococcus aureus, Listeria monocytogenes, and members of the bacterial genus Enterobacteriaceae (especially E. coli).

Viral meningitis

Viruses cause most meningitis infections in infants and young children. Although viral meningitis may often be mild, it is usually more severe in neonates and high-risk children. Some viruses can also cause severe cases of meningitis in older infants, children, and adults. One such very virulent virus is Herpes Simplex Virus (HSV).

Amebic meningitis

Amebic meningitis is caused by a single-celled protozoan organism (amoeba) called *Naegleria fowleri*. This tiny organism causes infection by migrating up the nose to the brain, where it embeds and multiplies. The ameba (*Naegleria fowleri*) is not contagious and does not spread from person to person. Instead, it gains access to the human nose, nasal passages, and sinuses when people swim in warm freshwater ponds, lakes, and rivers. *Naegleria fowleri* also inhabits pools, splash pads, tap water, and soil. Note that a person cannot get infected by drinking water contaminated with the amoeba because the amoeba does not gain access to the brain through the GI tract. Infection occurs only when the amoeba can travel up the nasal and sinus passages to the brain.

Parasitic meningitis

Parasitic meningitis does not occur as often as viral and bacterial meningitis. The parasites involved are primarily found in animals. People are infected by consuming contaminated foods or accidentally ingesting soil contaminated by the feces of infected animals.

Fungal meningitis

Several types of soil fungus cause fungal meningitis. These organisms can be introduced into the human body by inhaling suspended fungal spores. They can also be spread to patients during medical procedures if the equipment is not adequately sterilized or if infection control practices are breached.

Cause: Various causative agents could be involved – Bacteria (most commonly *Neisseria meningitidis*, *Hemophilus influenzae*, and *Streptococcus pneumoniae*), viruses, ameba, parasites, and fungi.

Mode of transmission: Bacterial, viral, and fungal meningitis are transmitted via the respiratory route through contaminated respiratory droplets. Amebic and parasitic meningitis are transmitted by the actual migration of the parasite through the nose, sinuses, or respiratory route to the meninges of the brain.

High-risk populations: The following pediatric populations have a considerably elevated risk of succumbing to a bacterial or viral meningitis infection:

- **Newborns and babies**: Their susceptibility is mainly due to the immaturity of their immune systems, which are not yet well developed. This allows these bacteria to breach the body's natural defense mechanisms to establish an infection and get into the bloodstream more easily.
- **Children who have frequent sinus infections**: Frequent sinus infections increase the likelihood of the sinus infectious agent finding its way to the brain coverings to establish an infection.
- **Children who have suffered recent severe head**

injuries and skull fractures **or who have just undergone brain surgery.**
- **Children with inner ear implants called cochlear implants.**
- **Unvaccinated children**: Children who are not up to date on recommended vaccinations

Signs and symptoms: For adults and older children, the three (3) classic symptoms of meningitis are fever, headaches, and the meningeal signs (Kernig sign and Brudzinski sign). However, for neonates, infants, and young children (the primary focus of this book), the above-mentioned three signs are often absent. For this population, the signs and symptoms of meningitis are a combination of any of the following presentations: lethargy, irritability, apathy, inconsolability, paradoxical inconsolability (occurs when the baby cries more when being held), shrill cry, poor feeding, fever, hypothermia, hypotonia, hypoglycemia, seizures, bulging fontanelles, paleness (pallor), jaundice (yellowing of the skin and mucous membranes), physiologic shock, apnea or bradypnea (slow or absent breathing rate), and intractable metabolic acidosis. In general, the following are frequently seen signs and symptoms in each pediatric age group:

- **Newborns:** They may present with febrile symptoms, reduced appetite, restlessness, or persistent crying or inconsolability. Because the typical signs and symptoms of meningitis are often subtle in newborns, you should call your pediatric PCP for medical advice if any of these symptoms are observed.
- **Infants and young children:** This population may present with symptoms of fever, vomiting, decreased appetite, irritability/fussiness/excessive crankiness,

excessive sleepiness, and a rash. For this population, seizures and fever may be the first manifestations of meningitis. It is essential to note that febrile seizures may have similar symptoms as described here, so you should check immediately with your pediatric PCP in doubt.
- **Older children:** This population may complain of headaches, back pain, and stiff necks and show signs of sensitivity to bright light (photosensitivity). A purplish rash can also occur on any part of the body. However, this rash is conventionally most visible on the lower legs, feet, forearms, and hands.

Diagnosis: To diagnose meningitis, your pediatric PCP will usually order lab testing of blood samples, swabs from the nose and/or the throat, and possibly cerebrospinal fluid taken from around the spinal cord. The process of collecting spinal fluid (spinal tap or lumbar puncture) is invasive. A special needle is inserted into the child's lower back to draw the fluid. The process will require numbing the area. The spinal fluid obtained is sent to the lab for analysis to determine whether the child has meningitis.

Treatment: Bacterial meningitis is treated with antibiotics. The pediatric PCP may begin with empirical antibiotics while waiting for the lab test results and switch to pathogen-specific antibiotics if the lab results indicate it is necessary.

Most cases of viral meningitis are self-resolving. Traditionally, a person with viral meningitis improves in about 7 to 10 days. The child with a mild infection can recover at home with sufficient bed rest, increased fluid intake, and over-the-counter painkillers.

Potential Complications: Meningitis in neonates, infants, and young children can lead to severe complications involving the nervous system, auditory deficiencies with possible deafness, seizure activity, immobility of the arms or legs, or learning difficulties. However, it is reassuring to note that when diagnosed early and treated correctly, 7 out of 10 children infected with bacterial meningitis recover without complications (AAP, 2023 July).

Prevention: Vaccines offer protection against some but not all meningitis infections. The meningococcal, pneumococcal, and Hib vaccines can protect against two of the most common bacterial agents that cause meningitis in infants and children: *Neisseria meningitidis* and *Hemophilus influenzae*. Also, the measles, mumps, influenza, and chickenpox (varicella) vaccines can help protect infants and children from the less common causes of viral meningitis. It is, therefore, essential to ensure your child receives these recommended vaccines when they are due.

Tips for Parents/Caregivers: For parents and caregivers of an infant diagnosed with infectious meningitis, it is crucial to maintain open communication with the child's healthcare provider and follow their guidance regarding medication schedules, monitor symptoms vigilantly, and adhere to any recommended precautions. Parents and caregivers should also ensure that the infant receives adequate rest and hydration and should be kept home away from daycare and school until complete recovery or as advised by the pediatric PCP. It is also crucial to keep track of any signs of worsening symptoms, such as high fever, severe headache, or changes in behavior, and seek immediate medical attention if they occur. Additionally, they should prioritize hygiene practices, including frequent handwashing and disinfection of commonly touched surfaces, to minimize transmission of the infection to other family members or caregivers. Providing emotional support and comfort to the infant during their recovery is essential, fostering a nurturing environment that promotes healing and well-being.

FEBRILE SEIZURES VS EPILEPTIC SEIZURES

Seizures in infants can be a terrifying experience for parents, often raising concerns about their child's health and well-being. Understanding the differences between infant febrile seizures and epileptic seizures is necessary for correct diagnosis and effective management. Febrile seizures occur frequently in the pediatric age group. They may fall into one of these two categories: (a) Simple febrile seizures are non-specific, last less than 15 minutes, and do not repeat within 24 hours. (b) Complex febrile seizures are protracted (persistent) and can happen more than once in 24 hours. They are also focal (specific) and tend to imply a more serious disease process, such as meningitis, tissue abscess, or brain inflammation (encephalitis) (Tejani, 2023).

Cause: **Febrile seizures** characteristically occur as a response to a sudden increase in body temperature, often due to infections such as the common cold, flu, or ear infections. They are more common in children between six months and five years old. Most febrile seizures in newborns and infants are linked to one of these three infections: otitis media, pharyngitis, or a viral infection (Tejani, 2023). On the other hand, **Epileptic seizures** occur as a consequence of deviant (irregular) electrical activity in the brain, which may be attributed to various factors such as genetic makeup, brain damage, or neurological deficits.

Mode of transmission: Both types of seizures are non-contagious and, therefore, cannot be passed from one person to another.

Signs and symptoms: Febrile seizures often manifest as generalized convulsions accompanied by a high fever. The child may lose consciousness and experience muscle stiffness, twitching, and jerking movements. Epileptic seizures can vary widely in presentation, from brief staring spells to full-body convulsions. Other symptoms may include repetitive movements, confusion, or loss of awareness. Unlike febrile seizures, there are different classifications and types of epileptic seizures based on clinical presentation and other factors.

Diagnosis: Diagnosing febrile seizures typically involves a complete medical history, comprehensive physical examination, and assessment of the child's fever. Laboratory tests, including blood analysis or a spinal tap, may be conducted to identify the underlying cause of the fever. Usually, febrile seizures will spontaneously resolve once the underlying cause is treated or eliminated. Also, the tendency to experience febrile seizures lessens as the child ages. Epileptic seizures may require electroencephalogram (EEG) testing, brain imaging scans, and neurological assessments to confirm the diagnosis and determine the underlying cause.

Treatment: Febrile seizures often do not require specific treatment beyond fever management with medications like acetaminophen or ibuprofen. However, it is essential to monitor the child's temperature and seek medical attention if the seizure lasts longer than a few minutes or is the first occurrence.

Prevention: Preventive measures for febrile seizures include fever control strategies such as tepid baths and appropriate clothing. Epileptic seizures may require antiepileptic medications to prevent future episodes, along with lifestyle modifications and seizure action plans. Most children with epileptic seizures have to see a neurologist periodically to oversee proper management.

Tips for Parents/Caregivers: For parents of children prone to febrile seizures, maintaining a fever management plan in consultation with their child's pediatric healthcare provider is crucial. This plan should include instructions on managing fevers, seeking medical help, and strategies for seizure first aid. Parents of children with epilepsy should educate themselves about their child's condition, including triggers, medications, and emergency protocols. It is imperative to create a nurturing environment for the child, ensuring they feel safe and understood both at home and outside of the home (daycare or school).

In summary, infant febrile seizures and epileptic seizures differ in their causes, symptoms, diagnosis, and management approaches. Parents can effectively support their children's health and well-being by understanding these distinctions and implementing appropriate preventive measures and seizure management strategies. Collaboration with healthcare professionals is vital to ensuring optimal care and minimizing the impact of seizures on the child's development and quality of life.

6

IMMUNOLOGICAL INFECTIONS

"There is nothing like a newborn baby to renew your spirit and to buttress your resolve to make the world a better place."

— VIRGINIA KELLEY

ALLERGIES

Respiratory allergies - Hay fever (aka Allergic rhinitis)

Allergic rhinitis, often referred to as hay fever, is a widespread allergic condition influencing millions worldwide. Comprehending the causes, symptoms, diagnosis, treatment, and preventive measures for allergic rhinitis is imperative for adequately managing this condition, especially in children. This section will help parents and caregivers better understand how to manage this common condition.

Cause: Allergic rhinitis occurs due to the immune system's exaggerated response to allergens such as pollen dust, mold, spores, dust mites, and pet dander. Exposure to these allergens activates the immune system to release biochemical substances like the Major Basic Protein (MBP) from eosinophils and histamine from mast cells and basophils. These substances induce inflammation and itching of the nasal passages, throat, and eyes.

Mode of transmission: Allergic rhinitis is an overreaction of the individual's immune system and, therefore, is non-contagious. It cannot be passed from one person to another.

Signs and symptoms: Typical symptoms of allergic rhinitis include sneezing, nasal congestion, runny nose, itching in the nose, eyes, or throat, and watery eyes. In children, symptoms may also include irritability, fatigue, difficulty sleeping, and impaired concentration, impacting their overall quality of life.

Diagnosis: Diagnosing allergic rhinitis involves a comprehensive evaluation of the child's medical history, allergy triggers, and symptoms. Allergy testing (blood tests or skin pricks) may be conducted to pinpoint specific allergens triggering the symptoms. A healthcare provider examines the nose and throat to confirm the diagnosis.

Treatment: Treatment options for allergic rhinitis aim to alleviate symptoms and reduce the body's allergic response to foreign particles. These may include over-the-counter or prescription antihistamines, nasal corticosteroids, decongestants, or nasal saline irrigation to relieve congestion and inflammation. Allergen immunotherapy involves administering allergy shots to the patient. This may be prescribed for children with chronic or severe symptoms.

Tips for Parents/Caregivers: Preventing allergic rhinitis symptoms involves minimizing exposure to known allergens. Parents can implement several strategies to help their child manage allergic rhinitis effectively. These strategies include:

- Keeping windows shut during allergy season and using air conditioning with HEPA filters effectively reduce indoor allergens.
- Encourage frequent handwashing to remove allergens and prevent the spread of germs.
- Clean and vacuum the home regularly to reduce dust mites, pet dander, and mold.
- Limit outdoor activities during peak pollen times, such as early morning or windy days.
- Discuss allergy medications with healthcare professionals and develop an action plan for managing flare-ups. By implementing these preventive measures and working closely with healthcare providers, parents can help their children lead healthier, more comfortable lives despite allergic rhinitis.

Food allergies

Food allergies in infants and young children pose significant challenges for parents and caregivers, requiring careful management to ensure the child's health and safety. Understanding the causes, signs, diagnosis, treatment, prevention, and proactive measures is crucial in navigating this complex condition. Keeping the child with food allergies safe and healthy at home, school, or daycare is of paramount importance, and this section will provide parents and caregivers with the necessary tips to achieve this.

Cause: Food allergies occur when the immune system mistakenly identifies specific (usually harmless) proteins in food as harmful substances, triggering an allergic reaction. Common allergenic foods include cow milk, eggs, peanuts, tree nuts, soy, wheat, and seafood (fish and shellfish such as shrimp and lobster). Genetic factors, environmental influences, and early exposure to allergenic foods may contribute to developing food allergies in susceptible individuals. An allergic food reaction usually happens shortly after the food is eaten and can vary from mild to severe (Healthy Children, 2018). Peanuts, tree nuts, and seafood are the most common causes of severe food allergic reactions (Healthy Children, 2018).

Signs and symptoms: The manifestations of food allergies can vary greatly, ranging from benign to severe reactions. Characteristic features include skin irritations such as itching, hives, rash, or eczema; gastrointestinal symptoms like vomiting, diarrhea, or abdominal pain; respiratory responses such as coughing, wheezing, or nasal congestion; and, in severe cases, anaphylaxis, a life-threatening allergic reaction marked by abnormal breathing pattern, facial and throat swelling, and an unusual dip in blood pressure. For easier understanding and monitoring of food allergic reactions, the signs and symptoms have been arranged according to systems in the table below:

Signs and symptoms of food allergies based on body systems	
Body system	Signs and Symptoms
Skin symptoms	• Hives (red spots that resemble mosquito bites) • Itchy skin rashes (also called atopic dermatitis, a type of eczema) • Swelling
Breathing symptoms	• Sneezing • Wheezing • Runny nose (rhinorrhea) • Throat tightness or itchiness
Stomach symptoms	• Nausea • Vomiting • Diarrhea
Circulation (blood-flow) symptoms	• Pale skin • Light-headedness • Loss of consciousness

Anaphylaxis is a significant and lethal allergic reaction involving multiple organs and body systems and requiring immediate medical intervention (refer to Chapter 6, Section 6.3 for details).

Food intolerance or **sensitivity** is a food-related illness rather than an allergy because the immune system does not cause the problem. This illness is usually related to digestive issues or other physiologic issues with food processing through the gastrointestinal system. Lactose intolerance, for example, occurs when a person has trouble digesting lactose (milk sugar), leading to stomach gas, bloating, stomach aches, and loose stools.

Diagnosis: Diagnosing food allergies involves comprehensively evaluating the child's medical history, symptoms, and potential triggers. Allergy testing, including skin prick, intradermal, patch, or blood tests, may help identify specific food allergens. Occasionally, oral food challenges and elimination diets performed under medical supervision may be required to confirm the diagnosis. Keeping a diet diary is also very useful to the healthcare provider in diagnosing a food allergy.

Treatment: Presently, there is no treatment for food allergies. Strict dietary elimination of the implicated food allergen remains the only effective therapy for food allergies (Sicherer, 2021). It is comforting, however, to recognize that food allergies are often outgrown during early childhood. In fact, it is estimated that 80 to 90 percent of egg, milk, wheat, and soy allergies go away by age 5 years (Healthy Children, 2018). The conventional treatment for food allergies is strictly avoiding the allergenic food(s) identified through diagnostic testing. Parents and caregivers must carefully read food labels, communicate dietary restrictions to schools and caregivers, and be prepared to administer emergency medications such as epinephrine in case of accidental exposure or anaphylactic reactions. Additionally, allergists may prescribe antihistamines or corticosteroids to manage milder allergic symptoms

Prevention & Tips for Parents/Caregivers: Preventing food allergies in infants and young children involves various strategies, including exclusive breastfeeding for the first six months of life, introducing solid foods gradually and one at a time, and delaying the introduction of highly allergenic foods until the child is developmentally ready, as advised by healthcare professionals. Parents should remain vigilant for signs of allergic reactions during food introduction and seek medical guidance if concerns arise. Additionally, fostering awareness and understanding of food allergies among family members, caregivers, and the child's support network is essential to ensure a safe and inclusive environment for the child.

Nuggets of Knowledge
Omalizumab (Xolair), innovative drug for food allergic reaction

Omalizumab (Xolair), a monoclonal antibody drug, was recently approved by the US Food and Drug Administration as monotherapy for treating food allergies. This approval may be a game changer in the management of severe food allergic reactions because it may now bring peace of mind to these patients and their families by reducing their risk of dangerous allergic reactions to accidental exposure.

While the drug does not cure food allergies, a phase 3, placebo-controlled trial found that after 16 weeks of treatment, two-thirds of the research participants were able to tolerate at least 600 mg of peanut protein (which is equal to about 2.5 peanuts) without experiencing moderate to severe allergic reactions (Ellis, 2024).

ANAPHYLAXIS

Anaphylaxis is a rapid and severe life-threatening type of allergic reaction involving multiple body systems and which requires immediate medical intervention. It is considered a medical emergency (AAP, 2019). According to the American Academy of Pediatrics, research has shown that a rising number of children have been treated in emergency departments for anaphylaxis in recent years. Being prepared and knowing the signs of an allergic reaction can save a child's life because anaphylaxis can be deadly if immediate help is not provided.

Causes: Any allergen (food, insect stings, medicines, and so on) can trigger an anaphylactic reaction. The most common food allergens that have been associated with triggering severe allergic reactions include peanuts, milk, eggs, tree nuts (walnuts, cashews, pistachios, and pecans), shellfish (shrimp and lobster), and fish (tuna, salmon, cod). The following insect stings are known to be linked with severe anaphylactic reactions: bees, wasps, fire ants, hornets, and yellow jackets). Medications that have the potential to cause anaphylactic reactions include the following classes: antibiotics, anti-seizure, aspirin, and non-steroidal anti-inflammatory drugs (NSAIDs). Peanuts are among the most common foods linked with allergic reactions in the United States. As an allergen suppression strategy for high-risk infants, the American Academy of Pediatrics encourages parents to try low-allergy-risk food options before introducing peanut-containing foods (AAP, 2019).

Symptoms: Although infants can present with the traditional signs and symptoms of anaphylaxis, that is, itching (urticaria), swelling (angioedema) of the lips, tongue, or airways, breathing difficulty (dyspnea) or difficulty swallowing, wheezing, and vomiting, they can also present with unconventional signs (Carlisle & Lieberman, 2021). These non-traditional signs of infant anaphylaxis may include irritability, fussiness, inconsolable crying, sudden drooling, unusual sleepiness, ear pulling, tongue thrusting, fussiness, and increased clinginess to the caregiver. Other non-classical signs of anaphylaxis that have been documented include skin changes (rash, redness, hives, and pale or bluish skin color), dizziness or fainting, coughing, chest tightness, sneezing, stuffy nose, runny nose, confusion, drowsiness, agitation, weak pulse, and other symptoms of shock (AAP, 2019).

Treatment: **Epinephrine** remains the recommended emergency treatment for symptoms of anaphylaxis. Epinephrine acts by rapidly reversing the life-threatening symptoms of anaphylaxis. When available, epinephrine should be given promptly, followed by placing a call to 911, and going to the emergency department. Epinephrine is packaged in auto-injector syringes, which makes administering (injecting) the medication easier. **The best place to inject epinephrine is in the muscles of the outer part of the thigh.**

Note: Children at risk for anaphylaxis should always carry at least two autoinjectors. This is because a second epinephrine dose may be needed if symptoms do not dissipate quickly.

Tips for parents and caregivers: Any caregiver for an infant or child with a life-threatening allergy should recognize anaphylactic signs and symptoms and know when and how to administer the lifesaving medication. The American Academy of Pediatrics proposes that parents of high-risk children or children with previous severe allergic reactions should have an *Allergy and Anaphylaxis Emergency Plan*. The family pediatrician or PCP can assist the family with creating and using their individualized plan and share it with anyone who cares for their child.

ASTHMA

Please refer to Chapter 1, section 1.13 for a detailed discussion on Asthma.

ECZEMA

Please refer to Chapter 8, Section 8.2, for a comprehensive discussion on eczema.

7

UROLOGICAL INFECTIONS

"Babies are always more trouble than you thought and more wonderful."

— CHARLES OSGOOD

URINARY TRACT INFECTION (UTI)

Your infant has been having an on-and-off fever for the past week, and you cannot seem to figure out why. Each time the fever came, you gave OTC Tylenol, and it subsided, only for it to return the next day. Yesterday, while spiking another fever, she began to have chills and then started vomiting. Since then, she has refused to eat, even shunning her favorite baby food. You also noticed that she appears to be wetting her diaper more frequently, and her urine seems darker, cloudy, and smells "off." Worried about these new additional symptoms, you schedule an office visit with your child's pediatric PCP. After asking you a bunch of questions, followed by examining the baby and performing a urine dipstick, the PCP announces that your baby "has a UTI". "A what?" you ask. "But she's just a baby!"

Does the above scenario or variations of it sound familiar? You bet! The majority of parents in my practice almost always respond to their child's UTI diagnosis with a puzzled or bewildered look, followed by variations of that ubiquitous question: "How can my baby have a UTI?"

So, let's talk about this infection to get a clearer picture of what is happening here.

First, what is a UTI?

In simple terms, a UTI is an infection of the urinary tract. UTIs are common infections resulting when bacteria (typically from the skin or rectal area) enter the urethra and migrate upwards to infect the urinary tract. UTI infections can affect various parts of the urinary tract, but the most prevalent site affected is the bladder (bladder infection, cystitis). If the bacteria can migrate far upwards, they may reach and infect the kidneys, causing another less prevalent but more severe UTI infection called pyelonephritis (kidney infection). UTIs are common in children, affecting 8 percent of girls and 2 percent of boys by age 7 years (CDC, 2021 May 3).

Cause: The most common causative pathogen of UTI in infants, toddlers, and children is *E. coli*, accounting for approximately 85 percent of cases (CDC, 2021 May 3).

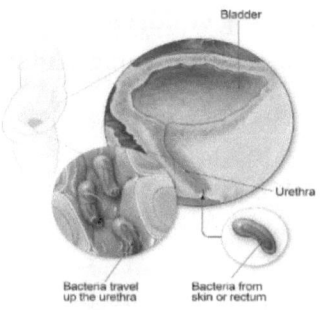
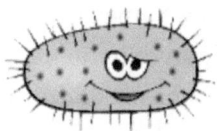

Risk factors: For school-aged children, delayed urination and chronic constipation are two of the greatest risk factors for developing a UTI (Rodgers, 2023). For other children, a structural or functional irregularity in the urinary tract may be the underlying reason for repeated UTIs. Some of the health-related problems that affect the bladder and various parts of the urinary tract are abnormal voiding patterns due to overactive or underactive bladder function, urinary tract obstruction; vesicoureteral reflux, and VUR (whereby urine back-flushes from the bladder to one or both of the ureters and sometimes even to the kidneys). VUR is common in infants and young children (NIDDK, 2018, June). Nevertheless, some children are predisposed to getting UTIs, just like some are predisposed to having ear infections. UTIs are generally more common in females because their urethras are shorter and closer to the rectum. This makes it easier for bacteria to enter the urinary tract (CDC, 2021, May 3).

Mode of transmission: For most children, the modes of transmission of UTIs include cross-contamination between the rectum and the urethra, mechanical transfer of germs as a result of poor hygiene practices by caregivers, and bacterial proliferation due to urinary stagnation (stasis) from structural or functional irregularities and inadequate hydration.

Signs and symptoms: Babies & young children: Common UTI symptoms seen in infants, toddlers, and young children less than 2 years of age are:

- Fever (may be the only sign present)
- Irritability or excessive fussiness
- Vomiting and/or diarrhea
- Poor appetite and poor feeding patterns
- Poor weight gain (especially for newborns).

Older children: For older children (ages 2 years and up), the symptoms of a UTI (bladder or kidney infection) may include the following:

- Pain or burning sensation with urination
- Dark, cloudy, bloody, or foul-smelling urine
- Frequent urination or intense urges to urinate
- Fever
- Flank pain (pain in the back or lower belly area)
- Frequent bed-wetting accidents occurring in a previously trained child

Diagnosis: For an infant or toddler under 2 years old with a UTI, it may be difficult to diagnose the infection because sometimes there are no symptoms, or the child may be too young to explain their feelings. In such situations, a urine test is the only way to determine with certainty whether the child has a bladder or kidney infection (UTI).

Treatment: The initial antibiotic treatment for a UTI should rely on the data for local antimicrobial susceptibility patterns specific to that region (location). For empirical coverage, however, the following antimicrobial agents are suggested: (a)

TMP/SMX (Bactrim or Septra); amoxicillin/clavulanate (Augmentin); and cephalosporins such as cefixime, cefpodoxime, cefprozil, or cephalexin in children 2-24 months of age. Antibiotic therapy should be 7-14 days in children aged 2-24 months. The CDC and the American Academy of Pediatrics (AAP) do not endorse antibiotic treatment of asymptomatic bacteriuria in children. Asymptomatic bacteriuria is the presence of bacteria in urine without any correlating clinical symptoms such as fever, painful urination, or flank pain. If an infant with UTI is febrile (has a fever), the CDC recommends undergoing renal and bladder ultrasonography during or following their first UTI, and any abnormal imaging results would require further testing for those infants (CDC, 2021 May 3).

For children who have an underlying abnormality that puts them at a higher risk for UTIs, a pediatric urologist or other specialists can treat any underlying structural or functional abnormality of the child's urinary tract. Treating these conditions may help prevent repeated bladder infections.

Prevention: For children with a normal urinary tract (no structural or functional abnormality), parents and caregivers can help them avoid UTIs by:

(a) encouraging and prompting timed voiding (for older infants and toddlers that have been toilet trained);

(b) changing diapers frequently for infants, and not allowing babies to sit in wet or dirty diapers for prolonged periods of time; parents and caregivers of infants should clean the genital area well during a diaper change, using gentle cleansers that do not irritate the skin.

(c) keeping the child hydrated by making sure they get enough to drink each day;

(d) avoid constipation in children by using a combination of adequate hydration and a fiber-rich diet. Why is this important regarding UTIs? The hard stools from constipation can press against the urinary tract and block urine flow, resulting in urinary stasis (pooling) in the bladder and ureters, allowing the bacteria to grow in these areas and causing UTIs. Therefore, helping your child have regular voiding and bowel movements can prevent constipation and UTIs.

(e) teaching children (especially female children) the proper techniques for cleaning after urinating. Teach the child to always wipe the genital area from front to back post-void or after having a bowel movement. This preventive tip is most crucial after a bowel movement in order to prevent the transfer of normal bacterial flora (especially *E. coli, Staph aureus,* and yeasts) from the lower intestinal tract into the urethra and bladder, where they cause opportunistic infections (NIDDK, 2017).

(f) providing loose-fitting clothing and cotton underwear for older toddlers, infants, and children. Wearing cotton underwear and loose-fitting clothes allows free circulation of air around the genitals, which keeps the area around the urethra dry and prevents the growth of bacteria.

For children with a structural or functional urinary tract abnormality, getting the child promptly treated for a related health problem may help prevent a UTI in the child.

Tips for Parents/Caregivers: Parents and caregivers should ensure that their older infants, toddlers, and children drink enough liquids. Keeping the body hydrated with more liquids may help flush bacteria from the urinary tract. You are encouraged to talk with your pediatric healthcare provider about how much liquid your child should drink and which beverages are best given to your child to help prevent a UTI (NIDDK, 2017).

Placing a warm heating pad on the child's back or abdomen may help ease the pain associated with bladder infection or kidney infection (UTI).

Hey there!

Just a moment, please.

I simply wanted to check in at this point and see how you're doing with **Newborn & Infant Infections Simplified**.

Are you enjoying the topics?

Have you learned any cool stuff yet?

Your thoughts mean a lot to me. Your feedback is immensely helpful for small, independent publishers like myself and also helps other moms, dads, and caregivers decide whether to try this book and other books by the author JK Karliese on Amazon.

If you've got a few minutes, kindly **scan the QR code** or **click the web link** below. It will take you directly to the book listing page on Amazon where you can share your thoughts, feedback, and any words of encouragement for the author and/or publisher. Just click the link below or open up your phone camera and scan the QR code to access the link that pops up.

Click here to help other parents with your review:

https://mybook.to/Newborn-Infections

OR: Scan this QR code with your phone camera:

Easy peasy. Thank you so much!

I truly appreciate you and would love you to follow my author page on Amazon for free ebooks, exclusive insights and tips, and early access to upcoming publications.

Join my active readers' community and make a difference today!

https://www.amazon.com/author/jk-karliese-books

8

SKIN (DERMATOLOGICAL) INFECTIONS

"I learned what is obvious to a child. That life is simply a collection of little lives, each lived one day at a time."

— *NICHOLAS SPARKS*

DIAPER RASH - MAY BE FUNGAL (CANDIDA SP.) OR BACTERIAL (STAPH SP.)

Diaper rash is a familiar and commonplace skin condition characterized by redness with or without skin breakdown. This irritation affects many infants and toddlers.

Cause: Diaper rash is typically caused by prolonged exposure to wetness, friction, or irritation from the baby's stool and urine. When a diaper is not changed promptly or if the baby has sensitive skin, the moist environment inside the diaper can irritate the skin, leading to redness, inflammation, and discomfort.

Mode of transmission: Diaper rash is a non-contagious medical condition and cannot be passed from one child to another.

Signs and symptoms: These often include redness and tenderness in the diaper area, along with possible bumps, scaling, or raw skin. Babies with diaper rash may exhibit increased fussiness or discomfort during diaper changes or when the affected area is touched. The rash can develop into open sores or blisters in more severe cases.

Diagnosis: Diagnosing diaper rash is usually straightforward and can be done by visually examining the affected skin area. The pediatric healthcare provider may also ask about the baby's recent diet, changes in skincare products, or any new medications that could be contributing to the rash. Sometimes, a healthcare provider may recommend testing for a fungal or bacterial infection if the rash is persistent or severe. The result of this testing will guide the provider in prescribing the appropriate cream/ointment to treat the identified organism. Note that the presence of bacteria or fungi with diaper rash is usually a secondary infection.

Treatment: Diaper rash treatment typically involves keeping the impaired skin area clean and dry, applying a protective skin barrier cream or ointment, and allowing the baby to have periods without a diaper to promote airflow and healing of the skin. Over-the-counter creams containing zinc oxide or lanolin can help create a protective barrier on the skin and aid in the healing process.

Prevention & Tips for Parents/Caregivers: Preventing diaper rash is the blueprint to keeping the baby comfortable and reducing the likelihood of recurrent rashes. Parents and caregivers can prevent diaper rash by adopting or modifying simple daily routines such as changing diapers frequently, using mild wipes, or simply rinsing the baby's bottom with water during changes and ensuring the diaper fits properly to minimize friction and moisture. Additionally, giving the baby some daily diaper-free time can help the skin breathe and heal.

In conclusion, diaper rash is a common skincare issue that many infants experience. However, parents and caregivers can effectively manage and prevent diaper rash for their little ones with prompt attention, proper care, and preventive measures. By maintaining good diaper hygiene practices, using gentle skincare products, and being attentive to changes in the baby's skin, families can help keep their baby comfortable and promote healthy skin in the diaper area.

INFANTILE ECZEMA (ATOPIC DERMATITIS)

Eczema (or Atopic Dermatitis) is a pervasive skin condition that causes dry, red, itchy skin. Infants and children with eczema tend to have more fragile skin than others. It is estimated that at least one in ten children has eczema. This segment aims to present parents with all they need to know about the condition, including tips for managing and preventing exacerbations.

Cause: The exact cause of eczema in infants is not fully unraveled, but both genetic and environmental factors are believed to play a role. A child's genotype may contribute to their likelihood of developing eczema, while environmental influences such as irritants, allergens, and dry weather can trigger or exacerbate symptoms. The most current scientific theory about the cause of eczema is "the filaggrin skin barrier theory."

The filaggrin skin barrier theory posits that an individual's skin barrier problems cause eczema. Many children with eczema do not have enough of a special protein called "filaggrin," found in the skin's outer layer. Filaggrin's functions are to help skin retain moisture and to help skin form a strong barrier between the body and the environment. Therefore, when there is too little of this protein, the skin is unable to retain sufficient moisture and has more difficulty holding in water and keeping out bacteria and environmental irritants (Stein, 2023).

Eczema often runs in families (a familial trait) and tends to occur with other allergic conditions such as asthma and allergic rhinitis (hay fever and seasonal allergies). Many infants and children with eczema also have food allergies. However, the foods themselves do not cause eczema.

Mode of transmission: Eczema is not contagious and cannot be passed from one person to another, even when they have a rash.

Signs and symptoms: Eczema typically manifests in infants as red or inflamed skin areas, skin dryness, itching, and the appearance of small, raised bumps. Babies with eczema may scratch their skin excessively, leading to further irritation and inherent skin infections. The most frequently affected skin areas are the cheeks, scalp, and creases of the elbows and knees.

What the child looks like: Eczema rashes present differently for each child. They can be all over the body or occur in clusters or just a few spots. The eczema rash often shows periods of worsening (called "exacerbations" or "flares") followed by periods of getting better (called "remissions"). The rashes may develop in different locations with each flare and as the infant gets older.

Babies & Infants: Eczema usually starts on the scalp and face in babies. Red, dry rashes may also appear on the cheeks, forehead, and around the mouth. It usually does not develop in the diaper area of babies and infants.

School-aged children and teenagers: Eczema rash is often found within elbow and knee creases, on the nape of the neck, and around the eye sockets in pre-school, school-aged, and older children.

Eczema can be especially uncomfortable for children and frustrating for their parents, especially when the itching makes it difficult to sleep.

Diagnosis: Diagnosing eczema in infants usually involves the healthcare provider performing a physical examination and enquiring about the baby's medical history and family history of eczema or other allergic conditions. In some cases, the pediatric PCP may recommend further testing (such as allergy tests) to identify triggers contributing to the infant's symptoms.

Treatment: Eczema treatment in infants typically involves a combination of gentle skincare practices and prescribed medications in more severe cases. Regularly moisturizing the baby's skin with fragrance-free, hypoallergenic creams or ointments can help maintain skin hydration and prevent flare-ups. A healthcare provider may prescribe topical corticosteroids or other anti-inflammatory medications to manage the inflammation and itching. Some children do outgrow eczema, usually by the age of four. For other children, they continue to experience the dry, sensitive skin associated with eczema as they grow into adulthood.

Prevention & Tips for Parents/Caregivers: Preventing eczema flare-ups in infants often involves identifying and avoiding triggers that worsen symptoms. Common triggers include harsh soaps, fragranced products, allergens like pet dander or dust mites, and sweat or overheating. Parents and caregivers can also help by dressing the baby in soft, breathable fabrics and maintaining a consistent skincare routine. Rough, stiff fabrics may tend to irritate fragile skin and trigger or exacerbate eczema symptoms in infants.

In conclusion, infantile eczema can be challenging to manage. However, with proper understanding, care, and guidance from the healthcare team, parents and caregivers can help their little ones find relief from eczema symptoms and improve their quality of life. Families can support their children's skin health and overall well-being by taking proactive steps to prevent flare-ups and following recommended treatment strategies.

CELLULITIS

Cellulitis is a skin condition attributed to bacterial agents. It can affect infants, presenting challenges for parents and caregivers. Understanding its causes, recognizing signs and symptoms, facilitating prompt diagnosis and treatment, and implementing preventive measures are crucial in managing cellulitis effectively in infants. This section will discuss all of these with the objective of preparing you to identify, understand, and successfully prevent this condition.

Cause: Cellulitis in infants typically occurs due to bacterial invasion through breaks or cracks in the skin. Common causative bacteria include Staphylococcus aureus and Streptococcus pyogenes. Factors predisposing infants to cellulitis include skin injuries, insect bites, diaper rash, or underlying conditions compromising the skin's integrity.

Transmission route: Cellulitis is transmitted by contact with broken skin.

Signs and symptoms: Signs and symptoms of cellulitis in infants may include **redness, warmth, swelling,** and **tenderness** at the affected site. The affected skin area may appear shiny, and infants may experience fever, fussiness, and irritability. In severe cases, cellulitis can progress to form an abscess formation or to become a systemic infection, necessitating urgent medical attention.

Diagnosis: Cellulitis in infants is diagnosed by a thorough physical examination by a healthcare professional, who assesses the affected area for characteristic signs and symptoms. Laboratory tests, which may include blood cultures, may be conducted to identify the causative bacteria and guide antibiotic therapy. In some cases, imaging studies like ultrasound or MRI may be necessary to evaluate the extent of infection.

Treatment: Cellulitis treatment in infants typically involves oral or intravenous antibiotics to eradicate the bacterial infection. The suspected causative organism and the severity of the infection often determine the choice of antibiotics. It is crucial to administer antibiotics as prescribed and complete the full course of treatment to prevent recurrence and antibiotic resistance. Supportive measures such as wound care and pain control may be adopted to promote healing.

Tips for Parents/Caregivers: Preventing infant cellulitis involves maintaining good skin hygiene and promptly addressing skin injuries or infections. Parents and caregivers should keep infants' skin clean and dry, avoid harsh soaps or irritants, and regularly inspect the skin for signs of injury or infection. Prompt treatment of minor cuts, scrapes, or insect bites with antiseptic agents and appropriate wound care can reduce the risk of cellulitis. Educating caregivers about the importance of skin protection and hygiene practices is essential in preventing cellulitis and promoting infant well-being. Moreover, seeking medical attention promptly for any signs of infection or worsening symptoms is crucial for the timely diagnosis and treatment of cellulitis in infants.

9

MISCELLANEOUS, GENERALIZED, AND NON-SPECIFIC INFECTIONS

"Children make your life important."

— NICHOLAS SPARKS

FEVER OF UNKNOWN ORIGIN (FUO)

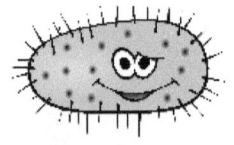

Fever is a problem that every parent or caregiver of a child has to deal with at some point in infancy and/or childhood. It is important to remember that fever is actually a sign or symptom of illness and is usually a good indication that the body is fighting off an infection. Determining the cause of your baby's fever is equally important so it can be treated properly and completely.

Before diving into the fever of unknown causes, let us start with the first things.

What parameters define a fever?

A child's normal temperature level varies depending on age, activity level, environment, and time of day. Body temperature is typically most elevated in the late afternoon and early evening hours and least elevated at night and in the early morning. Also, infants tend to have higher temperatures than older children (Healthy Children, 2021). The American Academy of Pediatrics (AAP) defines a true fever using the following parameters:

- **Rectal reading** above 100.4 degrees Fahrenheit (>38 degrees Celsius)
- **Oral reading** above 99 degrees Fahrenheit (>37.2 degrees Celsius)

Different types and brands of pediatric thermometers are available for parents/caregivers to use to measure their baby's temperature. However, using an ear thermometer for babies under 6 months old is not recommended since their ear canals (passages) are too small to allow an accurate reading (Healthy Children, 2021).

A fever of unknown origin (FUO) is a condition characterized by a persistent fever with an unidentified cause.

Cause: In general, the most frequent causes of fever in babies (newborns and infants) are ear infections, the common cold, urinary tract infections, throat infections, sinus infections, influenza infection (the flu), respiratory syncytial virus (RSV) infection, croup, pneumonia, and intestinal (bowel) related infections. The most serious conditions that cause fever in this pediatric population are blood infections (sepsis) and brain and spinal cord infections (meningitis). Both diseases are discussed extensively in other sections of this book. In general, elevated body temperatures in infants and children may also be linked to heat-related illness or heatstroke during the summer when there is a high likelihood of over-dressing babies and children in hot, humid weather.

The cause of FUO can be attributed to a myriad of factors, including infections, malignancies, autoimmune disorders, and inflammatory conditions. This makes diagnosing FUO challenging, as healthcare providers must conduct a thorough evaluation to identify the underlying issue.

Mode of transmission: The fever is non-contagious, but the underlying cause may be contagious, depending on the infectious agent involved.

Signs and symptoms: FUO traditionally presents with the following signs and symptoms: a high fever that lingers for a prolonged period, often occurring with other non-specific symptoms such as loss of appetite, weight loss (called "failure to thrive" in babies), irritability, lethargy, and excessive sweating. Since these symptoms are non-specific and can indicate various conditions, diagnosing FUO requires a comprehensive approach involving physical exams, blood tests, imaging studies, and sometimes even biopsies.

Diagnosis: Diagnosing FUO often involves a process of elimination whereby the pediatric PCP rules out common causes of fever through blood tests, imaging, and other diagnostic procedures. In some cases, further specialized tests may be required to pinpoint the underlying condition responsible for the fever.

Treatment: Treatment for FUO depends on the underlying cause. In cases where the cause is infectious, antibiotics or antiviral medications may be prescribed. For autoimmune disorders, immunosuppressive drugs may be necessary. If a malignancy is identified, treatment may involve surgery, chemotherapy, or radiation therapy. However, keeping the febrile infant hydrated and comfortable is one of the most important interventions in managing a fever.

Tips for Parents/Caregivers: Preventing FUO involves maintaining good overall health and seeking prompt medical attention for persistent unexplained fevers in children. Parents and caregivers must monitor a child's temperature regularly, ensure they receive recommended vaccinations, and seek medical advice if a fever persists for an extended period or is accompanied by concerning symptoms.

In conclusion, Fever of Unknown Origin presents a diagnostic challenge to providers due to the vast array of potential root causes and the associated non-specific symptoms. Healthcare providers must perform a meticulous evaluation to isolate the origin of the fever and commence appropriate treatment. By staying observant, pursuing medical guidance when necessary, and emphasizing preventive healthcare measures, parents and caregivers can help manage FUO efficaciously.

SEPSIS

Sepsis (also known as *septicemia* or *septicemia*) is a life-threatening condition resulting from the body's **extreme response** to an infection. Any infection can lead to sepsis, and without timely treatment, sepsis can rapidly progress to cause tissue damage, organ failure, and death (Owusu-Ansah, 2017). Sepsis can affect infants and poses significant risks to their health and well-being. Recognizing the causes, transmission routes, signs, and symptoms of sepsis, facilitating prompt diagnosis and treatment of the disease, implementing preventive strategies, and providing guidance for parents and caregivers are essential in managing sepsis effectively in infants.

Vulnerable (High-risk) populations: Although sepsis can affect anyone at any time, it does tend to occur more among certain high-risk groups within the population, particularly the very old, the very young, and those with chronic illnesses or immunocompromised status. Children (especially newborns and young infants) are more susceptible to developing sepsis compared to other pediatric age groups. Those with concealed health problems are also at increased risk. The American Academy of Pediatrics (AAP) reports that more than 75,000 infants and children develop severe sepsis annually in the United States, and nearly 7,000 of these children die (Owusu-Ansah, 2017). These numbers represent more fatalities than children who die from cancer.

Cause(s): Sepsis in infants typically arises from bacterial, viral, or fungal infections, commonly originating from the respiratory, gastrointestinal, or urinary tract. These infections can invade the bloodstream, resulting in widespread inflammation and organ dysfunction.

Mode of transmission: Infectious agents capable of causing sepsis to infants may be transmitted through a variety of routes, including direct contact with contaminated surfaces, respiratory droplets, or maternal transmission during childbirth.

Signs and symptoms: In infants, sepsis presentation may include fever (high body temperature), low body temperature (newborns and infants may present with low body temperatures rather than a fever), fast heart rate (tachycardia), rapid/fast breathing (tachypnea), shortness of breath, cold, clammy and pale hands and feet, lethargy, irritability/pain/discomfort, confusion, poor feeding, nausea, vomiting, diarrhea, and jaundice. In **severe cases**, infants may exhibit signs of shock, including **pale or mottled skin, weak pulse,** and **decreased urine output**. Early recognition of these symptoms is crucial for timely intervention and improved outcomes. It is typical for sepsis to be foreshadowed by an infection such as a urinary tract infection, a lower respiratory infection such as pneumonia, a skin infection (cellulitis), or a bone infection (osteomyelitis).

It is important to note that many of these signs and symptoms alone occur frequently in babies and children when they are sick, but when more than one of these signs and symptoms occur simultaneously or when a baby or infant appears to be sicker than usual, parents and caregivers should be alerted to seek medical intervention immediately.

Diagnosis: Diagnosing sepsis in infants involves a thorough clinical evaluation, including medical history, physical examination, and laboratory tests. Blood cultures, complete blood count (CBC), and inflammatory markers such as procalcitonin, erythrocyte sedimentation rate (ESR), and C-reactive protein (CRP) may assist in validating the presence of infection and establishing the severity of sepsis. Imaging studies like chest X-rays or ultrasounds may be conducted to pinpoint the source of infection and determine organ involvement.

Sepsis Workup: A 'sepsis workup' is medical lingo for the panel of tests used to diagnose the specific cause of a child's infection. It is important because it helps doctors and nurses determine what type of virus or bacteria is causing the infection. The sepsis workup may include blood tests, urine tests, spinal fluid analysis, and an X-ray or an ultrasound.

Neonatal sepsis: *Neonatal sepsis* is defined as sepsis occurring within a few months of birth (up to 90 days or 3 months). If the sepsis develops within the first hours or days after birth, it is called *early-onset neonatal sepsis*. However, when sepsis develops after the baby is one (1) week old, it is called *late-onset neonatal sepsis*. Clinical research has shown that premature babies tend to develop sepsis more often than infants who are not born prematurely (Owusu-Ansah, 2017).

Treatment: Detecting sepsis early and starting treatment immediately is often the difference between life and death (Owusu-Ansah, 2017). Parents and caregivers must pursue immediate medical intervention if they believe their child has an infection that is deteriorating. All cases of sepsis, whether confirmed or suspected, are treated in the hospital. Usually, these babies will need to be admitted to an intensive care unit (ICU). Fighting a septic infection is considered an emergency. Intravenous (IV) antibiotics will be given to fight the infection. Other potential medical interventions include IV fluids for stabilizing vital signs and addressing fluid imbalances, special heart and/or blood pressure medications (vasopressors), and medications to keep children calm and comfortable (antipyretics, analgesics, and sedatives). In some cases, the infants may even need a mechanical ventilator to help with breathing.

Prevention Tips for Parents/Caregivers: Preventing sepsis in infants involves implementing hygiene practices, vaccination, and early detection and treatment of infections. Parents and caregivers should practice good hand hygiene, including routine and proper handwashing with soap and water, following CDC protocol, particularly before handling infants or preparing formula. They should keep open wounds such as cuts and bruises clean until completely healed. Ensuring infants receive recommended vaccinations according to the immunization schedule helps protect them against vaccine-preventable infections. Promptly treating any signs of infection or illness in infants is crucial for reducing the risk of sepsis. Furthermore, educating parents and caregivers about the various presentations of sepsis and the importance of adequate and complete medical care can empower them to advocate for their infant's health and well-being effectively.

INFECTIONS IN PREGNANCY THAT MAY AFFECT THE NEWBORN AND INFANT

Group B Strep infection during pregnancy: For most pregnant women, infection by Group B Streptococcus does not cause any symptoms or harm. Nevertheless, for a small number of affected women, group B strep will infect the baby, usually during the baby's journey through the birth canal during labor or just before the start of labor. In these rare situations, the infection leads to a serious illness in the affected newborn (NHS, 2020). The above-described is most likely to occur in the following situations:

- The pregnant woman previously had GBS and is a current carrier.
- Early breaking of the bag of water prior to the onset of labor.
- Premature onset of labor (usually prior to 37 weeks of pregnancy).
- The pregnant woman experiences fever during or around the time of labor.

Given these factors, any pregnant woman who has had a GBS infection or who has had a baby with a GBS infection is offered intravenous antibiotics during labor to minimize the chances of transmitting the infection to the baby during birth. It is routine practice in the United States to test most women for GBS infection during the last few weeks of pregnancy to ascertain if they should be offered antibiotics during labor. If you have any concerns regarding GBS infection during or after your pregnancy, it is advised that you speak with your doctor, advanced nurse practitioner, or midwife.

Chicken Pox (Varicella zoster) infection during pregnancy: About 90 percent of the US population have been infected by the chicken pox virus in their lifetime and, therefore, are impervious to chickenpox infection (NHS, 2020). However, the remaining 10 percent who have never been exposed to chickenpox or who are not sure if they have had the disease must notify their obstetrics provider immediately if they come in contact with any person (child or adult) who has chicken pox. This is because having a chickenpox infection during pregnancy can be fatal or immensely hazardous for both the pregnant mother and the unborn baby.

What to do: If a pregnant woman or new mom suspects that they have been exposed to the chicken pox virus, they should inform their healthcare provider immediately. Usually, upon being informed, the healthcare provider will order a serological test to determine if the exposed pregnant woman is immune and, thus, the next steps to take. If a mother suspects their newborn infant has been exposed, they should also inform the pediatrician of the next steps.

Cytomegalovirus (CMV) infection during pregnancy: CMV belongs to the Herpesviridae family of viruses, which is also the family for chickenpox, cold sores, and genital sores viruses. CMV infection during pregnancy is very dangerous to the unborn baby because it can cause multiple problems, including the following: hearing loss, blindness or some form of visual impairment, developmental delays, learning difficulties, and epilepsy (NHS, 2020). The risk and severity of developing these problems are even greater if the pregnant woman has never had or been exposed to CMV before.

What to do: Because CMV is a ubiquitous virus (found everywhere in nature), it is very difficult to avoid getting infected. However, the risk of getting infected can be reduced by taking the following precautions:

- regular and consistent hand-washing with soap and warm water for at least 20 seconds, following the CDC's current guidelines for hand hygiene (CDC, 2022).
- avoid kissing babies, infants, and young children on the face
- avoid sharing food, utensils, cutlery, and drinking glasses and straws with young children

Animal-transmitted (zoonotic) infections that may harm the newborn or infant

Toxoplasmosis (*Toxoplasma gondii* - cats & sheep/lamb): Toxoplasmosis is caused by a unicellular parasite called *Toxoplasma gondii,* which causes severe neurological damage to the eyes, brain, and other organs (CDC, 2019). Cat feces (cat litter), lamb and sheep's blood, and body fluids (including milk) may contain this parasite.

What to do: To reduce the risk of getting infected with this dangerous parasite, it is advised that pregnant women avoid handling cat litter trays, gardening, or other soil-related activities and avoid contact with live sheep and lamb or with meat and milk from sheep and lamb. Any pregnant woman who experiences flu-like symptoms with swollen lymph nodes and with or without muscle aches and pains after contacting any of the above-listed sources should see their healthcare provider immediately. Newborns and infants should be kept away from contact with cat litter.

Hepatitis E (pigs): Ongoing research suggests that pigs may be a source of hepatitis E virus (HEV) infection (NHS, 2020). HEV infection is a very dangerous infection for a pregnant woman and the unborn baby because it attacks the liver, causing severe inflammation and damage (WHO, 2019). The virus is transferred to a host through the fecal-oral route, which means that eating infected and undercooked animal meat (including animal liver, especially pork) can lead to infection. There is currently no vaccine for the disease, but most cases are self-limiting.

What to do: The risk of infection among individuals (including expectant mothers) can be reduced by maintaining standard hygiene protocol, avoiding water and ice of unknown purity, properly cooking animal meat (especially pork liver) before consumption, and properly disposing of human and animal waste.

BLOOD-BORNE AND SEXUALLY-TRANSMITTED INFECTIONS (STIS) DURING PREGNANCY THAT MAY HARM THE NEWBORN/INFANT

Herpes infection during pregnancy: The causative agent for genital herpes is the Herpes Simplex Virus (HSV), an enveloped double-stranded DNA virus that belongs to the human Herpesviridae family of viruses and has two subtypes: HSV-1 and HSV-2 (Hammad & Konje, 2021). Both viruses can infect oral and facial areas and also the genital tract. However, HSV-1 is commonly associated with oral herpes, whereas HSV-2 is usually responsible for genital and anal herpes, although some cases of anal herpes have been attributed to HSV-1. All HSV viruses are lifelong viruses because they will persist in the infected person's body for life (CDC, 2023, April 4). According to a research publication by Hammad & Konje (2021), HSV infection is one of the most common sexually transmitted infections (STIs) among women of reproductive age, and it is estimated to affect about 2-3% of pregnant women. A person can become infected by genital herpes through having sex (genital contact) with an infected person or from receiving oral sex from someone who has cold sores (oral herpes). Initial genital herpes infection causes painful blisters or ulcers on the genitals. These symptoms can be treated with antiviral medication, but once infected with HSV, the virus is present in the body for life. The infected person will experience periods of dormancy during which there are no active lesions or symptoms and periods of outbreaks during which the virus is active and manifests its symptoms. After the initial infection, any subsequent outbreaks are typically less severe (NHS, 2020). HSV infection can be very dangerous for a newborn baby. Newborns that are infected by HSV experience severe morbidity that affects the skin, eyes, mucous membranes and mouth, and the central nervous system (CNS). Disseminated forms of the disease may occur and may be associated with mortality (Hammad & Konje, 2021).

During pregnancy, the immune system, which normally clears infections from gaining control in the body, becomes less effective. This makes it easier for women who have been previously infected with HSV to have an awakening/recurrence of the virus (also known as an outbreak). In most instances whereby infected women can pass the virus to their unborn baby, it occurs in utero during the third trimester because, at this time, there is a shedding of the awakened virus from infected genital areas - vulva, vagina, cervix, and perianal area. Mother-to-baby transmission of HSV is not common in early pregnancy, but when it occurs, it can cause congenital malformations (abnormal formation and development of tissues and organs in the unborn baby). If a pregnant woman gets infected for the first time with HSV during the third trimester, the risk of transmission to the baby is higher. For this reason, pregnant women are advised to avoid having sexual contact with an infected partner during an outbreak or whenever lesions are present.

What to do: Both subtypes of HS (HSV-1 and HSV-2) are capable of causing herpes disease in newborns and infants, and these herpes lesions can appear anywhere on the baby's body. HSV infections in newborn infants are very severe and may result in mortality (CDC, April 2023). Therefore, it is very important to protect the newborn infant from exposure to the virus by:

- proper handwashing before handling or feeding the baby
- avoid kissing the baby's face, especially kissing by anyone with a cold sore

For an HSV-infected mother, it is important to discuss with your healthcare provider when weighing the option of breast-feeding the baby.

HIV infection during pregnancy: The Human Immunodeficiency Virus (HIV) is a single-stranded RNA virus that belongs to the retroviridae (retrovirus) family of viruses. It has two subtypes (HIV-1 and HIV-2) that affect humans by attacking the immune system and can lead to Acquired Immune Deficiency Syndrome (AIDS) if left untreated (CDC, 2022 June).

HIV can be transmitted from an infected mother to the baby during pregnancy, birth, and breastfeeding (CDC, June 2022).

What to do: HIV testing is offered to pregnant women as part of the routine prenatal lab workup. Pregnant women who have already been diagnosed as HIV positive would need to be closely managed by a healthcare provider for the entire course of their pregnancy. In most cases, they would need to have the baby via Cesarean Section. Pregnant women and new moms who newly test HIV positive should consult with their healthcare provider (MD, APRN, CNM, Nurse Midwife) for HIV confirmation testing and to discuss the management of their pregnancy and birth in order to reduce the risk of infection for the baby. They will likely be advised not to breastfeed or chest feed the baby, as HIV can be transmitted to the baby in this way.

Hepatitis B infection during pregnancy: Infection by hepatitis B virus (HBV) in adults occurs through direct contact/exposure to blood and body fluids or through unprotected sexual contact. HBV infects the liver, and the majority of people with HBV will manifest no sign of illness, but they can be carriers of the virus and may infect others. HBV infection in a pregnant woman presents a significant risk to her infant at birth. If a pregnant woman is infected with HBV or gets infected during pregnancy, she can pass the infection on to the baby at birth (NHS, 2020, December 3). This transmission of the HBV infection from pregnant mother to baby is called "perinatal HBV transmission." It can be prevented by identifying HBV-infected pregnant women (that is, pregnant women with positive hepatitis B surface antigen [HBsAg]-positive immune screen results) and providing hepatitis B immune globulin (HBIgG) and hepatitis B vaccine to their infants within 12 hours of birth (CDC, 2020). Preventing perinatal HBV transmission is a crucial aspect of the national strategy to eradicate hepatitis B in the United States. This national strategy includes several guidelines, including the universal screening of pregnant persons for HBsAg during each pregnancy. This is the reason why every pregnant woman in the United States is offered a blood test for hepatitis B as part of prenatal care (NHS, 2020, December 3).

What to do: Babies who are determined to be at risk should be given the hepatitis B vaccine at birth to prevent infection, severe liver disease, and damage later on in life. This will be discussed in more detail in Chapter 10 under the topic, Vaccine-Preventable Infections of Newborns and Infants.

Hepatitis C infection during pregnancy: Hepatitis C infection is caused by the Hepatitis C Virus (HCV), which is a potentially fatal infection transmitted by direct contact with infected blood and targets the liver, causing both acute (short term) and chronic (long term) illness (NHS, 2020 December 3; WHO, 2023 December 18). Transmission is through contact with infected blood or body fluids, and this could occur through sharing needles or syringes as seen in illegal drug users, or from unsafe medical procedures such as blood transfusions with unscreened blood products, or by receiving invasive medical or dental interventions or procedures in countries where hepatitis C is rampant and infection control may be poor, or by having sex with an infected partner (NHS, 2020 December 3). It is important to note that many people with HCV infection show no symptoms and are oblivious that they are infected. Transmission of HCV infection from an infected pregnant mother to the fetus is possible, although the risk is much less significant than with hepatitis B or HIV. Symptoms of HCV infection include fatigue, loss of appetite, nausea, vomiting, abdominal pain, fever, dark-colored urine, and yellowing of the skin or eyes (jaundice). In babies, HCV infection typically manifests as jaundice, dark urine, and fever. These babies will require specialized care and treatment with antiviral medications. There is no vaccine for HCV infection.

What to do: If a pregnant woman suspects infection or exposure, she should inform her obstetrics healthcare provider immediately for the next steps. If it is suspected that an infant may have been exposed to HCV, the baby will likely be tested for HCV antibodies to determine its immune status, and if it is infected, it can be referred for specialist assessment.

Rubella (German Measles) infection during pregnancy: For the most part, rubella (German Measles) is not a common occurrence in developed countries such as the United States, Canada, and the UK, mostly due to the success recorded with the MMR vaccine. However, if a pregnant woman contracts rubella during the first trimester (within the first 4 months of pregnancy), it can lead to very serious implications, including birth defects and miscarriage (NHS, 2020 December 3). It is a good idea to know your immunization history, especially your MMR vaccination history, before getting pregnant because the MMR vaccine cannot be given during pregnancy.

What to do: If you are pregnant and unsure of your MMR vaccination history, you should contact your healthcare provider or midwife as soon as possible if:

- you come into contact with someone who has rubella
- you have a rash or come into contact with anyone who has a suspicious rash
- you have symptoms of rubella – which includes a characteristic red or pink spotty rash that starts on the face or behind the ears and spreads to the neck and body, usually within two weeks of having the following associated symptoms: fever, sore throat, cough,

sneezing, runny nose, sore red eyes, and headaches (NHS Choices, 2020).

Your healthcare provider will perform an evaluation and will likely order serological tests to check antibodies and antigens to help determine if you have been exposed to rubella.

Fifth Disease/Slapped Cheek Syndrome (Parvovirus B19) during pregnancy: Slapped cheek syndrome is also known as "Fifth Disease." It is a common, highly infectious, self-resolving disease in affected older children caused by Parvovirus B19 (NHS, 2017 October). Fifth, Disease is easily transmitted from person to person through secretions and airborne droplets and can be harmful to an unborn baby. Therefore, pregnant women are advised to avoid contact with young children showing the signs and symptoms of Fifth Disease. The disease typically resolves in affected older children within three weeks but can be more serious in infants and adults. Fifth Disease presents with the following signs and symptoms: a general feeling of unwellness initially (malaise), then fever, runny nose, sore throat, and headache, with the most significant sign being the appearance of a bright red rash on one or both cheeks (hence the name "Slapped Cheek Syndrome"). A few days after the appearance of the red cheek rash, a spotty rash may appear on the child's chest, arms, and legs. The rash can be raised and itchy and could be more difficult to see on dark-toned, brown, and black skin. The cheek rash and body rash typically fade within two weeks, but sometimes the body rash may persist for up to a week (NHS, 2017 October).

What to do: If you suspect your newborn infant is exposed, you should notify the pediatrician immediately. If the baby shows signs and symptoms, you should manage them as best as possible until you see the doctor. Keep the baby hydrated by breastfeeding or bottle-feeding often to help compensate for possible insensible fluid losses through secretions. You should keep track of the baby's temperature and may give Tylenol (following the manufacturer's recommended or pediatrician-approved dosage) to help alleviate the fever and headache.

10

ALL YOU NEED TO KNOW ABOUT FEVERS

"Fever is the protective mechanism, not the disease."

— RUDOLF VIRCHOW

For many new moms, figuring out their baby's fever is an uphill task. How do I figure out my baby's fever?

MEASURING THE BABY'S TEMPERATURE

A baby's temperature can be measured in several ways using different thermometers. Below are the thermometer options for measuring an infant's temperature:

- **Rectal** (between the buttocks): This method is most effective and preferred for infants three months and below. Research has proven that rectal temperature is

the most reliable temperature measurement method because it measures the core body temperature. A rectal temperature above 100.4^0F is considered a fever.
- **Temporal (temporal artery of the forehead):** The temporal temperature method measures the heat radiated from the temporal artery in the forehead. It is easy to use and noninvasive. A temporal temperature above 100.4^0F is considered a fever.
- **Tympanic:** The tympanic temperature is measured in the ear. This method is not recommended for babies under six months of age because their ear canals are very narrow at that age, making it challenging to properly insert the sensor probe of the thermometer. A tympanic temperature above 100.4^0F is considered a fever.
- **Axillary (underarm):** The axillary temperature is measured under the arm (in the armpit). This method is considered less precise for measuring an infant's temperature because it requires keeping the child still to obtain an accurate reading. An axillary temperature above 99^0F is considered a fever.
- **Oral:** The oral temperature is measured in the mouth and is not recommended for babies. An oral temperature above 100^0F is considered a fever.

WHAT IS A FEVER?

A fever is simply an abnormal increase/rise in body temperature. The cut-off value for labeling a thermometer reading a fever depends on the type of thermometer used. In general:

- A temperature greater than 100.4^0F is considered a

fever when using the rectal, temporal, and tympanic thermometers.
- A temperature reading of 99°F is considered a fever when using the axillary thermometer.
- A temperature of 100°F is considered a fever when using the oral thermometer.

HOW DO I TREAT MY INFANT'S FEVER?

Different factors cause fevers; therefore, a fever is treated based on its source or origin. Some fevers do not need treatment but rather simply require support as they resolve on their own.

Some crucial facts to keep in mind when it comes to managing fevers are as follows:

- Most pediatricians would recommend properly-dosed (weight-based dosage) **acetaminophen (Tylenol)** after age 2 months
- Most pediatricians recommend properly-dosed (weight-based dosage) ibuprofen (Motrin) after 6 months.

GENERAL PRINCIPLES FOR TREATING FEVERS:

- When a viral infection induces a fever, it will routinely run its course regardless of whether it is treated or not. However, most pediatric providers would recommend Tylenol or Motrin for comfort, following the above guidelines of over 2 months for Tylenol and over 6 months for Motrin.
- Fever caused by a bacterial infection will usually be treated with antibiotics. The pediatric provider may prescribe Tylenol or Motrin following the above-stated

guidelines to comfort the child before the antibiotic kicks in.
- Fever caused by inflammation or pain from a traumatic event or other factor is typically treated with Tylenol or Motrin, depending on the age guidelines.
- General fever guidelines for babies:

1. Keep the baby cool by removing blankets and unbundling clothing to allow air to get to the baby's skin. Use an air conditioner or fan when appropriate. Note that if the child starts to shiver after being uncovered or placed in an air-conditioned space, this signals that they are too cold, and the air temperature may need to be increased or a blanket cover provided.
2. Increase the child's fluid intake – this is necessary to replace the increased loss of body fluid through the skin during a fever. For babies, fluid intake can be increased via frequent feedings of breast milk or formula. Remember: do not force fluid on a baby, and do not give plain water to a baby less than 6 months old.
3. Treat the fever with properly dosed anti-pyretic: (1) OTC acetaminophen (Tylenol) for babies after 2 months. (2) OTC ibuprofen (Motrin) for babies after 6 months.

WHAT NOT TO DO IF YOUR INFANT HAS A FEVER

- Do not use aspirin to treat an infant's fever or discomfort.

<u>Rationale</u>: Aspirin has been linked with several serious side effects, including Reye syndrome.

- Do not use cool/cold water sponging to reduce an infant's fever.

Rationale: Cool or cold water can cause shivering and increase the child's temperature, which defeats the goal and worsens the child's condition.

- Never apply rubbing alcohol on an infant to treat a fever.

Rationale: Rubbing alcohol evaporates into the gaseous state easily and can be readily absorbed into the skin or inhaled through the respiratory tract, causing severe conditions which may include a coma.

FEBRILE CONVULSIONS/FEBRILE SEIZURES

Little Joey is 8 months old and has not been his usual active, playful self for a few days. After measuring an axillary temperature of 101 degrees Fahrenheit, his mom, Susan, decided to take him to the local children's emergency room, where he was subsequently diagnosed with an ear infection and prescribed antibiotics and fever medications. On the way home, his mom stopped by the pharmacy and picked up his new prescriptions. However, while settling him down in his playpen when they arrived home, Joey suddenly had an odd look on his face for a few moments. Then his body stiffened briefly, and his mouth and hands twitched for a few seconds simultaneously. His eyes rolled back in their sockets, and his body was arched stiffly in an unnatural position. His mouth was clenched tight, and a small amount of what looked like foamy saliva was seeping out of his clenched lips. He appeared to be unconscious. This happened so fast and unexpectedly that Susan was frozen for a few seconds. Then she lifted him quickly and began to yell his name, but he was completely unresponsive. It seemed like forever before he opened his eyes. It was extremely frightening, she stated, as she described the event to me later at the clinic. This is one mother's experience of a febrile seizure, and the scenario may sound familiar to other mothers who have had similar experiences.

Conventionally, febrile convulsions may last less than a minute —or perhaps just a few seconds, although it may seem like forever to a frightened parent. A high fever can trigger seizures between the ages of six (6) months and five (5) years. These are called "febrile convulsions". Febrile convulsions or febrile seizures in infants are usually associated with very high fevers and are as common as occurring in 2 to 5 out of every 100 children (Healthy Children, 2021). Typical manifestations include body stiffening, rolling back of eyes, involuntary twitching and jerking of arms and legs, and sometimes foaming or frothing at the mouth. Occasional loss of consciousness may also occur. Although these events may appear frightening to a parent or caregiver, they are generally not serious or permanent and do not cause severe or permanent damage to the brain or nervous system. Furthermore, they are not indicative of any type of neurological damage. Most times, febrile seizures disappear as the child gets older.

TYLENOL VS MOTRIN: MAKING THE RIGHT CHOICE FOR BABY

The two most popular medications prescribed for babies are pain relievers and fever reducers. Tylenol and Motrin belong in this category of medications. As stated earlier, acetaminophen (Tylenol; Panadol, Tempra) is recommended for babies at 2 months and older, whereas ibuprofen (Motrin; Advil) is recommended for babies at 6 months and older.

In general, both medications are dosed based on weight and may be used interchangeably for pain or fever, but it is worth noting that they work differently and have different side effects. Acetaminophen is best used for pain and fever relief but not for inflammation because it has no anti-inflammatory properties. Also, it is considered safe when dosed every 4 to 6 hours. Taking too much acetaminophen can result in deadly liver damage.

Ibuprofen, on the other hand, can also relieve pain and fever. However, it has the additional advantage of having anti-inflammatory properties, which makes it more suitable for certain types of pain/discomforts that involve some type of inflammatory manifestation, for example, fractures, skin traumas that involve a skin break, teething, and so on. Ibuprofen is usually dosed every 6 to 8 hours and is considered generally safe after 6 months. Its major disadvantage, however, is that it has the side effect of causing stomach pain/upset and also is not recommended for a child with bleeding disorders.

TO GIVE OR NOT TO GIVE?

Aspirin: The American Academy of Pediatrics advises against using aspirin to treat your child's fever or discomfort. Why? Aspirin has been linked with some significant adverse effects, which include stomach upset, gastrointestinal bleeding, and, most notably, Reye syndrome. Reye syndrome is a rare but serious and severe illness that causes swelling in the brain, confusion, and liver damage (AAP, 2022).

Cough & cold medicine: What is the AAP's recommendation for the use of over-the-counter (OTC) cough and cold medicines? According to the AAP, oral OTC cough and cold medicines can cause significant harm to young children. The perils of using these medicines far outweigh any help the medicines might have in reducing cold symptoms. Below are the AAP guidelines for these medications in children:

Children under 4 years: Over-the-counter cough and cold medicines are not endorsed for babies and young children under 4 years.

Children of age 4 to 6 years: Parents and caregivers may use cough medicines for their children **only if** recommended by the child's pediatric healthcare provider.

Children over 6 years: Cough medicines are safe when used correctly; simply ensure you adhere to the dosage instructions provided on the package regarding the correct amount of medication to administer.

Natural, herbal & organic remedies: Based on the AAP's recommendations and the FDA regulation, here is what you need to know about using natural, herbal, and organic remedies for your child:

- Not all natural, herbal, and organic therapies are safe. In fact. therapies are not safe simply because they are "natural." Although rare, side effects from natural therapies can and do occur. The AAP recommends that parents and caregivers check with their child's doctor before adding or changing a natural, herbal, or organic therapy. It is very helpful to bring all the products you give your child to your next medical appointment so

that you may review them with your child's pediatric PCP.
- Regarding whether they work, the AAP states that more research is needed to determine the efficacy of natural, herbal, and organic remedies. This statement applies to both conventional and natural/herbal/organic therapies. It is noted that these therapies may work for children with certain conditions but not for children with other conditions. To explain this concept using conventional therapy, we may recall the saying that although massage may help minimize stress, it is not a remedy for cancer.
- Insurance coverage is another crucial factor to contemplate when choosing complementary therapies (natural, herbal, and organic therapies and remedies). Coverage for complementary therapies is frequently more limited compared to conventional or traditional therapies. Parents and caregivers should double-check with their insurance company before accepting and scheduling these therapies for their infants.

OTC stool softener: The AAP recommends that the pediatric PCP be consulted before administering any OTC stool softeners to an infant.

TIPS FOR GIVING MEDICINE TO A BABY

An oral syringe is the best way to give liquid medicine to a baby.

General Tips

- Before giving medicine to your baby, be sure to read the

medication or prescription label and follow the instructions exactly.
- Always use the measuring devices (oral medication syringe, medicine dropper, measuring cup, or dosing spoon) that are included with the medication packaging instead of using a regular spoon from your kitchen. Why? Because regular kitchen spoons come in different sizes, which may end up causing you to give your baby too much or too little medicine.

Technique

- Hold the infant in an upright position on your lap.
- Using the medicine dropper or syringe, squirt some medicine into the inner lining of either cheek.
- Gently hold the baby's chin so their mouth stays closed and they can't spit it out.
- Stroke your hand down the baby's throat to encourage the swallowing reflex.
- Repeat the steps until you have given the full dose of the medication.

What to do if my baby doesn't like and won't swallow the medicine?

Sometimes, despite your best efforts, your baby refuses to take the medicine. They may clench their mouth shut or refuse to swallow the medicine and even spit it right out at you. Usually, the reason for this is that they do not like the taste of the medicine, or simply they find it uninteresting or a bother. Thus, most parents/caregivers ask: How do you give a baby medicine when they do not take it?

Here are some tips for giving medicine to an uncooperative baby:

- Mixing the medicine with a small amount of tasty liquid or soft food (such as apple juice, applesauce, pureed fruit, gelatin, or pudding) may make it more appealing to the baby. **Use only a small amount of the food or fluid**, and make sure your child eats it all to get the complete dose of the medicine.
- **Avoid mixing medicine in a baby's bottle of formula feed** — a baby who doesn't finish the bottle might not get the complete dose of the medication.

11

COMMON INJURIES & ACUTE EVENTS IN THE FIRST YEAR

"What good mothers and fathers instinctively feel like doing for their babies is usually best after all."

— BENJAMIN SPOCK

---

*I*njuries and acute events such as cuts, bruises, bites, burns, bleeding, choking, and so on are typically unavoidable in infancy and childhood, despite how careful parents and caregivers may be. Although every parent or caregiver would love for all injuries to be simple "boo-boos" that can be kissed away or fixed with a simple Band-Aid, the truth is that some injuries may require some form of first-aid intervention or focused and targeted treatment or even a visit to the emergency room. However, being knowledgeable and prepared about what to do can make a huge difference. This chapter aims to provide every parent and caregiver with the knowledge and skills required to make the appropriate intervention to treat common injuries and acute events that are encountered in the first year of life. The author's objective is that by the end of this chapter, you will be able to provide simple first aid for your child for minor emergencies and will also be able to know what to do to stabilize your child before you get to the emergency room, for more serious acute events. Without further ado, let's dive in.

QUICK TIPS TO HELP PREPARE FOR INFANT AND CHILDHOOD EMERGENCIES

The following quick tips should be part of your emergency contingency plan as the parent or caregiver of an infant or child:

- Discuss with your pediatrician: Consult with your pediatrician to create an action plan for handling various non-emergent, non-life-threatening injuries and an action plan for a serious emergency. The action plan should address the following:

1. What is considered an emergency versus a non-emergency
2. When to call your doctor's office: Request both the daytime clinic number and the after-hours number (nurse line).
3. When to call 911
4. When to call both your doctor's office and 911
5. What you should have handy at home as part of your first aid box

- Identify the nearest emergency room (ER) or hospital

emergency department (ED) to your home location and the quickest route to get there.
- Make sure that your house number is clearly visible from the street and that there is adequate lighting to make it visible at night.
- Keep a comprehensive list of all your emergency phone numbers: your spouse/significant other/partner's phone number, your pediatrician's office, pediatrician's after-hours emergency line, 911, the Poison Control Center hot line, the nearest ER, emergency medical service phone number (also accessible via 911); your family's health insurance carrier client line; your designated alternative emergency contact (close friend or relative); your job's phone number; your babysitter or child daycare number; and a trusted neighbor's phone number. These phone numbers should be saved in your phone, preferably in the "Favorites" folder, and programmed as speed dial numbers.
- Know the poison control line (**1-800-222-1222**) and display the poison control phone number sticker (or your bold printed copy) prominently in your home where all caregivers can easily see it.
- Keep first aid supplies in an adult-accessible but child-proof box and location.
- If you can afford it, have an extra car seat prepped and ready to go in case you must transport your child in a vehicle other than your family vehicle.
- Always have some cash reserve available at home. Also, have an emergency-ready purse/handbag at home, which should have cash, a credit card, a portable phone charger, an extra set of home keys, emergency phone numbers, and so on.

- Your child's personal biometric data and important medical information – Date of birth, weight, height, allergies, medications, medical implants such as pacemakers, immunization record, previous surgeries and hospitalizations, and chronic illness(es). All of these should be updated regularly
- Make sure your phone has all important apps preloaded, such as your child's pediatric hospital app and taxi/transportation apps (Yellow Cab, Uber, Lyft, Curb).

CUTS

a. Small cuts

Step 1. If the skin is broken, with or without bleeding, wash and rinse thoroughly with clean water and antiseptic soap (if soap is available). Ensure that all dirt and foreign materials are flushed out. If the skin is not broken, proceed to step 4.

Step 2. Dab the area dry with a sterile gauze pad, then apply an antiseptic spray or OTC antibiotic ointment.

Step 3. Cover with a Band-Aid or other absorbent bandage (many brands are available, such as Curad, McKesson, NexCare, Johnson & Johnson, and various store brands).

Step 4. Apply a cold compress if there is significant pain and swelling involved.

Step 5. After 24 hours in place, you may remove the bandage to expose the wound to air to heal. You have the option to re-apply a new bandage if there is a risk of the wound getting dirty or infected.

Signs of infection: The following are signs of possible wound infection and would require a doctor visit for the child: redness, warmth, swelling, an inordinate amount of pain, and possible drainage/oozing of yellow (pus) or white fluid.

b. Large cuts

For larger cuts that are bleeding profusely, follow these steps:

Step 1. Apply pressure to stem the blood flow using a gauze pad or a clean washcloth (you may also use a new diaper or even your fingers if there is no gauze pad or washcloth available). Continue to apply pressure and use more pads if bleeding persists until the flow of blood is reduced or stops.

Step 2. If the bleeding stops, apply a loose, non-stick bandage to the area and proceed to the doctor's office or emergency room. Do NOT apply anything else to a large/deep wound – no antiseptic rinse, no antibiotic cream. Keep the temporary bandage loose and not tight to promote circulation until you get to the pediatric provider.

For such large/deep cuts, the provider may use a skin glue (Dermabond) or stitches (sutures) to close the wound. Head wounds that occur at or near the face may require a follow-up appointment with a plastic surgeon for evaluation.

c. Large cuts with massive bleeding

For all skin wounds with massive bleeding (gushing or rhythmic pumping of blood out of the wound), these will require calling 911 for emergency medical attention.

BRUISES AND SCRAPES/ABRASIONS

Bruises: Bruises are black-and-blue marks resulting from a pressure injury to the skin. If the bruise is painful, apply cold compresses or ice packs for about 30 minutes to reduce the pain, swelling, and bruising. If the skin is broken, treat the bruise as an abrasion.

Scrapes/Abrasions: Scrapes and abrasions involve some amount of peeling of the top layer/layers of the skin in the affected area, exposing raw, red, and tender skin. The most common body areas affected by scrapes and abrasions are elbows and knees. These types of injuries are often associated with play or some type of physical activity.

What to do: (1) Wash or sponge the area with mild soap and water (antiseptic soap is preferred) to remove dirt and other foreign matter. (2) If the bleeding does not stop after a few minutes of the injury, apply mild pressure above the injury site/location. (3) Apply antiseptic spray or cream (example: triple antibiotic cream) (4) Cover the area with a loose gauze dressing or a large Band-Aid bandage such that the dressing/bandage is loose enough to allow air circulation around the wound (5) Note that a dressing or bandage may not be necessary if there is only scraped skin without bleeding.

SPLINTERS & SLIVERS

Splinters and slivers are caused when small pieces of an object (especially wood) are embedded in the skin.

What to do: Clean the affected body part (usually fingers and toes) with an alcohol prep pad and allow it to dry. If the splinter or sliver is visible, attempt to remove it with a tweezer (if it is large enough) or try easing it out with a sewing needle if it is very tiny. Do not attempt to remove a splinter or sliver with your bare hands because you risk the splinter/sliver getting stuck in your own fingers. After successfully removing the splinter or sliver, rewash the site with warm, soapy water for 15 minutes, 3 times a day for a couple of days. Be sure to consult the pediatric provider if the remains are embedded in the infant's skin or if the area starts showing signs of infection – warmth, redness, swelling, and pain). A deeply embedded splinter or sliver would likely require a tetanus shot if the baby's DTaP vaccination is not current.

PUNCTURES/PUNCTURE WOUNDS

Puncture wounds go straight into the skin at a vertical or near-vertical angle. They are perforating wounds. Small puncture wounds are typically caused by sharp objects such as nails, needles, pens, pencils, and thumbtacks. Deep puncture wounds are associated with knives, sticks, and rods.

What to do: (1) For small puncture wounds, soak the wound in warm, soapy water for 15-20 minutes, then call your pediatric provider on the next steps. (2) For deep/large puncture wounds, stem any blood flow and take the baby to the ER immediately. Do not remove the object (knife, stick, rod, pipe) if it is still embedded in the skin. Instead, pad or stabilize the object to prevent it from moving around in the skin while the child is transported to the ER. Keep the child as calm and still as possible to prevent the injury from worsening. Deep puncture wounds would likely require a tetanus shot if the baby's DTaP vaccination is not up to date.

LACERATIONS

Treat same as for cuts and puncture wounds discussed (sections 11.2 and 11.5)

SCALDS (MOIST HEAT) AND HEAT EXHAUSTION/HYPERTHERMIA/HEATSTROKE

Scalds:

Scalds are caused by moist heat such as hot water or hot steam.

What to do: (1) Apply cool running tap water (not iced water or ice cubes/chips/blocks) to the burn for at least 20 minutes and up to three hours after the burn. (2) Do not apply Vaseline, burn ointments, or other grease-based ointments to the burn. (3) Cover the burn with dry dressing and call your pediatric provider or take the child to the ER if the scalded skin area is larger than the child's palm.

Prevention: (1) Never leave a baby unattended in a tub. (2) The hot water heater in your home should be set no higher than 120°F. This will reduce the risk of scalding accidents. Water at 140°F is capable of causing third-degree burns in an infant within 3 minutes of contact. This is due to the thinness and fragility of the infant's skin. (3) Parents residing in apartment buildings where they have no control of the water temperature can purchase anti-scald safety devices from plumbing stores. These devices will slow water flow from a faucet to a trickle when the water temperature reaches a high, unsafe level for the human skin. (4) Always turn the handle of cooking utensils inwards or sidewards, away from the front of a stove where a toddler can easily reach them.

Heat exhaustion/Hyperthermia and Heat stroke:

Every year, it seems as though the summer is a little (or a lot) hotter than the year before. Pediatric emergency rooms continue to see increasing numbers of children being brought in for heat exhaustion, heat stroke, dehydration, and other heat-related complications. It is, therefore, important for parents and caregivers of little ones to be knowledgeable and prepared for heat-related issues in infants.

Heat exhaustion (also known as **mild hyperthermia**) results from a high core body temperature above normal. In heat exhaustion, the core body temperature can reach up to 105^0F. It is the most common form of heat injury in the United States during summer.

Signs and symptoms of heat exhaustion: Heat exhaustion presents with the following signs and symptoms in infants: excessive sweating, irritability, thirst, refusal of food, nausea, vomiting, decreased urine output, darker urine color, and elevated body temperature.

What to do: (1) Remove the child from the hot area into a cool, air-conditioned environment. (2) Remove excessive clothing and expose as much skin to air as possible. (3) Give and encourage frequent sips of cool fluids – cooled formula for younger infants and cooled water and fruit juices for older infants 6 months and above. (4) Apply cool compresses to the body using towels or washcloths.

Heat stroke (also known as **severe hyperthermia**) is the most serious heat-related condition that occurs when the body is unable to manage its temperature due to a rapid rise in the core temperature, such that the body's sweating mechanism collapses, and the body is unable to cool itself down. This typically occurs suddenly and rapidly after the child has been overheating for a while without any intervention. The core body temperature can elevate up to 106°F or greater within 10 to 15 minutes during a heat stroke. Without immediate emergency intervention, heat stroke can lead to lasting disability or death.

Signs and symptoms of heat stroke: (1) Hot, dry skin OR damp skin from profuse sweating (2) Very high body temperature (fever) of $106°F$ and above (3) lethargy OR agitation (4) confusion (5) convulsions/seizures (6) altered mental status or loss of consciousness. Heat stroke can be injurious if treatment is stalled or deferred.

What to do: (1) Call 911 (2) Remove all clothing (3) Move infant to a shade or cool environment (4) Wrap the infant in a towel soaked in cold tap water (5) Keep replacing cold, wet towel with a fresh one after few minutes of use on the baby's skin (6) Offer cooled breastmilk or formula in a bottle, if the baby is conscious, awake, and alert. Do not give anything by mouth if the baby is comatose, convulsing, or has altered mental status. (7) If there is a delay in getting an ambulance, rush the child to the nearest ER (8) If breathing stops or pulses cannot be felt at any point while reviving the baby, begin infant CPR immediately.

BURNS

a. Dry heat/flame burns

For minor (1st degree burns): (1) Immerse burned body part (usually fingers, hands, arms, legs, feet, toes) in cool water (not cold water) of about $50-60°F$ and hold under the running cool water for about 15-30 minutes or until the baby does not appear to be in pain anymore. (2) Pat the skin dry with a soft towel (do not apply ice, butter, grease, or burn ointment because they could worsen the skin damage). (3) Cover the burn with a loose, non-adhesive bandage, a gauze pad, or a cloth bandage. (4) Notify your pediatric provider for further instructions if pain persists after several hours.

For moderate (2nd deg222ree burns) and major (3rd degree burns): Second (2nd) degree burns appear raw and blistered. Third (3rd) degree burns appear white or charred black. Take the child to the ER for second-degree and third-degree burns, any burns on the face and genitals, and any large burns that are the size of the child's hand or larger.

b. Sunburn

Follow these steps for treating sunburn on an infant: (1) Apply cool water compresses for about 10 to 15 minutes at a time and up to 3 or 4 times each until the redness of the sunburned skin subsides. (2) Apply any baby-safe cooling sunburn cream or spray in between the cool compress treatments. You may also use a gentle moisturizing cream instead of a sunburn spray. (3) If there is pain, you may give a pediatrician-approved OTC acetaminophen (Tylenol). For babies older than 6 months, giving ibuprofen (Motrin) may be a better option due to its anti-inflammatory properties. (4) Severe sunburns involving skin blistering would require scheduling the child to see the pediatric provider.

Caution: Avoid applying Vaseline, baby oil, or other ointments to a burn. The grease seals in heat and seals out the air required for the burn to heal.

c. Chemical burn

Chemical burns are caused by corrosive and caustic chemicals, such as caustic soda (lye) in some hair relaxers and cleaning agents, pipe drain cleaners, floor cleaners, hydrochloric acid, organic acids in cleaning supplies and some home remedies, and so on. These chemicals can cause very serious burns, especially when they involve the soft mucous membranes of the oral (mouth, throat) and nasal cavities.

What to do: (1) Using rubber gloves and a clean, soft, dry cloth, gently brush off dry chemical residue or wet chemical from the skin. (2) Immediately flush the affected area with large amounts of clean water. (3) Call and notify the child's pediatric provider AND the Poison Control center (1-800-222-1222, if in the United States). (4) If the chemical has been swallowed, treat the infant as you would treat swallowed poisons after calling Poison Control (do not give the infant anything to eat, drink, or induce vomiting; and do not give any medications without the directions of Poison Control). When calling the Poison Control center, be prepared to provide details of the chemical swallowed.

d. Electrical burn

- Disconnect the electrical power source first before touching the baby
- Alternatively, use a dry, non-metallic object such as a wooden stick or ruler, a broom, a cushion, or even a book to separate or dislodge the child from the electrical power source (Do NOT use your bare hands to remove the baby from the power source).
- If the baby is not breathing and has no pulse, dial 911 and then begin infant CPR with rescue breaths right away.
- If the baby is breathing and has a pulse, call your pediatric provider immediately or take the infant to the ER as soon as possible.

BITES

a. Animal bites

We love our pets and would do almost anything for them. To us, they are as much family as our kids, and we keep up with their health and well-being just as we do for every other member of our household. If everyone were like-minded, that would be the case. The following are important tips regarding managing animal bites:

- Wash the wound thoroughly but gently with copious amounts of water.
- Control bleeding (if present) by applying pressure or bandaging above the wound site. This also prevents serious germs from disseminating throughout the body via the blood supply.
- Do not apply ointments, solutions, or lotions to the wound. Do not apply anything to the wound.
- As much as possible, try to avoid moving the affected body part unless it is absolutely necessary.
- After washing, dab dry with gauze and loosely cover the wound site with gauze until you get to the ER.

Rabies is the most serious infection that can arise from an animal bite wound. Rabies infection, while not common in humans, is almost always deadly when it occurs. Most household pets in the United States are vaccinated against rabies. The situation may be different in other countries. Regardless of the vaccination status information provided by the pet owner (if the offending animal is not yours), it is advisable to request to see actual proof of vaccination. Obtain as much information as you can about the animal and provide all of this information to your child's pediatric provider and the Animal Control department. In most cases where the skin is broken, the provider will prescribe prophylactic (preventive) antibiotic treatment. Continue to monitor the wound after seeing the pediatric healthcare provider, and call the provider immediately if you observe the following signs of infection: redness, swelling, tenderness, and disproportional or increasing pain.

Although most animal bites affecting infants are associated with domestic pets, there are rare occasions whereby non-domestic animals may be involved, such as coyotes (especially in Texas), raccoons, bats, and so on. Most non-domestic animals that attack and bite unprovoked are rabid, and such bites require emergent attention.

b. Human bites

In some cases, a baby may be bitten by another child. If the skin is unbroken (intact), routinely clean the area and inform the pediatric provider's office. If the skin is torn or appears compromised in any way, wash the bite thoroughly but gently with clean, flowing water. Stop any bleeding by applying pressure above the bite site. Avoid manipulating the wound or applying any antibiotic ointment, solution, cream, or spray. Dab the cleaned wound dry with gauze, then cover it loosely with fresh, clean gauze and call the pediatric provider's office or take the child to the ER. In this situation, prophylactic antibiotics will likely be prescribed as a preventive measure against infection.

c. Snake bites

Snake bites are extremely rare occurrences among infants. The few cases seen are associated with outdoor activities such as camping. A bite from a poisonous snake species could be fatal if not treated promptly. The four main venomous snake species in the United States are rattlesnakes, copperheads, coral snakes, and cottonmouth snakes (also known as water moccasins). Fortunately, anti-venom is available for these snakes in the United States if administered immediately. The most concerning implication of a poisonous snake in an infant is the fact that due to the baby's size/weight, even a very small amount of venom can be fatal. Below are the most important tips for managing a snake bite:

- Call 911 and then call the poison control helpline.
- Avoid moving the affected area. Keep the baby and the affected limb as still as possible to reduce the spreading of the venom through the blood.
- Quickly immobilize the limb with a splint.
- Apply firm pressure with a tourniquet, rope, or cloth above the bite area. Check the pulse distal to (beneath) the bite area to ensure circulation is not completely cut off. If you anticipate a delay in the arrival of help, loosen the tourniquet such that a finger can slide under it – this slows down circulation from the bite to other parts of the body without completely cutting off the blood circulation.
- Keep the affected limb/body part at a level below the heart.
- If available, you can apply a cool compress to minimize the pain but do not apply ice to the area.
- Do not give the baby any medicine unless directed by the medical provider or the poison control center

For bites from non-poisonous snake species, treat the bite as you would treat a deep cut or a puncture wound. Then, notify the pediatric provider for further instructions.

d. **Insect bites/stings**

The most common insect bites are spiders, dog ticks, mosquitoes, bees, wasps, hornets, fire ants, and deer ticks (typically after a family camping trip).

- **Minor, mildly painful bites**: For mildly painful bites, such as bites from fire ants, ticks, wasps, or some bee species, wash the site with soap and cool water, apply a cold compress if swelling is present, and give the baby acetaminophen or ibuprofen if the pain is significant.
- **Painful bites**: For very painful bites such as spider bites, irrigate the area with cool water and wash with soap, then apply a cold compress and call the Poison Control Center.
- **Itchy bites**: For itchy insect bites such as mosquito bites, apply calamine lotion or other anti-itch medication. Depending on the child's age, the pediatric provider may prescribe an antihistamine such as diphenhydramine (Benadryl).
- **For honey bee stings, wasp stings, or other insects with stingers**: (1) Gently remove the stinger with tweezers, your fingers, or scraping horizontally using a credit card or the blunt edge of a table knife. (Avoid pinching the stinger when removing with your fingers to avoid injecting more venom into the wound). (2) Wash the area with soap and cool water. (3) Apply a cold compress pack or make one by wrapping ice in a towel. (4) You may give a pediatrician-approved pain reliever if needed.

- **Poisonous insect bites**: Some more common poisonous insect bites are associated with the brown recluse spider, tarantula, the black widow spider, or a scorpion. For these cases: (1) take note of the insect's appearance (if a spider). This will help the Poison Control Center to determine if it is a poisonous species. (2) Call 911 and the Poison Control Center. (3) Keep the child still and immobilize the area if it is possible to do so. (4) Observe the child for any symptoms and hypersensitivity reactions.
- **For ticks**: (1) Use a blunt tweezer or your gloved fingers to remove the tick immediately if you know how to do so without squeezing, crushing, or puncturing the insect open. Place the extracted tick on a sheet of paper and take a picture, then save the tick to show the pediatric provider if possible. (2) Wash the area with soap and cool water, (3) Notify your pediatric primary care provider for further instructions.

For all insect stings, observe the child for signs of an immediate-type hypersensitivity reaction over the next 24 hours and monitor for delayed hypersensitivity response over the next 3 to 7 days. Some indicative signs of a hypersensitivity reaction are sudden, generalized swelling (especially of the face), shortness of breath, generalized macular rash, redness and inflammation of the bite/sting area, and severe pain. These are mostly associated with stings from bees, wasps, and hornets.

CONVULSIONS/SEIZURES

Infant convulsions (seizures)) may be caused by identifiable or non-identifiable factors. Some of the identifiable causes of seizures are family history/genetics, ingestion of certain prescription medications, ingestion of toxic substances, electric shock, and high fevers (febrile seizures). Certain disease conditions, such as meningitis, encephalitis, epilepsy, brain tumors, and cerebral palsy, are also associated with seizures and convulsive episodes.

What to look for: The following are some common signs and symptoms of seizures to watch for – stiffening of the body, sudden collapse, rolling up of eyes to reveal the whites of the eyes, uncontrolled stiff jerking movements, which usually will immediately follow stiffening and collapse, and foaming or drooling from the mouth. For most seizures, there is no obvious impairment of the airway, but for the more serious cases, impaired breathing effort has been observed. Febrile seizures (febrile convulsions) are associated with very high fevers in babies. Febrile seizures are discussed in Chapter 5 under the subtitle "Febrile seizures versus Epileptic seizures."

What to do: Follow these steps to help your baby during a seizure:

1. Move the baby to a flat surface with a wide, uncluttered area, such as the room's carpeted floor or the middle of an adult bed (not a crib). Clear the immediate area around the baby from clutter.
2. Loosen any tight clothing, especially around the neck and chest.
3. Lay the baby sideways with the hips elevated higher than the head by placing a pillow beneath the hip.
4. Do not attempt to clean the foam or drool from the mouth or place anything in the mouth while the seizure occurs.

5. Time the seizure from beginning to end and write the total time down. Also, write down everything you observed during the seizure. Try to recall the baby's activities or behavior immediately before the seizure and the post-seizure appearance and response.
6. Call your baby's provider to inform and provide the details of the seizure activity.

When to call 911 for a seizure: (1) If the baby stops breathing or has no pulse during or after the seizure, call 911 (or have someone nearby call 911) and begin infant CPR. (2) If the seizure lasts more than 2 minutes or appears to be severe, call 911 (3) Also call 911 if there appear to be multiple seizures back-to-back.

EXTREME COLD/EXPOSURES

a. Frostbite

The CDC defines frostbite as a type of freezing weather injury caused by prolonged exposure to freezing temperatures with resultant numbness and discoloration of the affected areas, which frequently involves body extremities such as the fingers, toes, nose, ears, cheeks, and chin. Severe cases of frostbite can result in permanent damage to the body and possible amputation of the affected body part. Early signs of frostbite include the skin of the affected body part being very cold and stiff, and appearing white or yellow-gray in color; swelling of the affected area; and pain. As the frostbite progresses to severe, the skin is not only very cold but now appears pale, waxy, and very hard/stiff.

Risk factors for frostbite: The following infants are prone to experiencing frostbite:

- Infants with innate (preexisting) blood circulation problems – examples are babies born with cardiovascular defects.
- Infants that are often improperly dressed during winter
- Infants living in households with socioeconomic challenges
- Infants living in abusive homes.

What to do: Early recognition of the signs of frostbite is critical. The parent or caregiver should get the baby indoors as soon as possible. If you are unable to get the infant indoors immediately, place them under your clothing next to your skin until you can get them indoors. Once inside the house, the rewarming process should be gradual, not a "quick thaw." Immerse the affected body part in tepid water (slightly warmer than the body temperature). If it is not possible to immerse the body part (for example, nose, cheeks, chin, ears), apply tepid-warm compresses to the affected area with a washcloth. Continue the immersion or warm compresses until the normal skin color returns. Remember to continue adding warm water to the soaks to maintain the tepid temperature (approximately 102^0F). Once the baby's skin color in the affected area returns, nurse the baby or give warmed formula or fluids. If you have someone to help besides yourself, you can nurse or feed the baby while the other person is applying the soaks or warm compresses.

It is important to remember that frostbitten skin may become red and swollen as it is rewarmed and will be prone to blistering. With that in mind, be gentle with the skin when applying the warm compresses, and when drying—gently pat the skin to dry. Be sure to notify the provider's office once the baby is rewarmed and settled. Usually, an ER visit is not necessary unless the case is severe in a child with a pre-existing health condition.

What not to do: (1) Do not re-warm the frostbitten skin with a stove, heater, radiator, heat lamp, heating pad, or open fire. (2) Do not dip the affected part in hot or very warm water for a quick defrost. (3) Do not rub or massage the affected body part to restore warmth.

Frostnip is a milder and less severe form of frostbite in which the affected body part is cold and pale without getting to the waxy, stiff, and numb stage. Frostnip takes less time to rewarm and causes less pain and swelling.

Prevention: (1) Be prepared during winter – dress infants and children appropriately for being outdoors during winter; layering clothing can make much difference; do not neglect those body parts that have prolonged exposure to the atmosphere (ears, lips, nose, fingers). (2) Prepare your home and car for winter storms or other winter emergencies. Preparation may include having an emergency kit with supplies such as a flashlight, batteries, wool gloves, a wool cap, and a spare blanket.

b. Hypothermia

Hypothermia is caused by prolonged exposure to very cold temperatures. This causes rapid heat loss from the body at a faster rate than it produces, using up the body's stored heat energy

and causing the core body temperature to drop to abnormally low levels. Hypothermia is particularly dangerous because very low core body temperature affects brain function.

Risk factors for hypothermia in infants: (1) babies who sleep in cold bedrooms. (2) babies who are kept outdoors for prolonged periods during cold winter weather

Signs and symptoms of hypothermia in infants: (1) cold, bright red skin (2) low energy (lethargy) (3) shivering (4) sleepiness (4) irritability

Signs of severe hypothermia in infants: (1) shivering stops (2) floppy (loss of muscle control (3) declining consciousness

What to do: Hypothermia is considered a medical emergency.

- Call 911 or transport the child to the nearest ER.
- Remove wet clothing and wrap the infant completely in a warm blanket. Alternatively, you could place the infant skin-to-skin next to your chest and abdomen and wrap both of your in a warm blanket.
- Nurse the baby or feed formula while they are still wrapped next to your skin or in a warm blanket while you await the arrival of EMS
- Turn up the heater if in a car or at home
- For a baby showing signs of severe hypothermia and who may be unconscious and may not seem to have a pulse or to be breathing, begin CPR even if they appear to be dead and continue CPR until EMS arrives.

FOREIGN OBJECTS & INJURIES FROM FOREIGN OBJECTS IN BODY CAVITIES

1. Foreign object in the eye: This could be an eyelash or a grain of sand. The following techniques may be able to remove the offending material from the eye. For all of these techniques, you must have another person available to hold and calm the baby. (a) Irrigate (flush) the affected eye with copious amounts of clean or sterile tepid (body temperature) water, then dab dry with a clean towel and check to see if the object is still there. (b) Wash and dry your hands or use sterile gloves and moisten a cotton ball; then, while using your non-dominant hand to hold the baby's eyelid open, use the moistened cotton ball in your dominant hand to attempt gently removing the foreign object from the eye while someone is holding the baby very firmly. You can only use this technique at the corners of the eye, beneath the lower eyelid, or perhaps from the white part of the eye. Do NOT attempt using a cotton ball or any other item to touch the pupil of the eye. (c) Try pulling the upper eyelid down over the lower eyelid for a few seconds each time until the foreign object is removed. If the object remains after the above attempts, cover the affected eye with a small, lint-free gauze pad and proceed to your pediatrician's office, the urgent care clinic, or the emergency room.

2. Foreign object in the ear: The parent/caregiver's first response should be to try dislodging the object from the ear if they feel comfortable doing so and have the necessary equipment. Below are suggested techniques for removing a foreign object from a child's ear.

- **For a non-metal (plastic or wood object)** that is not deeply- embedded in the ear (that is, it can be seen): You **must** have someone to hold the baby still. Place a drop of quick-drying glue to the end of a paper clip or other thin rod and touch the glue end of the paper clip/rod to the object in the ear (do not touch it to the ear). Allow a few minutes to dry, then gently pull back on the paper

clip/rod, and the object should come out stuck on the clip/rod.
- **For a metal object**: Hold a strong magnet at the entrance to the ear canal (without inserting the magnet into the ear canal) and allow the object to be pulled out onto the magnet.
- **For a live insect**: Shine a flashlight into the ear and try to lure the insect out if it's not stuck in ear wax.

Parents and caregivers who do not feel comfortable trying the above techniques, do not have the equipment described above for attempting these removals, or have tried the techniques unsuccessfully should take the baby to the pediatrician's office, the pediatric urgent care clinic, or the ER.

3. Foreign object in the throat/mouth: If your baby is choking on food or some other foreign object and he/she can breathe, cry, and cough, your first response would be to allow and encourage them to keep coughing. However, if the baby continues coughing for more than 2-3 minutes and possibly begins to change color in the face, call 911, and while waiting for help to arrive, begin implementing the emergency rescue protocol (back slaps and chest thrusts) for a choking infant as taught by the American Heart Association (AHA) in its Basic Life support (BLS) class. (Parents and caregivers are encouraged to enroll in a CPR/BLS training class to receive this basic but very important skill).

4. Foreign object in the nose: You should suspect a foreign object in the infant's nose if: (a) the baby is having difficulty breathing, (b) there is bloody nasal discharge, or (c) there is foul-smelling non-bloody or bloody discharge from the nose.

What to do: If you can reach the object, try to remove it with your fingers (do not probe with your fingernails or use tweezers or any other instrument). If you are unable to extract the object, take the baby to the emergency room.

NOSEBLEEDS

A nosebleed is a sudden free outflow of blood from one or both nostrils that usually self-resolves within a few minutes. Most nosebleeds are caused by unintentional trauma, such as picking the nose or sticking sharp objects into it, or by very dry and cold atmospheric air.

To stop a nosebleed in an infant: To stop a nosebleed in an infant, you will need a soft cold compress or ice chips wrapped in a soft baby pillowcase or cloth.

- Keep baby upright and leaning slightly forward. Have someone keep the baby calm with distractions or toys.
- Using the cold compress, gently and firmly pinch the nostrils shut by pinching and applying pressure to the top of the nose. Hold the pressure for 10 minutes. (Do not worry about suffocating the baby because the pinching will cause the baby to breathe through the mouth rather than the nose.)
- After 10 minutes, release the nose, remove the cold compress, and check to see if the bleeding has stopped.
- If the nosebleed persists after 2 cold compresses, call your pediatrician's number or take your child to the nearest emergency department.
- If bleeding has not stopped, repeat the process again.

Caution:

- Do not lay the infant down or lean them back because this will allow blood to flow down his throat, which could induce vomiting.
- Do not allow the baby's head to bend forward (looking down) because it would make the bleeding worse.
- Do not put tissue or gauze into your child's bleeding nose
- Once the bleeding stops, supervise the infant not to rub, pick, or put objects in their nose for 2 to 3 days. This will allow the broken blood vessel(s) to heal. If the bleeding continues after the second cold compress attempt, it is best to call your pediatrician or take your child to the nearest emergency department (*How to Stop a Nosebleed*. (n.d.).

Prevention:

- If the air inside your home is dry, especially during winter and spring, you may run a cool mist humidifier in your child's room at night.
- Do not smoke in the home or around your child.
- Monitor your infant to ensure that he/she is not picking their nose.
- Apply saline nasal drops or spray to the nostrils as directed by your child's healthcare provider.
- Apply petroleum jelly to the inside of your infant's nostrils several times a day to help protect the mucous membranes from dry air by keeping them moisturized.
- Discuss with your child's pediatrician about the possibility of allergies being the cause of the nosebleed.

Note: Call the child's pediatric healthcare provider for the following situations: If an injury to the head or face caused the nosebleed, or the nosebleed does not stop or resumes again after cold compresses, or there is a large amount of blood, or the child feels faint/weak/ill, or if there is bleeding from other parts of the body, or there is an object stuck up in the child's nose.

FRACTURES OR BROKEN BONES

Signs that an infant may have a broken bone or fracture include extreme pain reaction and inconsolable crying when the affected limb or area is touched; inability to move that part of the body; inconsolable crying not alleviated by feeding or diaper changes while the baby maintains a stiff position; and swelling or discoloration of the affected area.

1. **For simple fractures (broken bones) of arms, legs, or fingers**: (a) Use a firm padded object (such as a ruler, wooden spoon, small thick book, or magazine) to splint and immobilize the injured part of the body. Use a bandage, strip of cloth, neck tie, neck scarf, or any strip of cloth to secure the splint without being so tight to impede blood circulation (A good way to check if it is too tight is to check the blood flow to the finger or toes at the distal part (lower end) of the affected area. (b) Next, apply an ice pack to the area to reduce swelling. (c) next, take the child to the ER right away.
2. **Compound (complex) Fractures**: These are more serious broken bones, usually involving a break in the skin. If the bone is poking through the broken skin, do NOT touch it. Step 1. Apply a tourniquet about an inch or two above the break to control blood loss if there is a

lot of bleeding. **Step 2.** Cover the broken skin area of the injury with a sterile gauze, or you can use a brand-new diaper. **Step 3.** Take the child to the nearest emergency immediately.

ELBOW DISLOCATIONS (ALSO KNOWN AS "NURSEMAID'S ELBOW)

Elbow dislocations are also known as "Nursemaid's Elbow". They are not normally seen in newborns and infants but rather associated more with older infants, toddlers, and small children. This occurrence pattern is due to the nature of the injury – for young children, they are typically caused by tugging on the hands of small walking children by adults in a hurry; for older infants and toddlers, they are caused by adults playing with toddlers by holding the hands and swinging them around and around for fun, or by tossing the toddlers into the air and catching them on their arms and under-arms as they descend. Regardless of how it is caused, an elbow dislocation is painful and uncomfortable for the child. Common symptoms include persistent crying and inability or unwillingness to move the affected arm by the child. The good news is that an experienced ER medical provider easily corrects it.

What to do: Follow these steps to manage elbow dislocations.

Step 1. If pain is severe, you may give Tylenol or another pediatrician-approved pain reliever. **Step 2.** Next, apply a splint to immobilize the arm and then apply an ice pack. **Step 3.** Lastly, take the child to the emergency room right away.

HEAD INJURIES

For head injuries, it is important to understand first of all that due to the high vascularity of the scalp in general (there are many blood vessels in the scalp), much bleeding is seen with cuts or bruises to the head regardless of how small or superficial the injury actually is. Also, head bruises tend to swell up pretty quickly, and it is not uncommon to find a large egg-sized bump after a minor impact injury to the head.

Head injuries in children are considered to be more serious if it involves any of the following scenarios:

- Falling onto a hard surface from a height equal to or greater than the child's height (Murkoff & Widome, 2018).
- A hit to the head with a heavy object
- Blows to the sides of the head tend to do more damage in children than blows to the front and/or back of the head.

a. Superficial head injuries: Cuts and bruises to the scalp

As stated previously, due to the high vasculature of the scalp, these tend to bleed and swell easily. They are treated the same way you would treat a regular cut, bruise, scrape, or abrasion to the skin.

For small cuts:

Step 1. If the skin is broken, with or without bleeding, wash and rinse thoroughly with clean water and antiseptic soap (if soap is available). Ensure that all dirt and foreign materials are flushed out. If the skin is not broken, proceed to step 4.

Step 2. Dab the area dry with a sterile gauze pad, then apply an antiseptic spray or OTC antibiotic ointment.

Step 3. Cover with a Band-Aid or other absorbent bandage (many brands are available, such as Curad, McKesson, NexCare, Johnson & Johnson, and various store brands).

Step 4. Apply a cold compress if there is significant pain and swelling involved.

Step 5. After 24 hours in place, you may remove the bandage to expose the wound to air and allow it to heal. If the wound becomes dirty or infected, you can reapply a new bandage.

Signs of infection: The following are signs of possible wound infection and would require a doctor visit for the child: redness, warmth, swelling, an inordinate amount of pain, and possible drainage/oozing of yellow (pus) or white fluid.

For larger and/or deeper cuts:

For larger cuts that are bleeding profusely, you will want to proceed as follows:

Step 1. Apply pressure to stem the blood flow using a gauze pad or a clean washcloth (you may also use a new diaper or even your fingers if there is no gauze pad or washcloth available). Continue to apply pressure and use more pads if bleeding persists until the flow of blood is reduced or stops.

Step 2. If the bleeding stops, apply a loose, non-stick bandage to the area and proceed to the doctor's office or emergency room. Do NOT apply anything else to a large/deep wound – no antiseptic rinse, no antibiotic cream. Keep the temporary bandage loose and not tight to promote circulation until you get to the pediatric provider.

For such large/deep cuts, the provider may use a skin glue (Dermabond) or stitches (sutures) to close the wound. Head wounds that occur at or near the face may require a follow-up appointment with a plastic surgeon for evaluation.

Note that head wounds with massive bleeding (gushing or rhythmic pumping of blood out of the wound) will require calling 911 for emergency medical attention.

b. Serious head trauma

Serious head traumas usually involve a hard blow to the head or a bad fall landing on the head. These may also be seen in babies who are involved in motor vehicle accidents (MVAs). Some have been associated with child abuse. Fortunately, these are not very common in babies. It is not unusual for a baby or child to initially appear to be fine after a serious head trauma because the symptoms may not manifest for several days. It is, therefore, imperative for the parent or caregiver to monitor a child very closely for the first 6 hours after a head trauma or injury and then continue monitoring over the next 24 hours. A brief loss of consciousness or drowsiness of no more than 2 to 3 hours after a head injury is considered okay and nothing to worry about.

Below are signs and symptoms of serious head trauma and would require calling 911 immediately if your baby shows any or a combination of these:

- **Non-arousable (prolonged loss of consciousness or difficulty being woken up)**: It is recommended that for the first 24 hours after a head injury, you check the baby every 1-2 hours during daytime naps and 2-3 times overnight. With each check, touch the baby and try to wake them up. If the baby is easily arousable, that is ok. However, if the baby is unresponsive and you are unable to wake the sleeping baby within 24 hours of a head injury, you should quickly check for breathing (up and down movement of the abdomen with breaths) and a brachial pulse (inner part of the elbow) and call 911. Be prepared to tell the 911 operator a brief background of the problem, the current condition of the baby, and your location. For example:

911 operator: 911, what is your emergency?

Parent: My baby fell off the bed and landed on his head this morning and now, I cannot wake him up. He is breathing, but his pulse is very weak. We live at 123 Oak Lane, and I need an ambulance.

- **Vomiting**: sudden onset of vomiting
- **"Raccoon eyes" (periorbital ecchymosis)** – black and blue discoloration appearing around the eyes or behind the ears. This is usually caused by a "basal skull fracture", that is, a fracture of the bottom part of the skull where the brain rests.
- **Unresponsive pupils**: Lack of pupillary response when light is shined into the eyes. This means that the pupils of the eyes do not shrink when you shine a pen light into them, and they also do not grow larger when the penlight is removed.
- **Unequal pupil size**: When the pupils of both eyes are observed and compared, they are not of the same size—one is more open (larger) than the other. Pupils are normally the same size.
- **Oozing of blood or watery fluid (serum) from nose and ears**: Blood or serum (blood without the blood cells) oozing from the baby's nose and ears.

- **Depressed skull area**: A depression or indentation in the skull
- **Absence of depression in swollen wound site**: There is a large swelling at the injury site, and you cannot detect a depression or indentation through that swelling.
- **Inability to move a limb (an arm and/or a leg)**: The baby's inability to move an arm and/or a leg, usually on one side of the body, is a cause for concern.
- **Dizziness or Impaired balance and coordination**: This is dizziness or a lack of balance that persists more than an hour post-injury. It is more easily observed in a toddler or child who can stand and walk than a newborn or infant.
- **Unusual and Persistent pallor**: This is paleness that persists for more than a few minutes post-injury.
- **Convulsions**: Convulsions or other seizure-like activity occurring after a head injury in a child with no prior history of convulsions is a serious cause for concern.
- **Atypical behavior**: The baby is behaving unusually, for example, unusual eye-rolling, clumsy or uncoordinated movements; appears confused or dazed, appears not to recognize familiar faces, and so on.

What to do: (1) After calling 911 for help, try not to move the baby, especially if you suspect that there may be a neck injury. (2) Talk gently and calmly to the baby and keep the baby lying quietly on a flat surface with the head turned to one side. (3) Do not offer any food or drink if the baby is awake and conscious. (4) Begin CPR if the baby is not breathing and/or does not have a pulse. (*Note: This author highly recommends that all parents and caregivers take the CPR certification course.*)

INFANT CHOKING EMERGENCY

Disclaimer: This section provides general information and guidance on infant choking and does not replace a formal approved course on infant basic life support (BLS) and emergency resuscitative care. The author highly recommends that parents/caregivers undertake formal training on these infant emergency resuscitative concepts, such as those courses approved by the American Heart Association (AHA) and the Red Cross.

The first sign of choking in an infant is usually coughing, which is the body's natural way of attempting to clear the airway or dislodge an obstruction from the throat or airway.

If a baby (infant) is choking and coughing, allow him/her to cough for 2-3 minutes. If after 2 to 3 minutes, the baby continues to cough, proceed with the following steps:

Step 1. Assess the baby for the following signs and symptoms:

- the baby continues to cough, but no sounds come out
- the baby begins to struggle for breath, makes high-pitched crowing sounds, and ceases to cry
- the baby begins to turn blue around the lips, mouth, and fingertips/fingernails
- the baby stops breathing, becomes motionless, and may or may not have a pulse

Step 2. Call 911 (if alone) or ask someone else nearby to call 911 (if another person is nearby) for emergency medical assistance. *If the baby is unconscious, skip to step 7 after step 2.*

Step 3. Positioning for back slaps: Position the baby on your dominant forearm face-up with the infant's head resting on your hand. Place your other hand (non-dominant) hand on top of the baby so that the baby's jaw rests between and is supported by your thumb and fingers. Turn the baby over on your arm such that he/she is now face down, supported on your forearm. Lower the arm holding the baby onto your thigh so that the baby is upside down with the baby's head positioned lower than the chest and the rest of the body.

Step 4. Give back slaps (back blows): Administer back blows (forceful slaps) in a downward direction between the baby's shoulder blades using the heel of your free dominant hand and with sufficient force aimed at dislodging the foreign object from the throat and out the mouth. After giving 5 back slaps, proceed to Step 5 (positioning for chest thrusts).

Step 5. Positioning for chest thrusts: Next, turn the baby from the facedown position used for back slaps to a faceup positioning with the back of the baby's head and nape of the neck supported between the thumb and other fingers on your non-dominant hand. Lower the non-dominant arm that is supporting the baby onto your opposite thigh. Ideally, the baby's head should be lower than the chest because this will assist in dislodging the foreign object from the throat or airway.

Step 6. Give chest thrusts: Locate the correct place to give chest thrusts – the breastbone (located at the center of an imaginary line running across the baby's chest from one nipple to the other. Administer chest thrusts by using the pads of 2 or 3 fingers to push down (depress) the breastbone at the center of the chest to a depth of about one and a half (1.5 inches), which is about One-third the depth of the baby's chest, then releasing the chest to recoil to its normal position. One complete depress and release motion is considered one chest thrust. Perform a total of 5 chest thrusts, then re-position again to do back blows.

Maintain a back-and-forth repetition of 5 back blows followed by 5 chest thrusts until the object is dislodged, and the airway is cleared, allowing the baby to cough, cry, and breathe OR become unconscious. If, at this point, the baby becomes unconscious, perform step 2 (call 911), then return to step 7 to continue.

Step 7. Perform a foreign body check ("finger sweep"): Open the baby's mouth and look for the foreign object. If you can see a foreign object and it is easily removable, use one finger to sweep across the inside of the mouth (finger sweep) to remove the object.

Step 8. Give 2 rescue breaths: Gently tilt back the baby's head while lifting the chin (head tilt-chin lift) – this opens up the unconscious baby's airway. Place your mouth over the baby's mouth to form a seal and give 2 rescue breaths. Successfully delivered rescue breaths will cause the baby's chest to rise and fall with each rescue breath. If there is no chest rise and fall with your rescue breaths, reposition the baby's head by adjusting the head-tilt chin-lift position, and try again. If repeat rescue breaths do not produce any chest rise and fall, begin infant CPR right away as you await the arrival of EMS.

Remember: For unconscious, unresponsive, and non-breathing babies, skip steps 3-6 after steps 1-2, and proceed with step 7 (performing a foreign-body check followed by a finger sweep if an obstructing object is visible).

(Images: Back blows, Chest thrusts, Finger sweeps)

11.19Infant Anaphylaxis Emergency

Epinephrine is the recommended emergency treatment for infant anaphylaxis. It quickly reverses the life-threatening symptoms of anaphylaxis. The general recommendation for treating an anaphylactic emergency is as follows: When available, epinephrine should be given immediately to the infant or child experiencing anaphylactic symptoms, followed by a call to 911 and a trip to the emergency department.

What to do after giving an infant or child epinephrine (Epi):	
Action	Details, Explanations & Rationales
Note what time the 1st **dose** of Epi was given	This is information that will be useful for the EMTs when they arrive
Call 911	Call 911 and ask for an ambulance with epinephrine. When they arrive, tell the rescue EMT squad when the epinephrine was last given.
Stay with the child	Stay with the child and continue to monitor symptoms. Be prepared to reposition the child if it appears that the airway is compromised.
Give a 2nd **dose** of Epi, if...	**Give a second dose of epinephrine** if symptoms worsen, continue, or do not improve in 5 minutes.
Keep the child lying on his/her back, but...	Keep the child lying on his/her back, but if the child vomits or has trouble breathing, the keep the child lying on his or her **side.**
If the child is awake & stable, you may give other Rx medications...	You may give other prescribed medications, such as the child's bronchodilator/inhaler or an antihistamine, but **never replace Epi with another medicine during anaphylactic emergencies.**

BREATHING EMERGENCIES & LOSS OF CONSCIOUSNESS

Following is an abridged summary of what to do to provide cardiopulmonary resuscitative (CPR) care for an infant experiencing an emergency. Be advised that the summary below is NOT a certification for CPR.

How to provide CPR on an infant (newborn to one year old)

You Arrive on the Scene

Step 1. Check the scene for safety.

Actions:

(1) Check the infant for consciousness.

(2) Gently tap the infant's shoulder or tap/flick the bottom of the heel and shout out loud enough to arouse the infant.

Step 2. If No Response

Actions:

(1) Call 911 immediately.

(2) If the infant is lying prone on his or her stomach, turn the infant over onto his or her back (supine position). The infant must be lying supine on a hard, flat surface while performing CPR.

Step 3. Check for Breathing and Signs of Life

Actions:

(1) Watch the infant's chest for any normal breathing movement. **Look for signs of life and breathing for no more than 10 seconds.**

Step 4. If No Breathing or Signs of Life

Actions:

Begin CPR

Begin CPR as follows:

a. Place two or three fingers of the dominant hand on the center of the infant's breastbone, just below the nipple line.

b. Push down firmly to compress the chest 1½ inches in depth and release. Repeat 30 times.

c. After giving compressions 30 times, give 2 breaths: Tilt the infant's head back slightly by placing one hand on the forehead and lifting up on the infant's chin with two fingers of the other hand. Cover both the infant's nose and mouth with your mouth and give two small, slow breaths, watching for a rise of the infant's chest.

d. Continue with 30 compressions / two breaths and 30 compressions / two breaths in repeating cycles.

Step 5. Continue CPR until another rescuer takes over, you see signs of life, or help arrives.

(*CPR for Infants*, 2019)

Note: Comprehensive coverage of CPR and other emergency resuscitative care is beyond the scope of this book. The author recommends that the reader enroll in an infant CPR course to gain the full practical advantage of this topic.

12

VACCINE-PREVENTABLE INFECTIONS OF NEWBORNS AND INFANTS

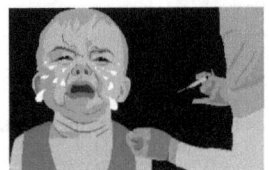

"Preventing childhood diseases is not just a health issue, it's an investment in our future [because] healthy children today build a stronger society tomorrow".

— BILL GATES

It is estimated that approximately 6.6 million children die each year, and about fifty percent of these deaths are attributed to infections, including pneumonia and diarrhea, which could be prevented by vaccination (Greenwood, 2014). Scientists and medical professionals generally agree that vaccination has made the most significant contribution to global health of any human intervention, aside from the introduction of clean water and sanitation. This view is supported by the fact that death from smallpox and measles was rampant in the pre-vaccination period, with up to half of the population dying from the former during epidemics (Greenwood, 2014). The development and application of vaccination as a public health mechanism is credited to Edward Jenner and his experiments with cowpox in 1796. Since then, the vaccine development process has evolved and improved over many centuries, with the United States and Europe leading the way in embracing the disease-prevention strategy. In fact, according to Andre et al. (2008), vaccination has greatly reduced the burden of infectious diseases, and only clean water, also considered a basic human right, performs better.

The Centers for Disease Control and Prevention (CDC) is a globally recognized authority in public health that plays a fundamental role in developing and broadcasting vaccination guidelines to ensure optimal protection against a wide array of potentially life-threatening infections. According to the CDC, vaccination remains one of the most effective strategies in preventing infectious diseases, especially by shielding the vulnerable population of newborns and infants who have yet to develop a robust, mature immune system (CDC, 2023). The World Health Organization (WHO) agrees by stating that immunization is one of modern medicine's greatest success stories and, therefore, expanding access to immunization is crucial to achieving the WHO's Sustainable Development Goals (SDGs) because in addition to preventing sickness and death associated with infectious diseases such as diarrhea, measles, pneumonia, polio and whooping cough, effective immunization strategies also result in broader gains in education and economic development (WHO, 2019).

This chapter draws upon the latest research findings, clinical studies, and epidemiological data to offer insights into the significance of timely vaccinations in establishing a robust immune defense during the critical stages of infancy. The information provided in this chapter is grounded in the authoritative guidelines and evidence-based immunization recommendations provided by the CDC. The CDC's Advisory Committee on Immunization Practices (ACIP) regularly reviews and streamlines clinical immunization guidelines to replicate the most current scientific advancements and epidemiological trends. By integrating these guidelines into this chapter, the author hopes to empower parents, healthcare practitioners, and policymakers with the knowledge required to make informed decisions regarding vaccinating newborns and infants.

Despite the historical and scientific evidence supporting the efficacy of immunization, there are individuals and groups with strong opposing views. The anti-vaccination campaign is not a new phenomenon. Its origin dates back to the very origins of immunization, with a history of diverse and sometimes surprising supporters, including Alfred Russel Wallace, the co-discoverer of evolution (Greenwood, 2014). Today, the "anti-vax" campaign boasts prominent and influential societal figures, including politicians, sports superstars, musicians, socialites, and prominent actors and actresses, to mention but a few.

The position of the publishers of this book regarding the conundrum of "to vax" or "not to vax" is non-judgmental. While we recommend immunization and other scientifically proven infection prevention methods, we understand and respect every family's religious, cultural, and personal beliefs, especially the right of each parent/guardian to make decisions they feel are best for their child/ward.

CDC Recommendations for Infant and Childhood Immunization

The CDC advises that infants and children should be vaccinated against diphtheria, *Hemophilus influenzae type b* (Hib), hepatitis A and hepatitis B viruses, human papillomavirus, influenza, mumps, measles, rubella, Neisseria meningitidis, pertussis, polio, rotavirus, Streptococcus pneumoniae, tetanus, and varicella (CDC *Yellow Book*, 2024). For the purposes of this book, however, the discussion will be limited to only those vaccines that are recommended for newborns and infants. Therefore, the following vaccines will not be covered here: HPV vaccine and Neisseria meningitis vaccine.

Vaccine Information Statements (VIS)

Vaccine Information Statements (VISs), formerly known as Vaccine Information Sheets, are information sheets produced by the CDC that explain the vaccine's benefits and risks to the vaccine recipients (Vaccine Information Statement, 2019). A United States federal law titled the National Vaccine Childhood Injury Act requires that healthcare providers (both public and private providers) who order and administer vaccines must give the appropriate VIS to the patient, their parent, or their legal guardian/representative before each/every dose of the specific vaccines. It is important to remember that the appropriate VIS must be given **before the vaccination and before each dose** if it is a multi-dose series. The VIS must be given **regardless of the age** of the recipient/patient. More facts about VISs, including where to find and how to use them, can be found on the CDC website: https://www.cdc.gov/vaccines/hcp/vis/about/facts-vis.html#law.

Next, we will delve into the various vaccine-preventable illnesses of newborns and infants and how to handle them.

HEPATITIS B

Hepatitis B is a viral infection that remains a significant public health concern, particularly in newborns and infants.

Cause: The causative organism of hepatitis B infection is the hepatitis B virus (HBV), an enveloped, partially double-stranded DNA virus assigned to the Hepadnaviridae family of viruses (Chang, 2007).

Target: The Liver. HBV primarily targets the liver, resulting in a spectrum of liver diseases that range from acute infection to chronic conditions. It is pertinent to note that newborns and infants are at heightened risk of illness and death from HBV due to their developing immune system, which makes them more susceptible to the long-term effects of hepatitis B infection.

Mode of transmission: HBV is disseminated among the population through contact with *infected blood or body fluids*, as occurs during pregnancy or delivery, through sex, or by injection drug use (IDU), with the most notable risk for lingering infection occurring during perinatal infection, Conners et al (CDC Recommendations, 2023). HBV infection can be transmitted either vertically (also known as perinatally, from mother to child during pregnancy or childbirth) or horizontally from an infected person to the child through exposure to infected blood and body fluids (Chang, 2007). Furthermore, exposure to contaminated instruments during medical procedures or unsafe injections can contribute to transmitting the virus in healthcare settings. Perinatal transmission from highly infectious mothers to their neonates is a medically significant route for HBV infection (Chang, 2007) and is the route of concern for this discussion. The primary medium or source of transmission of concern for newborn and infant HBV infection is through contact with infected blood and other bodily fluids.

Signs and symptoms: The signs and symptoms of hepatitis B in newborns and infants may vary significantly. Some may not show any symptoms at all (that is, these babies remain asymptomatic). In contrast, others may exhibit the following: jaundice, dark urine, pale stools, and, in severe cases, liver failure. Moms need to remember that an infected baby may not show symptoms immediately. This emphasizes the importance of timely diagnosis of the disease and intervention.

What the child looks like: The symptomatic infant appears pale with a yellowish tinge to the skin (jaundice) and passes dark-colored urine and pale-colored stools.

Diagnosis: Serological screening tests that detect viral markers in the blood are used to diagnose HBV in newborns and infants. These markers include hepatitis B surface antigen (HBsAg) and antibodies to hepatitis B antigens such as anti-HBs and anti-HBc. To confirm a preliminary positive test, molecular techniques such as polymerase chain reaction (PCR) may be used to detect the presence of viral DNA.

Treatment: There is currently no available efficacious treatment for children with chronic HBV infection and who have normal alanine aminotransferase (ALT) liver enzyme, but for children with elevated ALT enzyme that is greater than 2 times the upper limit of the normal range, ***interferon-α*** or ***nucleoside analogue therapy*** can be used to reduce the viral load (Chang, 2007). Generally, treatment for hepatitis B in newborns and infants is primarily supportive because the immune system often clears the infection spontaneously. In cases of chronic infection, antiviral medications may be considered under the supervision of a healthcare professional. Regular monitoring is crucial to assess the progression of the infection and determine the need for intervention.

Prevention/Vaccine: Prevention is the most cost-effective method for successfully controlling HBV infection and its complications (Chang, 2007). Prevention of hepatitis B in newborns and infants is achieved through vaccination with the Hepatitis B vaccine (Hep B vaccine), which is a critical component of routine childhood immunization programs. The Hep B vaccine is administered in a series of doses, with the first dose given shortly after birth. The vaccine plays a dual role: it protects infants from acquiring the infection, and it helps prevent the development of chronic hepatitis B and its associated complications.

The ACIP Recommendations for HBV testing and immunization:

The ACIP recommendation for Hepatitis B Virus testing for pregnant women and immunization for infants is quoted as follows:

"ACIP recommends testing all pregnant women for hepatitis B surface antigen (HBsAg), and testing HBsAg-positive pregnant women for hepatitis B virus deoxyribonucleic acid (HBV DNA); administration of HepB vaccine and hepatitis B immune globulin (HBIG) for infants born to HBV-infected women within 12 hours of birth, followed by completion of the vaccine series and postvaccination serologic testing; universal hepatitis B vaccination within 24 hours of birth, followed by completion of the vaccine series." (Schillie et al, 2018).

> **Box 1:**
>
> **Hepatitis B virus screening and testing recommendations — CDC, 2023**
>
> **Universal hepatitis B virus (HBV) screening**
>
> - HBV screening at least once during a lifetime for adults aged ≥18 years (new recommendation)
> - During screening, test for hepatitis B surface antigen (HBsAg), antibody to HBsAg, and total antibody to HBcAg (total anti-HBc) (new recommendation)
>
> **Screening pregnant persons**
>
> - HBV screening for all pregnant persons during each pregnancy, preferably in the first trimester, regardless of vaccination status or history of testing*
> - Pregnant persons with a history of appropriately timed triple panel screening and without subsequent risk for exposure to HBV (i.e., no new HBV exposures since triple panel screening) only need HBsAg screening
>
> **Risk-based testing**
>
> - Testing for all persons with a history of increased risk for HBV infection, regardless of age, if they might have been susceptible during the period of increased risk†
> - Periodic testing for susceptible persons, regardless of age, with ongoing risk for exposures, while risk for exposures persists†
>
> * **Source:** Schillie S, Vellozzi C, Reingold A, et al. Prevention of hepatitis B virus infection in the United States: Recommendations of the Advisory Committee on Immunization Practices. MMWR Recomm Rep 2018;67(No. RR-1):1–31.
>
> † Susceptible persons include those who have never been infected with HBV (i.e., total anti-HBc negative) and either did not complete a HepB vaccine series per Advisory Committee on Immunization Practices recommendations or who are known to be vaccine non-responders.

ROTAVIRUS

Rotavirus is a highly contagious virus that most often infects infants and young children, causing severe diarrhea and vomiting. According to the World Health Organization (WHO), this disease is of significant public health importance because it is a leading cause of severe gastroenteritis in newborns and infants with the potential to cause severe dehydration and morbidity in this vulnerable population. Also, according to the Centers for Disease Control and Prevention (CDC), rotavirus is a leading cause of severe diarrhea in infants and young children worldwide, which results in an estimated 128,500 deaths annually (CDC, 2021).

Cause: The infection is caused by Rotavirus. LeClair & McConnell (2023) describe Rotavirus as a double-stranded RNA virus that has a spiral-shaped ("wheel-shaped") appearance when viewed under an electron microscope. It is considered to be the leading cause of acute gastroenteritis in the world and the leading cause of severe gastroenteritis in children less than 5 years of age (LeClair & McConnell, 2023).

Target: The Rotavirus targets and attacks the gastrointestinal system (tummy), also known as the GI tract or gut. Infected persons will release particles of the virus in their feces (poop). When unwashed hands that have touched poop or when toys and other objects that have touched poop are placed in or around the mouth of a child, the child can become infected. A person with rotavirus can infect others before they start having symptoms. However, an infected person is most infectious to others when they have started showing symptoms and during the first three days after recovery (CDC, 2021).

Mode of transmission: The rotavirus is transmitted through the fecal-oral route, typically by ingestion of fecal-contaminated food, water, or fomites (including objects like toys and play areas).

This typically happens when:

- unwashed hands that are contaminated with poop are placed in the mouth or used to prepare food
- a person touches contaminated objects or surfaces and then puts their finger(s) in the mouth

- a person eats contaminated food or drinks contaminated water (this is not a standard method of transmission of this particular virus)

With this in mind, thorough handwashing is the most essential cornerstone for reducing the risk of contamination and infection by rotavirus. For bottle-fed infants, the parent or caregiver should hand-sanitize with alcohol-based hand sanitizer or perform vigorous handwashing with soap and water for at least 20 seconds before preparing the baby's food. Hands should be washed with soap and water after diaper changes. Further proactive efforts to prevent infection include washing or wiping toys and other surfaces in the infant's play area with germicidal wipes. Packing a potable bottle of alcohol-based hand sanitizer and germicidal wipes in your baby's diaper bag is advised as a proactive preventative measure. Also, dirty diapers should be wrapped appropriately and properly disposed of immediately. If you are unable to dispose of a poopy diaper right away, be sure to wrap it up in a plastic bag and place it in another sealable plastic bag, and hold it in a separate compartment of your diaper until you are able to dispose of as soon as possible.

Signs and Symptoms: Symptoms of rotavirus infection include watery diarrhea, vomiting, fever, and abdominal pain. These symptoms can lead to severe dehydration very quickly in newborns and infants, with serious and sometimes fatal consequences if not treated promptly and aggressively (CDC, 2021). Symptoms typically start about two days after a person is exposed to rotavirus, and the vomiting and watery diarrhea that follows can last between three to eight days (CDC, 2021).

What the child looks like: The infected baby appears pale, weak, and irritable. Babies may show signs of abdominal pain by flexing their legs and arms forward in a protective posture towards the abdomen. They may also cry out when the belly is touched or during movement. The most significant symptoms are vomiting and watery diarrhea, and should be a signal to take the child to the emergency room right away. The CDC reports that incidences of rotavirus infection in infants and children are seen more during the winter and spring seasons (January through June).

Diagnosis: To diagnose rotavirus infection, the parent or caregiver is asked to collect a stool (poop) sample from the baby in a labeled specimen container, and the sample is sent to the lab to test for the presence of the virus. Any one of several testing methods may be used to test for the virus in the lab, and these include enzyme immunoassay (which is the most common testing method used today), latex agglutination, electron microscopy, or by viral culture *[Rotavirus Workup: Laboratory Studies.* (n.d.)]. This testing is crucial because it helps confirm the diagnosis and guides the healthcare team in making treatment decisions.

Treatment: Currently, there is no effective treatment for rotavirus infection. According to the World Health Organization (WHO), the primary treatment for rotavirus infection is focused on preventing and treating dehydration caused by diarrhea and vomiting. These symptoms are managed by supportive measures and interventions such as oral rehydration therapy (ORT), which helps replace lost fluids and electrolytes, or by giving intravenous (IV) fluids for severe cases.

Prevention/Vaccine: Although good hygiene practices like handwashing and cleanliness are important and encouraged, they are not enough to control the spread of the disease. Rotavirus vaccination is the best way to protect your child from contracting the rotavirus infection. Currently, two rotavirus vaccines are approved and licensed by the FDA for infants in the United States. They are:

- RotaTeq® is given in three doses at ages 2 months, 4 months, and 6 months
- Rotarix® is given in two doses at ages 2 months and 4 months

The rotavirus vaccines are given by mouth – drops of the vaccine are placed in the baby's mouth.

The CDC's schedule recommendation for the rotavirus vaccination is 3 doses in infancy at 2, 4, and 6 months of age (CDC, 2023, November 16). Research has shown the rotavirus vaccine to be highly effective in reducing the severity and hospitalizations associated with the disease. Since the vaccine was developed and used in many countries, the associated disease burden has significantly reduced worldwide. However, the author encourages parents and caregivers to discuss and compare the benefits versus the potential risks of vaccination with their healthcare provider to make informed decisions.

POLIOMYELITIS ("POLIO")

Polio (also known as poliomyelitis) is a disabling and life-threatening disease that can find its way to and infect the spinal cord (and sometimes the brain), possibly causing serious symptoms that may eventually result in some degree of paralysis. Polio is caused by the poliovirus. Most people infected with the poliovirus show no symptoms at all. In contrast, others may experience minor symptoms such as sore throat, fever, tiredness, nausea, headache, or stomach pain and eventually recover without complications. A smaller group of people, however, will develop the following more serious symptoms that affect the brain and spinal cord: (a) Paresthesia (a feeling of pins and needles in the legs), (b) Meningitis (an infection of the sheet-like covering of the spinal cord and/or brain), (c) Paralysis (numbness and immobility of parts of the body), or (d) weakness in the arms, legs, or both.

The most severe and significant symptom associated with poliomyelitis disease is paralysis because it can lead to permanent disability and death. Sometimes, improvements in the limb paralysis associated with polio infection may occur over time. However, it has also been documented that in some other reported cases, infected individuals have developed new muscle pain and muscle weakness or flaccidity 15 to 40 years after the initial polio infection or exposure. Furthermore, some polio victims suffer chronic fatigue for the rest of their lives. These long-term sequelae of polio are collectively called "post-polio syndrome."

Cause: The causative agent for polio is the poliovirus, a highly contagious virus that primarily affects the nervous system. The poliovirus enters the body through the oral route (the mouth), typically through ingestion of contaminated food or water or by contact with an infected person's feces.

Target Organ/Tissues: The poliovirus primarily targets the spinal cord and the brainstem by disrupting motor neurons responsible for muscle movement. This results in muscle weakness, paralysis, and potentially life-threatening complications such as respiratory failure.

Mode of Transmission: The poliovirus is transmitted primarily through the fecal-oral route. This means that the virus is spread through the ingestion of contaminated food, water, or objects/surfaces (fomites). Person-to-person transmission can also occur through direct contact with respiratory droplets (from sneezes, coughs, and so on) from an infected individual.

Epidemiological Distribution: Polio has been eliminated from the United States since the introduction of the polio vaccine in 1955. Prior to that, It was very common in the United States, paralyzing and killing thousands of people every year. Although it has been eliminated from the United States, it still occurs in other parts of the world, especially in developing regions like South Asia and Africa.

Signs and Symptoms: Most polio infections are asymptomatic or cause mild flu-like symptoms. However, when symptoms are present, they may start with a mild fever and a painful (sore) throat about 6 to 20 days after exposure to the virus. Children may also briefly feel discomfort or numbness in their back, neck, and legs. An infected person is most contagious 7 to 10 days before symptoms appear, and they are capable of infecting others for another 7 to 10 days. Notably, in a small percentage of polio cases, the virus attacks the nervous system, leading to paralysis. Paralysis causes severe muscle pain. In general, symptoms of paralytic polio include the following: muscle pain, stiffness, weakness, and characteristic paralysis that typically affects the legs more than the arms.

What the Child Looks Like: In severe cases of paralytic polio, affected children may exhibit muscle wasting, deformities, and difficulty walking or standing. They may also experience respiratory distress if the muscles responsible for breathing are affected, leading to shallow breathing or even respiratory failure.

Diagnosis: The pediatric PCP diagnoses polio using a combination of clinical evaluation, medical history, and laboratory tests. Physical examination may reveal signs of muscle weakness or paralysis, particularly asymmetrical limb involvement (one limb involved to a different extent than the other). Laboratory tests, including throat swabs, stool samples, or cerebrospinal fluid analysis, may also be performed to detect the presence of the poliovirus.

Treatment: There is currently no cure for polio. While some children may fully recover from the disease, others may face lifelong disabilities or even death. Although there is no cure for polio infection, it can be prevented by vaccination with the polio vaccine. The best way to protect yourself and keep the United States polio-free is to maintain high herd immunity (group protection) in the population against polio through vaccination.

Prevention/Vaccine: The best protection against polio is the polio vaccine. In the United States, the inactivated polio vaccine (IPV) is the only vaccine recommended. By trained health workers, IPV is given as an intra-muscular shot (injection into a muscle). The polio vaccine can be administered either as a single vaccine or as part of a combination vaccine (whereby several vaccines are combined together into one shot). In other words, the polio vaccine may be given simultaneously with other vaccines with no significant negative effects.

Polio Vaccine schedule for kids: According to the CDC's recommended vaccination schedule, children should get four (4) doses of polio vaccine at 2 months, 4 months, 6–18 months, and 4–6 years of age.

DIPHTHERIA

Cause: Diphtheria is a bacterial infection caused by the organism *Corynebacterium diphtheriae*, which produces toxins that affect the respiratory system. The toxins released by the bacteria cause inflammation and the formation of a thick, grayish membrane in the throat and nose, leading to airway obstruction and other complications.

Target: Diphtheria is a disease that primarily affects/targets the respiratory system, particularly the throat and upper airways. The toxins produced by the bacteria can also damage other organs, including the heart and nervous system, leading to serious complications such as myocarditis and neuropathy

Mode of Transmission: Diphtheria is spread through respiratory droplets or direct contact with an infected person's respiratory secretions. It can also be transmitted indirectly by contacting contaminated objects or surfaces (fomites). Crowded living conditions, poor hygiene practices, and lack of vaccination contribute to the spread of the disease.

Signs and Symptoms: Symptoms of diphtheria can vary depending on the seriousness of the infection. Initially, individuals may experience sore throat, fever, and swollen glands in the neck. As the infection progresses, a thick, grayish membrane may develop in the throat, causing difficulty breathing, swallowing, and speaking. In severe cases, diphtheria can lead to complications such as myocarditis, paralysis, and even death.

Following infection, diphtheria can induce mild fever, sore throat, and chills in the affected child after a few days. Fatigue, accompanied by a nasal discharge (rhinorrhea) and a thick gray membrane covering the throat, may also develop. If not treated quickly, the infection can spread a toxin called the C. diphtheriae toxin throughout the body. This toxin causes very serious problems, including difficulty swallowing, paralysis, and heart failure.

What the Child Looks Like: Due to the systemic effects of the infection, children with diphtheria may appear pale, weak, and lethargic. A characteristic grayish membrane in the throat and nose is a hallmark feature of diphtheria. As the disease progresses, affected children may exhibit signs of respiratory distress, including rapid breathing, cyanosis (bluish discoloration of the skin), and difficulty swallowing.

Diagnosis: Diagnosing diphtheria involves a combination of clinical evaluation, laboratory tests, and microbiological culture of samples from the throat, nose, or skin lesions. The presence of the characteristic membrane in the throat and identification of Corynebacterium diphtheriae bacteria or their toxins in culture specimens confirm the diagnosis.

Treatment: Prompt treatment of diphtheria is essential to prevent complications and reduce the spread of the disease. Treatment typically involves (a) administering antibiotics to eliminate the bacteria and (b) administering antitoxin to neutralize the toxins produced by the bacteria. Supportive care is imperative for managing diphtheria, including respiratory support, hydration, and monitoring for complications, which may be necessary, particularly in severe cases.

Prevention/Vaccine: Vaccination is the most effective strategy for preventing diphtheria. The diphtheria vaccine is typically administered in childhood as part of the combination vaccine known as the DTaP (diphtheria, tetanus, and acellular pertussis) vaccine. Thanks to this vaccine, there are currently very few cases of diphtheria in the United States AAP. 2015). Booster doses of the vaccine, often combined with tetanus and pertussis vaccines (Tdap), are recommended for adolescents and adults to maintain immunity against diphtheria. Vaccination protects individuals from diphtheria, helps prevent outbreaks, and helps maintain community herd immunity. Regular vaccination following recommended schedules is crucial for comprehensive protection against diphtheria and its potentially devastating consequences.

TETANUS

Tetanus is also known as "lockjaw" which comes from the rigidity or clenching of the muscles around the jaw of an infected person/child that prevents the affected individual from opening his or her mouth or swallowing. It's a severe and potentially deadly infection triggered by a toxin produced by the bacterium Clostridium tetani, commonly found in soil and capable of contaminating wounds. Any open wound, regardless of size, presents a potential entry point for tetanus infection. However, the risk is higher with deep puncture wounds or those contaminated with dirt, feces, or soil. A child who sustains an injury from a soiled garden tool or debris propelled by a lawnmower might contract tetanus if they have not received adequate immunization. Similarly, a newborn could be at risk of infection if the umbilical cord is exposed to contamination during cutting with an unsterilized tool.

Tetanus is **not contagious** and cannot be spread from person to person. Because healthcare providers frequently prescribe tetanus immunizations, tetanus is very rare in the United States, with only a few dozen cases reported each year (AAP, 2015 November). These are usually non-immunized individuals or those who have not kept up with the recommended booster dose every 10 years.

Cause: Tetanus is a potentially life-threatening bacterial infection caused by the bacterium *Clostridium tetani*, commonly found in soil, dust, and manure. The bacterium produces a potent neurotoxin that affects the nervous system, leading to severe muscle spasms, rigidity, and possibly death.

Target: The target organs of tetanus infection are nerves and muscles, especially those controlling voluntary movement. The neurotoxin released by *Clostridium tetani* binds to nerve endings, interfering with neurotransmitter release and causing uncontrolled muscle contractions.

Mode of transmission: Tetanus is typically transmitted by introducing Clostridium tetani spores into the body through puncture wounds, lacerations, or other types of open wounds contaminated with soil or animal feces. These spores can germinate in anaerobic (oxygen-deprived) environments such as deep wounds, allowing the bacteria to proliferate and produce the powerful and potentially deadly toxin.

Signs and symptoms: Signs and symptoms of tetanus infection may include muscle stiffness, particularly in the jaw (lockjaw), neck, and abdominal muscles, difficulty swallowing, muscle spasms, fever, sweating, elevated blood pressure, and rapid heart rate. As the disease progresses, severe spasms can lead to respiratory failure and death if left untreated.

Symptoms of tetanus usually develop gradually over the first 1 to 2 weeks after a child's wound has been contaminated with spores of the tetanus bacteria. The affected child experiences twitching, clenching, or cramping of the jaw muscles (lockjaw), a headache, and generalized irritability. Furthermore, they undergo muscle tightening, pain, and spasms that escalate in intensity and extend to other areas of the body, such as the neck, shoulders, and back.

What the child looks like: Children affected by tetanus may exhibit muscle rigidity, clenched fists, and arching of the back due to muscle spasms. Their facial expression may appear fixed and drawn, and they may experience difficulty opening their mouth or swallowing.

Diagnosis: Diagnosis of tetanus is primarily based on clinical symptoms and history of exposure to contaminated wounds. Laboratory tests, such as wound cultures, may be performed to identify the presence of Clostridium tetani bacteria. However, diagnosis is often made based on clinical presentation and the characteristic symptoms of tetanus.

Treatment: Treatment for tetanus infection involves wound care to remove contaminated tissue, antibiotics to eradicate the bacteria, and administration of tetanus immunoglobulin to neutralize the circulating toxin. Symptomatic treatment includes muscle relaxants to alleviate spasms, sedatives to control agitation and supportive measures such as mechanical ventilation if respiratory muscles are affected.

Prevention/Vaccine: Preventive vaccination is crucial in preventing tetanus infection. The tetanus vaccine, typically administered as part of the combined tetanus-diphtheria-pertussis (Tdap) vaccine series, provides immunity against tetanus. Booster doses are recommended every 10 years to maintain immunity throughout life. Prompt wound care and tetanus vaccination following injury are essential preventive measures to reduce the risk of tetanus infection.

Preventive tips for parents/caregivers: If your child has a wound that may have been contaminated with soil, it is crucial to contact your pediatric PCP as soon as possible, especially if you are unsure about the child's immunization status.

Successful treatment of tetanus infection is possible if the disease is detected and managed quickly. If your child's pediatrician confirms or strongly suspects a tetanus infection, immediate hospitalization is likely, with placement in an intensive care unit. Treatment may involve prescribing antibiotics like metronidazole (Flagyl) or penicillin, along with an antitoxin medication. (AAP, 2015).

PERTUSSIS (WHOOPING COUGH)

Cause: Pertussis (commonly known as whooping cough) is a **highly contagious** respiratory infection that primarily affects the respiratory tract, particularly the airways, and lungs, leading to characteristic symptoms and complications. Pertussis is caused by the bacterium *Bordetella pertussis*. Whooping cough may begin like a common cold, but unlike a cold, the coughing can last for weeks or months.

Target: The target organs of pertussis infection are the respiratory tract's organs, including the trachea (windpipe) and bronchi (airways). Bordetella pertussis bacteria attach to the respiratory epithelial cells, releasing toxins that damage the airway linings and cause inflammation.

Mode of Transmission: Whooping cough is transmitted through respiratory droplets expelled when an infected person coughs, talks, or sneezes. Close contact with an infected individual, particularly in crowded or poorly ventilated environments, increases the risk of transmission. Pertussis is highly contagious. Infected individuals can disseminate the bacteria to others during the initial catarrhal (cold-like) stage and throughout the illness's paroxysmal (coughing) stage.

Signs and Symptoms: Signs and symptoms of whooping cough infection typically progress through three stages: (a) the catarrhal stage, characterized by mild respiratory symptoms similar to the common cold; (b) the paroxysmal stage, marked by severe, uncontrollable coughing fits often accompanied by a characteristic "whoop" sound as the child gasps for air; and (c) the convalescent stage, during which symptoms gradually subside but coughing may persist for weeks.

What the Child Looks Like: Children affected by pertussis may appear distressed and out of breath during coughing fits, with flushed or cyanotic (blue) skin due to oxygen deprivation. They may exhibit fatigue, poor feeding, and difficulty breathing during coughing episodes, and younger infants may experience apnea (brief pauses in breathing) or vomiting after coughing fits.

Diagnosis: The diagnosis of pertussis is primarily based on clinical symptoms and a history of exposure to infected individuals. Tests such as polymerase chain reaction (PCR) or culture of respiratory secretions might be conducted to verify the presence of Bordetella pertussis bacteria in the laboratory.

Treatment: Whooping cough is treated with antibiotics, typically macrolides such as azithromycin or clarithromycin, which eradicate the bacteria and reduce the severity and duration of symptoms. Treatment also involves providing supportive care, including adequate hydration, rest, and monitoring for complications such as pneumonia or dehydration, which is essential, particularly in infants and young children.

Prevention by Vaccination: The most important preventive measure against whooping cough is vaccination, and the CDC recommends whooping cough vaccination for everyone (CDC, 2019). The pertussis vaccine is typically administered in childhood as part of the combined diphtheria-tetanus-pertussis (DTaP) vaccine series. Booster doses, such as the tetanus-diphtheria-acellular pertussis (Tdap) vaccine, are recommended for adolescents and adults to maintain immunity and prevent transmission. Vaccination of pregnant individuals during each pregnancy is also recommended to provide passive immunity to newborns during the vulnerable period before they can receive their own vaccinations. Vaccination of close contacts, including family members and caregivers of infants, helps protect vulnerable individuals and prevent the spread of pertussis within communities.

Prevention by other means: Other preventive measures against pertussis (whooping cough) include:

- **Preventive antibiotics**: Preventive antibiotics, also known as post-exposure prophylaxis (PEP), are medicines given to someone who has been exposed to harmful bacteria in order to help prevent them from getting sick. For people exposed to whooping cough, the CDC recommends preventive antibiotics only if they: (a) Live with the person who has been diagnosed with whooping cough, or (b) if they are at increased risk for serious disease (for example, babies, people with certain medical conditions), or (c) if they will have close contact with someone who is at increased risk for serious disease (for example, women in their third trimester of pregnancy, people who work with or care for high-risk individuals).
- **Practicing good hygiene**: The CDC recommends practicing good hygiene to prevent the spread of whooping cough germs and other respiratory illnesses. Some of the ways to achieve that are (a) covering your cough or sneeze and (b) washing your hands often (practicing good hand hygiene). Proper hand washing following the CDC's hand hygiene guidelines includes

washing your hands often with soap and water for at least 20 seconds or using an alcohol-based hand sanitizer if soap and water are unavailable (CDC, 2019).

- **Temporary natural immunity from exposure**: Previous exposure to the whooping cough germs confers a temporary immunity. People who have gotten sick with whooping cough at some point do have some natural immunity (protection) against future whooping cough infections. But this protection is temporary. It is important to remember that getting sick with whooping cough does not provide lifelong protection. This is why getting vaccinated is recommended by the CDC for lasting protection against the disease, even if you have had whooping cough before (CDC, 2019).

HEMOPHILUS INFLUENZAE TYPE B INFECTIONS

Haemophilus influenzae type b (Hib) can cause a variety of infections. Most *Haemophilus influenzae type b* infections usually affect children under age 5 years but can also affect adults with certain medical conditions. Hib bacteria can cause mild illnesses such as ear infections or bronchitis. They can also cause severe illnesses such as blood infections (sepsis). Severe Hib infections are called "invasive Hib disease" and require in-patient treatment in a hospital. Prior to the introduction of the Hib vaccine, Hib disease was the primary cause of bacterial meningitis in children under 5 years old in the United States. (see Chapter 5, section 5.1 for a detailed discussion on meningitis infections).

Cause: Haemophilus influenzae type b (Hib) infection is caused by the bacterium *Haemophilus influenzae type b*, a gram-negative bacterium commonly found in the respiratory tract. While it can cause various infections, including pneumonia and meningitis, Hib primarily targets the respiratory tract and can spread to other organs through the bloodstream.

Target: The target organs of Hib infection are the respiratory tract, particularly the upper airways, and lungs, as well as the meninges (lining of the brain and spinal cord) in cases of invasive disease such as meningitis. Hib bacteria can also infect the lungs, blood, joints, and other tissues, leading to various clinical manifestations.

Mode of Transmission: Hib is transmitted through respiratory droplets expelled when an infected person coughs, sneezes, or talks. Close contact with an infected individual, particularly in crowded or poorly ventilated environments, increases the risk of transmission. Infants and young children are particularly susceptible to Hib infection, with the highest risk of severe disease occurring in those under five years of age.

Signs and Symptoms: Signs and symptoms of Hib infection vary depending on the site of infection. In cases of respiratory tract infection, symptoms may include fever, cough, difficulty breathing, and ear pain (otitis media). Invasive diseases, such as meningitis or septicemia, may present with more severe symptoms, including high fever, irritability, lethargy, vomiting, stiff neck, and seizures.

What the Child Looks Like: Children affected by Hib infection may appear unwell, with signs of systemic illness such as fever, irritability, poor feeding, and lethargy. In cases of invasive disease, they may exhibit specific symptoms related to the affected organ or tissue, such as neck stiffness in meningitis or joint pain in septic arthritis.

Diagnosis: Hib infection is diagnosed using a combination of clinical evaluation, medical history, and laboratory tests.

Laboratory tests, such as blood cultures, cerebrospinal fluid analysis, or imaging studies, may be performed to confirm the presence of Hib bacteria and assess the extent of infection.

Treatment: Treatment of Hib infection typically involves antibiotics, such as third-generation cephalosporins or ampicillin, to eliminate the bacteria and prevent complications. Supportive care is essential in managing Hib infections, especially in severe cases. It would include adequate hydration, fever management, and monitoring for complications such as meningitis or pneumonia.

Prevention/Vaccine: Preventive vaccination is crucial in preventing Hib infection and its potentially life-threatening complications. The Hib vaccine, typically administered as part of the routine childhood immunization schedule, provides immunity against Hib bacteria. Multiple doses of the vaccine are recommended to ensure adequate protection, with booster doses given as needed to maintain immunity throughout childhood. Vaccination of infants, starting at two months of age, helps protect against invasive Hib disease and reduces the risk of transmission within communities. Additionally, catch-up vaccination may be recommended for older children or individuals at increased risk of Hib infection.

CDC Vaccination guidelines for the Hib vaccine:

The Hib vaccine is usually given in three (3) or four (4) doses (depending on manufacturer/brand).

Infants: They get their first dose of the Hib vaccine at two (2) months of age and will usually finalize the series at 12–15 months of age.

Children between 12 months and 5 years of age: If they have not previously been completely vaccinated against Hib, they may need one (1) or more doses of the Hib vaccine.

Children over 5 years old and adults: Conventionally, this group does not typically receive Hib vaccine, but it might be advised for older children or adults whose spleens have been damaged or removed, including people with sickle cell disease, before surgery to remove the spleen, or following a bone marrow transplant. Hib vaccine may also be recommended for people 5 through 18 years old living with HIV.

The Hib vaccine can be administered either individually or as part of a combination vaccine, which combines more than one vaccine into one shot.

It is okay to give the Hib vaccine simultaneously with other vaccines.

STREPTOCOCCUS PNEUMONIAE

Cause: *Streptococcus pneumoniae* is a bacterium commonly found in the respiratory tract. It is a leading cause of various infections in young children, including pneumonia, meningitis, and otitis media. The bacteria can also invade the bloodstream, causing invasive pneumococcal disease. According to Olarte & Jackson (2021), in their investigative article on Streptococcus pneumoniae published in the journal *Pediatric in Review*, *Streptococcus pneumoniae* continues to be the most common cause of vaccine-preventable death in children worldwide.

Target: The primary target organs or tissues of Streptococcus pneumoniae infections are the respiratory tract (particularly the lungs and sinuses), the middle ear, the bloodstream, and the meninges (membranes) covering the brain and spinal cord.

Mode of Transmission: *Streptococcus pneumoniae* infection is transmitted through respiratory droplets expelled when an infected person coughs, sneezes, or talks. Close contact with an infected individual or contact with contaminated surfaces or objects may also facilitate disease transmission.

Signs and Symptoms: The signs and symptoms of *Streptococcus pneumoniae* infection typically vary depending on the site of infection. Common manifestations include fever, cough, chest pain, shortness of breath, headache, stiff neck, and altered mental status. In children, symptoms may include irritability, poor feeding, vomiting, and difficulty breathing

What the Child Looks Like: Children affected by *Streptococcus pneumoniae* infection may appear febrile and lethargic (tired and weak in appearance), with respiratory distress, such as rapid breathing or retractions (visible sinking of the skin between the ribs or under the ribcage during inhalation), indicating pneumonia or meningitis. In severe cases, they may exhibit signs of sepsis, such as pale or mottled skin, reduced urine output, and altered mental status.

Diagnosis: Diagnosis of *Streptococcus pneumoniae* infection often involves a combination of clinical evaluation, medical history, and laboratory tests. Laboratory tests, including blood cultures, cerebrospinal fluid analysis, and imaging studies such as chest X-rays, may be performed to confirm the diagnosis and to assess the extent of infection.

Treatment: Treatment of *Streptococcus pneumoniae* infection typically involves antibiotics, such as penicillin or cephalosporins, to eradicate the bacteria and prevent complications. In cases of invasive pneumococcal disease, hospitalization, and intravenous antibiotics may be necessary, along with supportive measures to manage symptoms and prevent complications.

Prevention/Vaccine: Preventive vaccination is essential in preventing *Streptococcus pneumoniae* infection and its complications. The incidence of invasive pneumococcal disease has significantly decreased with pneumococcal conjugate vaccines (Olarte & Jackson, 2021). The **pneumococcal conjugate vaccine (PCV)** and **pneumococcal polysaccharide vaccine (PPSV)** effectively provide immunity against pneumococcal disease. Vaccination against pneumococcal disease is recommended as part of routine childhood immunization schedules, with booster doses recommended for high-risk groups, such as older adults and individuals with certain medical conditions. Vaccination of close contacts, including family members and caregivers, also helps prevent the spread of *Streptococcus pneumoniae* within communities and protects vulnerable individuals.

INFLUENZA (FLU)

Influenza, more commonly known as "the flu," is a contagious respiratory illness caused by influenza viruses. It primarily affects the upper airway, including the nose and throat, but can also affect organs and structures of the lower respiratory tract, which includes the bronchial tree and the lungs, and can lead to a wide range of symptoms from mild to severe. The following population groups are more likely to suffer severe cases of the flu or to develop serious health complications from a flu infection: babies and young children; individuals with certain health conditions (such as asthma, COPD, diabetes, heart disease, and chronic kidney disease); and the elderly.

Cause: Influenza is caused by the influenza virus. There are two main types of influenza (flu) viruses: A and B. The influenza A and B viruses are responsible for the seasonal flu epidemics we experience yearly.

Target organs or tissues: Seasonal influenza infection targets the respiratory tract, particularly the upper and lower airways including the structures associated with them. Influenza viruses invade the respiratory epithelial cells, causing inflammation and damage to the mucous membranes.

Transmission route: The flu virus is transmitted from person to person through respiratory droplets expelled when an infected person coughs, sneezes, or talks. The virus can also spread by touching contaminated surfaces or objects and touching the mouth, nose, or eyes.

Signs and Symptoms: The signs and symptoms of seasonal influenza infection typically include fever, cough, sore throat, runny or stuffy nose, muscle or body aches, headache, fatigue, and occasionally vomiting or diarrhea, particularly among the pediatric population (children).

What the Child Looks Like: A child with a flu infection may appear lethargic, with flushed cheeks and watery eyes. They may experience respiratory symptoms such as coughing, sneezing, nasal congestion, and systemic symptoms such as fever, chills, and body aches.

Diagnosis: The diagnosis of seasonal influenza infection is often based on clinical symptoms and a history of exposure to individuals with influenza-like illness. Rapid influenza diagnostic tests (RIDTs) may be performed to confirm the presence of influenza viruses, although these tests may have limitations in sensitivity and specificity.

Treatment: Treatment of seasonal influenza focuses on symptom management and supportive care. Antiviral medications such as oseltamivir (Tamiflu) or zanamivir (Relenza) may be prescribed to reduce the severity and duration of symptoms, particularly in individuals at high risk of complications.

Prevention/Vaccine: Preventive vaccination reduces the risk of seasonal influenza infection and its associated complications. The influenza (flu) vaccine is updated annually to match circulating virus strains and is recommended by the CDC for all individuals aged **six months and older**. Vaccination offers protection against influenza viruses and reduces the likelihood of severe illness, hospitalization, and death. Vaccination of close contacts, including family members and caregivers, also helps prevent the spread of influenza within communities and protect vulnerable individuals, such as young children, older adults, and individuals with underlying health conditions.

MUMPS (PAROTITIS)

Mumps is a highly contagious disease caused by a virus that causes swelling of the salivary glands (parotitis), hence the characteristic puffy cheeks and tender, swollen jaw of affected individuals (CDC, 2019). The salivary glands are scientifically known as the parotid glands.

Cause: Mumps is caused by the mumps virus, which belongs to the Paramyxoviridae family of viruses. It primarily affects the salivary glands, leading to the characteristic facial swelling commonly associated with the disease, but it can also involve other organs and tissues, causing a range of symptoms.

Target: The salivary glands, particularly the parotid glands located on the sides of the face, are the target organs or tissues of mumps infection. The mumps virus infects and inflames the salivary glands, leading to swelling and tenderness.

Mode of Transmission: Mumps is transmitted through **respiratory droplets** expelled when an infected person coughs, sneezes, or talks. Close contact with an infected individual or contaminated surfaces or objects may also facilitate transmission.

Signs and Symptoms: The signs and symptoms of mumps typically include fever, headache, muscle aches, fatigue (tiredness), loss of appetite, and swelling and tenderness of one or both parotid glands, resulting in a characteristic "chipmunk-like" appearance. In some cases, mumps infection can lead to complications such as meningitis, encephalitis, orchitis (inflammation of the testicles), or oophoritis (inflammation of the ovaries).

Some long-term severe complications of mumps

- orchitis (swelling of the testicles) in males
- oophoritis (swelling of the ovaries) and/or mastitis (swelling of the breasts) in females
- encephalitis (swelling of the brain)
- meningitis (swelling of the tissue covering the brain and spinal cord)
- loss of hearing (temporary or permanent)

What the Child Looks Like: Children affected by mumps may exhibit swollen and tender cheeks due to parotid gland swelling. They may experience pain or discomfort when chewing or swallowing and appear fatigued or irritable due to systemic symptoms such as fever and muscle aches.

Diagnosis: The diagnosis of mumps is often based on clinical symptoms and a history of exposure to individuals with mumps-like illness. Laboratory tests, such as viral culture or polymerase chain reaction (PCR) testing of saliva or throat swabs, may be performed to confirm the presence of the mumps virus.

Treatment: The basis for treating mumps is primarily supportive and focuses on relieving symptoms. Bed rest, adequate hydration, and over-the-counter pain relievers such as acetaminophen or ibuprofen may help alleviate fever, pain, and discomfort. In severe complications, hospitalization and specialized care may be necessary.

Prevention/Vaccine: Preventive vaccination reduces the risk of mumps infection and its associated complications. The measles, mumps, and rubella (MMR) vaccine effectively provides immunity against mumps. Vaccination is typically administered in two doses, with the first dose given at 12-15 months of age and the second dose at 4-6 years of age. Vaccination of close contacts, including family members and caregivers, also helps prevent the spread of mumps within communities and protects vulnerable individuals from infection.

1st Dose MMR – age 12-15 months

2nd Dose MMR – age 4-6 years

MEASLES (RUBEOLA)

Measles, also known as rubeola, is an exceptionally transmissible infection caused by a virus that proliferates in the nose and throat mucus of an infected person and can spread to others through contact with tiny respiratory droplets that are suspended in the air during coughing and sneezing by the infected person. The measles virus can survive for up to two hours in respiratory droplets suspended in an airspace or on objects after an infected person leaves the area. Measles is so contagious that if one person gets infected, up to 90 percent of the people close to that person who are not immune will also become infected (CDC, 2019).

Cause: Measles is caused by the measles virus, which is a member of the viral Paramyxoviridae family. It primarily affects the respiratory system, causing many symptoms and potential complications.

Target: The target organs or tissues of measles infection are the **respiratory tract**, including the lungs and airways, as well as **the skin** and **mucous membranes**. The measles virus infects respiratory epithelial cells, leading to systemic spread and multi-organ involvement.

Mode of Transmission: Measles is transmitted through respiratory droplets, which are expelled when an infected person coughs, sneezes, or talks. The virus can also spread by direct contact with respiratory secretions, contaminated surfaces, or objects. The infectivity period for measles ranges **from four days before through four days after the rash appears**

Signs and Symptoms: Measles signs and symptoms typically include high fever, cough, runny nose (rhinorrhea/coryza), and red, watery eyes (conjunctivitis), followed by a characteristic rash that spreads from the face to the trunk and extremities. The rash comprises tiny, red spots that may coalesce into larger patches, usually persisting for several days. Tiny white spots known as **"Koplik spots"** may appear inside the mouth (on the inner cheek linings or on the roof of the mouth), usually two to three days after symptoms begin.

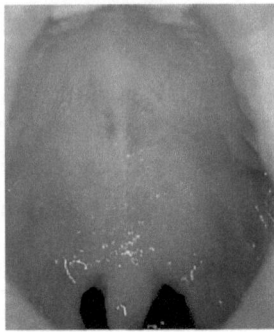

(Rubeola) - Measles' Koplik spots on upper palate

What the Child Looks Like: Children affected by measles may exhibit a feverish appearance, with flushed cheeks and photophobia (sensitivity to light). They may experience respiratory symptoms such as coughing and sneezing and systemic symptoms such as fatigue, irritability, and poor appetite.

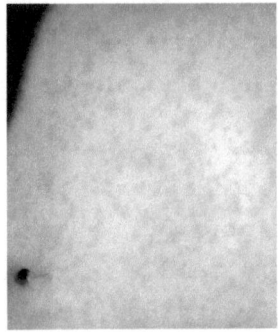

Rubeola (Measles) rash - after 3 days

Diagnosis: Diagnosis of measles is often based on clinical symptoms and history of exposure to individuals with measles-like illness. Laboratory tests, such as serological testing or polymerase chain reaction (PCR) testing of respiratory or blood specimens, may be performed to confirm the presence of the measles virus

Treatment: Measles treatment is primarily supportive and focuses on relieving symptoms. Bed rest, adequate hydration, and over-the-counter medications such as acetaminophen or ibuprofen may help alleviate fever, pain, and discomfort. In severe cases or complications, hospitalization, and specialized care may be necessary.

Prevention/Vaccine: Preventive vaccination is crucial in reducing the risk of measles infection and its associated complications. The measles, mumps, and rubella (MMR) vaccine effectively provides immunity against measles. Vaccination is typically administered in two doses, with the first dose rendered at 12-15 months of age and the second dose at 4-6 years of age. Vaccination of close contacts, including family members and caregivers, also helps prevent the spread of measles within communities and protects vulnerable individuals from infection.

RUBELLA (GERMAN MEASLES)

Rubella, otherwise known as German Measles, is a very communicable viral infection. Most people who get rubella usually experience a mild illness, with symptoms that can include a mild fever, inflamed and painful throat, and a peculiar rash that starts on the face and spreads to the rest of the body. Rubella infections can be severe and capable of terminating a pregnancy or causing severe birth defects in a developing baby if a woman is infected while she is pregnant. The best protection against rubella is the MMR (measles-mumps-rubella) vaccine.

Cause: Rubella is caused by the Rubella virus

Target: Rubella initially attacks and replicates in the upper respiratory tract (specifically, the nasopharynx) and nasopharyngeal lymphoid tissue, and then the virus spreads to regional lymph nodes (Lee & Bowden, 2000). It also affects the skin (rash).

Transmission Route: Rubella typically spreads through respiratory droplets from an infected person, making it highly contagious, especially in crowded environments such as schools and daycare centers. The virus can also be passed from a pregnant woman to her unborn child, potentially leading to severe birth defects known collectively as "congenital rubella syndrome."

Signs and Symptoms: The signs and symptoms of rubella can vary but commonly include a mild fever, sore throat, swollen lymph nodes, and a characteristic red rash that starts on the face and spreads to the rest of the body. It is important to note that some individuals, especially children, may not display any symptoms at all, which can make the virus difficult to detect without proper testing

What the Child Looks Like: The typical infant/child with rubella (German Measles) will have a mild fever, sore throat, swollen lymph nodes, and a diagnostic red rash that starts on the face and spreads to the rest of the body (top to bottom rash development).

Diagnosis: Rubella diagnosis usually involves a physical examination, blood tests to detect the presence of the virus or antibodies, and possibly a throat swab or a skin biopsy. Accurate diagnosis is crucial, especially in pregnant women, to prevent potential complications and birth defects.

Treatment: Treatment for rubella is typically supportive, focusing on managing symptoms such as fever and discomfort. Rest, hydration, and over-the-counter pain relievers may be recommended to help alleviate symptoms. However, no specific antiviral medication is available to treat rubella itself.

Prevention/Vaccine: The most effective way to prevent rubella is through vaccination. The best protection against rubella is the MMR (measles-mumps-and rubella) vaccine. The MMR vaccine protects against measles, mumps, and rubella and is endorsed by the CDC for children and adults who have not been previously vaccinated. This vaccine effectively prevents rubella infection and its complications, including the risk of congenital rubella syndrome in pregnant women. Most children who get the MMR vaccine will be protected against rubella.

VARICELLA (CHICKENPOX)

Varicella (Chickenpox) is a highly contagious disease that causes an itchy, blister-like rash that first appears on the chest, back, and face and then spreads over the entire body. The illness is highly contagious, such that if one person becomes infected, it is probable that up to 90 percent of individuals in close proximity who lack immunity will also contract the disease. Chickenpox can pose severe risks and potentially be life-threatening, particularly for infants, adolescents, adults, pregnant women, and individuals with compromised immune systems. Before the development of the Varicella vaccine, about 4 million people got chickenpox each year in the United States, and about 100-150 of these infected people died (CDC, 2019 November 12).

Cause: Chickenpox (Varicella) is caused by the Varicella-Zoster Virus (VZV), a member of the herpesvirus family. Chickenpox primarily affects the skin and mucous membranes, leading to characteristic symptoms and skin lesions.

Target: Target organs or tissues of varicella infection are the skin, respiratory tract, and nervous system. The varicella-zoster virus infects respiratory epithelial cells, leading to systemic spread and skin involvement, resulting in characteristic vesicular lesions (vesicular rash).

Mode of Transmission: Varicella is transmitted through respiratory droplets expelled when an infected person coughs, sneezes, or talks. It can also be transmitted by direct physical contact with skin lesions or respiratory secretions from an infected person.

Signs and Symptoms: The signs and symptoms of varicella typically include fever, headache, fatigue, and loss of appetite. This is followed by the appearance of a pruritic (itchy) rash consisting of small, red spots that progress to vesicles (fluid-filled blisters) and eventually crust over. This characteristic fluid-filled rash is called a vesicular rash. The varicella (chicken pox) rash typically begins on the face, scalp, or trunk and spreads to other body parts.

What the Child Looks Like: Children affected by varicella may appear febrile with flushed cheeks and fatigue. They may experience discomfort and itching due to the rash, which can lead to intense scratching, potentially tearing the skin and creating an avenue for secondary bacterial infections. The rash may be accompanied by systemic symptoms such as fever and malaise.

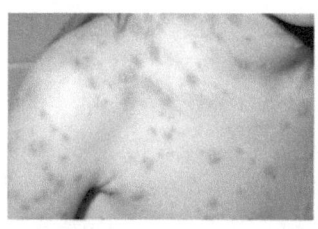 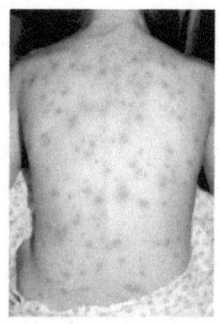

Varicella (Chickenpox) rash - trunk - front view   Varicella (Chickenpox) rash - trunk - back view

Diagnosis: The diagnosis of varicella is often based on clinical symptoms and the characteristic appearance of the rash, as described above. Laboratory tests, such as viral culture or polymerase chain reaction (PCR) testing of vesicular fluid or throat swabs, may be performed to confirm the presence of the varicella-zoster virus.

Treatment: The treatment of varicella is primarily supportive and focuses on relieving symptoms. Bed rest, adequate hydration, and over-the-counter medications such as acetaminophen or ibuprofen may help alleviate fever, pain, and discomfort. Antihistamines or calamine lotion may be used to relieve itching.

Prevention/Vaccine: Preventive vaccination is crucial in reducing the risk of varicella infection and its associated complications. The varicella vaccine, usually administered as part of the combined measles-mumps-rubella-varicella (MMRV) vaccine series, provides immunity against varicella. Vaccination is recommended for all children aged 12-15 months and again at 4-6 years of age. Vaccination of close contacts, including family members and caregivers, also helps prevent the spread of varicella within communities and protects vulnerable individuals from infection.

HEPATITIS A

Hepatitis A virus is a highly contagious, short-term liver infection. Hepatitis A infection can cause a person to be ill for a few weeks and up to several months, but will eventually recover completely without any lasting liver damage (CDC, 2021 February 17). It is only in very rare cases that hepatitis A infection can cause liver failure and possibly death.

Cause: Hepatitis A infection is caused by the Hepatitis A virus (HAV).

Target: HAV targets the liver

Transmission route: Hepatitis A virus is found in the stool and blood of infected people; therefore, it is spread through the fecal-oral route or by close personal contact with an infected person. In the United States, Hepatitis A infection is chiefly spread through the ingestion of contaminated food or water or close contact with an infected individual. Children are particularly susceptible to hepatitis A due to their lower immune system defense mechanism compared to adults, thus making them more vulnerable to the virus. The hepatitis A virus (HAV) can persist outside the body for several months. However, heating food and liquids to temperatures of 185°F (85°C) for a minimum of 1 minute can effectively destroy the virus. Parents and caregivers need to be aware that exposure to freezing temperatures does not eliminate the virus.

Signs and Symptoms: The signs and symptoms of hepatitis A in children can vary quite a bit but often include fatigue, abdominal pain, loss of appetite, nausea, vomiting, and jaundice (yellowing of the skin and eyes). Children infected with hepatitis A may also exhibit flu-like symptoms such as fever, muscle aches, and diarrhea.

What the Child Looks Like: As described above.

Diagnosis: Diagnosing Hepatitis A in children typically involves ordering blood tests to detect specific antibodies or viral particles in the bloodstream. Doctors may also conduct liver function tests to assess the liver's overall health and function. Early diagnosis is crucial to prevent the spread of the virus and ensure timely treatment.

Treatment: The treatment plan for hepatitis A in children is primarily supportive care, focusing on rest, hydration, and monitoring of symptoms. In severe cases, hospitalization of the child may be necessary to provide intravenous fluids and supportive care. No particular antiviral medication is approved for treating hepatitis A, but most cases resolve on their own with time and proper care.

Immunity: Once an infected person recovers from hepatitis A, they will have developed antibodies that will protect them for life against the disease (CDC, 2021, February 17).

Prevention/Vaccine: Vaccination is the best way to prevent hepatitis A in children. The hepatitis A vaccine is recommended for all children and is typically administered in two doses several months apart. Vaccination not only shields children from acquiring the virus but also aids in halting the transmission of hepatitis A within the community.

CDC AND AAP RECOMMENDED IMMUNIZATION SCHEDULE

(BIRTH TO 18 MONTHS)

The most recent version (2024 version) of the CDC and AAP recommended immunization schedule from birth to 18 years is available for viewing and printing at the following website:

https://www.cdc.gov/vaccines/schedules/downloads/child/0-18yrs-child-combined-schedule.pdf

A condensed version is provided in this book.

CDC AND AAP RECOMMENDED IMMUNIZATION SCHEDULE

Printable Newborn/Infant Vaccination Schedule (arranged by the disease)

Hepatitis B vaccine – 3-dose series:|| At Birth; At 2-3 months; At 6-18 months

Rotavirus vaccine – 3-dose series:|| At 2 months; At 4 months; At 6 months

Hib vaccine – 3-dose series:|| At 2 months; At 4 months; At 6 months

PCV – 3-dose series:|| At 2 months; At 4 months' At 6 months

Diphtheria (DTaP) – 5-dose series:|| At 2 months; At 4 months' At 6 months; At 15-18 months; At 4-6 years.

Tetanus (DTaP) – 5-dose series:|| At 2 months; At 4 months; At 6 months; At 15-18 months; At 4-6 years.

Pertussis (DTaP) – 5-dose series:|| At 2 months; At 4 months; At 6 months; At 15-18 months; At 4-6 years.

IPV – 3-dose series:|| At 2 months; At 4 months'; At 6-18 months

Influenza virus: Annually, beginning from 6 months

Mumps (MMR) vaccine: 2-dose series:|| 1st dose at 12-15 months; 2nd dose at 4-6 years

Measles (MMR) vaccine: 2-dose series:|| 1st dose at 12-15 months; 2nd dose at 4-6 years

Rubella (MMR) vaccine: 2-dose series:|| 2-dose series:|| 1st dose at 12-15 months; 2nd dose at 4-6 years

Varicella (Chicken pox): 2-dose series: 2-dose series:|| 1st dose at 12-15 months; 2nd dose at 4-6 years

Hepatitis A vaccine: 2-dose series with minimum of 6 months between them:|| Example: At 12-24 months; Then, at 18-42 months

Covid-19 vaccine: Minimum of 6 months of age. For the unvaccinated
- 2-dose series of the Moderna brand
- 3-dose series of the Pfizer brand

Key:

PCV – Pneumococcal Conjugate Vaccine

DTaP – Diphtheria, Tetanus, & acellular Pertussis

IPV – Inactivated Polio Virus vaccine

MMR – Mumps Measles Rubella vaccine

CDC AND AAP RECOMMENDED IMMUNIZATION SCHEDULE

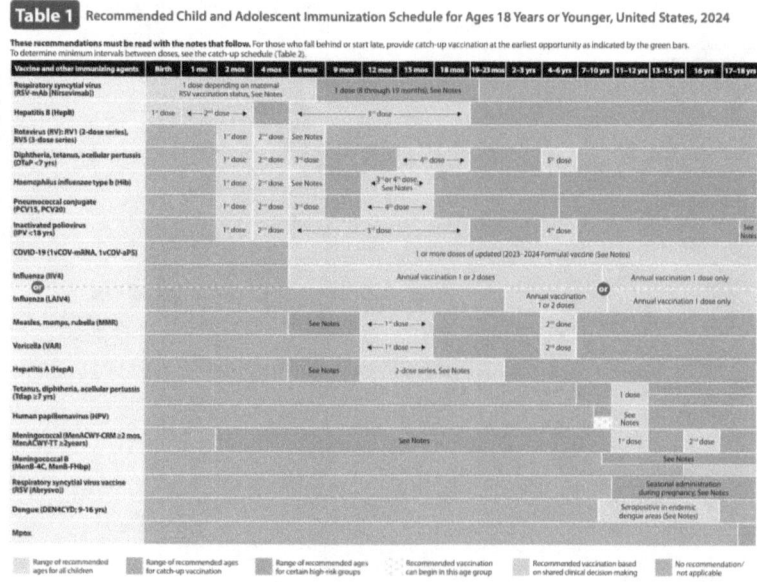

Table 1. Recommended Child and Adolescent Immunization Schedule for Ages 18 Years or Younger, United States, 2024

Table: CDC & AAP Recommended Immunization Schedule Summary

Age	At Birth	2 Months	1-2 Months	4 Months	6 Months	6-18 Months	6 Months & Up	12-15 Months	12-24 Months	15-18 Months	18-42 Months	4-6 years
Hep B	X		X			X						
Rotavirus		X		X	X							
Hib		X		X	X							
PCV		X		X	X			X				
IPV		X		X		X						X
DTaP		X		X	X					X		X
Influenza							X					
MMR								X				X
Varicella								X				X
Hep A								X		X		

CDC AND AAP RECOMMENDED IMMUNIZATION SCHEDULE

Table 2: Handy Vaccination Summary Card (0-18 Months)

Newborn:

- Hepatitis B (birth)

2 months:

- DTaP (Diphtheria, Tetanus, Pertussis)
- IPV (Polio)
- Hib (Hemophilus influenzae type b)
- PCV13 (Pneumococcal conjugate vaccine)
- Rotavirus

4 months:

- DTaP
- IPV
- Hib
- PCV13
- Rotavirus

6 months:

- DTaP
- IPV
- Hib
- PCV13
- Rotavirus
- Influenza
- Hepatitis B (if not given at birth)

12 months:

- MMR (Measles, Mumps, Rubella)
- Varicella (Chickenpox)
- Hepatitis A (first dose)

15 months:

- PCV13 (booster dose)

18 months:

- DTaP
- Hib

Special vaccines:

-Covid-19: given @ 6 months & up

-Annual vaccination 1 or 2 doses

CONCLUSION & RECOMMENDATIONS

What a journey! I hope you've learned a lot along the way and enjoyed reading it as much as I enjoyed writing it.

To summarize our journey through this manual, "Newborn and Infant Infections Simplified" is an essential handbook for parents and caregivers navigating the challenges of caring for newborns and infants. This comprehensive guide provides in-depth information on the causes, symptoms, diagnosis, treatment, prevention, and available immunizations for common infections and minor emergencies that affect young children.

The book begins by exploring the various causative agents of infections in newborns and infants, including bacteria, viruses, and fungi. Next, it delves into how these pathogens can enter the human body and cause respiratory, gastrointestinal, skin, and more illnesses. Through clear and concise explanations, the book guides parents and caregivers to better understand the factors contributing to their infant's health concerns.

CONCLUSION & RECOMMENDATIONS

As the narrative progresses, "Newborn and Infant Infections Simplified" addresses the signs and symptoms parents should watch for in their newborns and infants, emphasizing the importance of early recognition and prompt medical attention. From fever and cough to rash and irritability, the book equips parents with the knowledge to identify potential infections and minor emergencies, empowering them to take proactive measures to safeguard their child's well-being. You will gain knowledge and skills to manage the most common illnesses and emergencies of infanthood confidently.

Furthermore, "Newborn and Infant Infections Simplified" provides invaluable guidance on diagnosing, treating, and preventing common infections and minor emergencies in newborns and infants. It covers a range of topics, including when to seek medical care, home remedies for mild ailments, and the role of vaccinations in preventing serious illnesses. With practical tips and expert advice, this book is a trusted resource for parents seeking to navigate the complexities of newborn and infant healthcare with confidence and peace of mind. It is authored by an experienced advanced practice medical professional and backed by the most recent findings from medical research. It is recommended that you combine the information in this book with the expert guidance of your child's pediatric primary care provider to achieve the best results for your child. The ultimate objective is your peace of mind as a parent during this vulnerable stage of your child's growth and development.

RESOURCES FOR PARENTS & CAREGIVERS

Community Resources

- Your State Department of Health and Human Services

Important Online Resources

- **CDC Immunization Schedules**: The printable format for the complete and most current revised edition (2024 revision) of the CDC immunization schedules for birth through 18 years is available on this website: https://www.cdc.gov/vaccines/schedules/downloads/child/0-18yrs-child-combined-schedule.pdf
- **Vaccine Information Statements** (VISs): For in-depth information regarding the origin and uses of VISs, visit the following CDC web page: https://www.cdc.gov/vaccines/hcp/vis/about/facts-vis.html#law
- **Correct Hand Hygiene Protocol per CDC:** Visit the following website to read the current CDC hand hygiene guidelines and download printable health

promotion materials and fact sheets: https://www.cdc.gov/hygiene/personal-hygiene/hands.html
- **American Academy of Pediatrics' HealthyChildren.org website:** provides tips on how to manage common infant and childhood illnesses. https://www.healthychildren.org/
- **Poison Control Hotline**: (1-800-222-1222)

Thank You...FREE Gift for you!

I hope you have enjoyed this free ebook companion to your book purchase. If you loved or learned from *Newborn & Infant Infections Simplified*, **kindly leave us a review** through your Amazon purchase account. Your feedback/review means so much to small, independent authors and publishers like us.

Click below to leave a review:

https://mybook.to/Newborn-Infections

Whether you are a new mom of a neonate or a seasoned mom of an older infant, please be reassured that our team is available to support you and your growing family with resources that cater to every need that you may have. I encourage you to check out the various books that we offer: CPR and emergency care for newborns and infants, log books for vital signs such blood pressures, prayer books for pregnancy; post-partum self-care manuals; relaxation techniques curated for moms; books for baby care and baby health, pregnancy guide book for expectant dads; and so much more!

Check out the author profile page of JK Karliese on your Amazon Marketplace, to preview and shop other publications by the same author and for more tips and strategies! **Click the link below:**

https://www.amazon.com/author/jk-karliese-books

Scan the QR code below for a **FREE gift** and to subscribe for other books by JK Karliese

BIBLIOGRAPHY

Alper, B. (2019, February 2). *Uremia: Background, Pathophysiology, Etiology.* Medscape.com. https://emedicine.medscape.com/article/245296-overview

Amdani, Shahnawaz & Makhoul, M. (2023). *Cardiomyopathy in Children & Teens.* HealthyChildren.org. Retrieved March 14, 2024, from https://www.healthychildren.org/English/health-issues/conditions/heart/Pages/Pediatric-Cardiomyopathy.aspx?_gl=1

American Academy of Pediatrics (2015). *Diphtheria.* HealthyChildren.org. Retrieved March 22, 2024, from https://www.healthychildren.org/English/health-issues/vaccine-preventable-diseases/Pages/Diphtheria.aspx?_gl=1

American Academy of Pediatrics (2015). *Natural Therapies and Children: FAQs.* HealthyChildren.org. Retrieved March 21, 2024, from https://www.healthychildren.org/English/health-issues/conditions/treatments/Pages/Natural-Therapies.aspx?_gl=1

American Academy of Pediatrics (2015 November 11). *Tetanus.* HealthyChildren.org. Retrieved March 22, 2024, from https://www.healthychildren.org/English/health-issues/vaccine-preventable-diseases/Pages/Tetanus.aspx?_gl=1

American Academy of Pediatrics (2019). *Anaphylaxis in Infants & Children.* HealthyChildren.org. https://www.healthychildren.org/English/health-issues/injuries-emergencies/Pages/Anaphylaxis.aspx?_gl=1

American Academy of Pediatrics (2022). *Treating Your Child's Fever.* HealthyChildren.org. Retrieved March 20, 2024, from https://www.healthychildren.org/English/health-issues/conditions/fever/Pages/Medications-Used-to-Treat-Fever.aspx?_gl=1

American Academy of Pediatrics (2023, July 31st). *Meningitis in Infants and Children.* HealthyChildren.org. Retrieved from https://www.healthychildren.org/English/health-issues/conditions/head-neck-nervous-system/Pages/Meningitis.aspx?_gl=1

American Academy of Pediatrics. (2023, August 21). *Safe sleep.* www.aap.org. https://www.aap.org/en/patient-care/safe-sleep/

American Academy of Pediatrics (2024). *Croup in Young Children.* (n.d.). HealthyChildren.org. Retrieved February 16, 2024, from https://www.healthychildren.org/English/health-issues/conditions/chest-lungs/Pages/Croup-Treatment.aspx?_gl=1

American Academy of Pediatrics (2024). (2024). Aap.org. https://publications.

BIBLIOGRAPHY

aap.org/pediatrics/article-abstract/127/4/e898/65104/Risk-Factors-for-Hand-Foot-and-Mouth-Disease-and

American Academy of Ophthalmology (2023, April 25). *Conjunctivitis: What Is Pink Eye?* https://www.aao.org/eye-health/diseases/pink-eye-conjunctivitis#:~:text=Conjunctivitis%E2%80%94often%20called%20%E2%80%9Cpink%20eye

American Lung Association. (2023). *Pneumonia symptoms and diagnosis.* Www.lung.org; American Lung Association. https://www.lung.org/lung-health-diseases/lung-disease-lookup/pneumonia/symptoms-and-diagnosis

American Lung Association (n.d.). *Learn About Asthma.* Www.lung.org. Retrieved from https://www.lung.org/lung-health-diseases/lung-disease-lookup/asthma/learn-about-asthma

Andre, F., Booy, R., Bock, H., Clemens, J., Datta, S., John, T., Lee, B., Lolekha, S., Peltola, H., Ruff, T., Santosham, M., & Schmitt, H. (2008). Vaccination greatly reduces disease, disability, death and inequity worldwide. *Bulletin of the World Health Organization, 86(2)*, 140–146. https://doi.org/10.2471/blt.07.040089

Botgros, A., & MacMahon, E. (2021). Erythrovirus B19 infection. *Medicine, 49(12)*, 785-789. https://doi.org/10.1016/j.mpmed.2021.09.012

Carlisle, A., & Lieberman, J. (2021). Clinical Management of Infant Anaphylaxis. *Journal of Asthma and Allergy, 14*, 821. https://doi.org/10.2147/JAA.S286692

Centers for Disease Control and Prevention. (2017). *2017 Combined Recommended Immunization Schedule for Children and Adolescents Aged 18 Years or Younger, United States.* https://www.cdc.gov/vaccines/schedules/downloads/child/0-18yrs-child-combined-schedule.pdf

Centers for Disease Control and Prevention. (2018, December 3). *Diagnosis and Treatment | Listeria |* Www.cdc.gov. https://www.cdc.gov/listeria/diagnosis.html#:~:text=Listeriosis%20is%20usually%20diagnosed%20when

Centers for Disease Control and Prevention. (2019). *About Flu.* Centers for Disease Control and Prevention. https://www.cdc.gov/flu/about/index.html

Centers for Disease Control and Prevention. (2019). *About Kawasaki Disease.* Centers for Disease Control and Prevention. Retrieved from https://www.cdc.gov/kawasaki/about.html

Centers for Disease Control and Prevention. (2019). *Haemophilus Influenzae Type b. Vaccine Information Statement.* (2019). CDC. https://www.cdc.gov/vaccines/hcp/vis/vis-statements/hib.html

Centers for Disease Control and Prevention. (2019). *Toxoplasmosis - General Information - Frequently Asked Questions (FAQs).* CDC. https://www.cdc.gov/parasites/toxoplasmosis/gen_info/faqs.html

Centers for Disease Control and Prevention. (2019). *E. coli (Escherichia coli).* CDC. https://www.cdc.gov/ecoli/

Centers for Disease Control and Prevention. (2019). *Mumps.* Centers for Disease Control and Prevention. https://www.cdc.gov/mumps/index.html

BIBLIOGRAPHY

Centers for Disease Control and Prevention. (2019). *Pertussis*. Centers for Disease Control and Prevention. https://www.cdc.gov/pertussis/about/signs-symptoms.html

Centers for Disease Control and Prevention. (2019). *Pneumonia*. CDC. https://www.cdc.gov/pneumonia/index.html

Centers for Disease Control and Prevention. (2019, January 4). *Conjunctivitis*. Centers for Disease Control and Prevention. https://www.cdc.gov/conjunctivitis/about/causes.html

Centers for Disease Control and Prevention. (2019, January 4). *Protect Yourself From Pink Eye*. Centers for Disease Control and Prevention. https://www.cdc.gov/conjunctivitis/about/symptoms.html

Centers for Disease Control and Prevention. (2019, February 8). *Hypothermia|Winter Weather*. Centers for Disease Control and Prevention. https://www.cdc.gov/disasters/winter/staysafe/hypothermia.html

Centers for Disease Control and Prevention. (2019, April 26). *Flu Symptoms & Complications*. Centers for Disease Control and Prevention. https://www.cdc.gov/flu/symptoms/symptoms.htm

Centers for Disease Control and Prevention. (2019, September 6). *Asthma FAQs*. Centers for Disease Control and Prevention. https://www.cdc.gov/asthma/faqs.htm

Centers for Disease Control and Prevention. (2019, December 12). *Rubella | German Measles | Home | CDC*. (2019, December 12). Www.cdc.gov. https://www.cdc.gov/rubella/

Centers for Disease Control and Prevention. (2019, November 12). *Chickenpox | Home | Varicella | CDC*. (2019, November 12). Www.cdc.gov. https://www.cdc.gov/chickenpox/

Centers for Disease Control and Prevention. (2020). *Perinatal Transmission*. Centers for Disease Control and Prevention. https://www.cdc.gov/hepatitis/hbv/perinatalxmtn.htm

Centers for Disease Control and Prevention. (2020, June 4). *Kawasaki Syndrome*. Retrieved from https://www.cdc.gov/kawasaki/

Centers for Disease Control and Prevention. (2021). *Rotavirus*. Centers for Disease Control and Prevention. https://www.cdc.gov/rotavirus/index.html

Centers for Disease Control and Prevention. (2021, February 17). *Hepatitis A FAQs | CDC*. Centers for Disease Control and Prevention. https://www.cdc.gov/hepatitis/hav/afaq.htm#A1

Centers for Disease Control and Prevention. (2021, April 26). *Suffering from a sinus infection?* Centers for Disease Control and Prevention. https://www.cdc.gov/antibiotic-use/sinus-infection.html

Centers for Disease Control and Prevention. (2021, May 3). *Pediatric Outpatient Treatment Recommendations | Antibiotic Use | CDC*. Www.cdc.gov. https://www.cdc.gov/antibiotic-use/clinicians/pediatric-treatment-rec.html

BIBLIOGRAPHY

Centers for Disease Control and Prevention. (2021, May 7). *Suffering from a sore throat?* Centers for Disease Control and Prevention. https://www.cdc.gov/antibiotic-use/sore-throat.html

Centers for Disease Control and Prevention. (2021, July 1). *Ear Infection.* Centers for Disease Control and Prevention. https://www.cdc.gov/antibiotic-use/ear-infection.html

Centers for Disease Control and Prevention. (2022, June 30). *About HIV.* Centers for Disease Control and Prevention; CDC. https://www.cdc.gov/hiv/basics/whatishiv.html

Centers for Disease Control and Prevention. (2022, July 14). *Keeping Hands Clean | CDC.* Www.cdc.gov. https://www.cdc.gov/hygiene/personal-hygiene/hands.html

Centers for Disease Control and Prevention. (2023, March 9). *Rhinoviruses: Common Colds | CDC.* Www.cdc.gov. https://www.cdc.gov/ncird/rhinoviruses-common-cold.html

Centers for Disease Control and Prevention. (2023, April 4). *Herpes simplex virus (HSV).* Centers for Disease Control and Prevention. https://www.cdc.gov/breastfeeding/breastfeeding-special-circumstances/maternal-or-infant-illnesses/herpes.html#:~:text=Importantly%2C%20both%20types%20of%20virus

Centers for Disease Control and Prevention. (2023, November 16). *Immunization Schedules for 18 & Younger.* Centers for Disease Control and Prevention. https://www.cdc.gov/vaccines/schedules/hcp/imz/child-adolescent.html#table-1

Centers for Disease Control and Prevention. (2023, December 5). *Pediatric Pneumonia Update.* Www.cdc.gov. Retrieved from https://www.cdc.gov/respiratory-viruses/whats-new/pediatric-pneumonia-update.html

Centers for Disease Control and Prevention. (2024). *Sore throat image.* Retrieved from https://www.cdc.gov/antibiotic-use/community/images/sore-throat-lg.jpg?_=05512?noicon

Centers for Disease Control and Prevention. (2024). *Strep throat image.* Retrieved from https://www.cdc.gov/groupastrep/diseases-public/strep-throat.html

Chang, M.-H. (2007). Hepatitis B virus infection. *Seminars in Fetal and Neonatal Medicine, 12*(3), 160–167. https://doi.org/10.1016/j.siny.2007.01.013

Cincinnati Childrens (2022). *Myocarditis in Children | Symptoms, Causes, Treatment & Prognosis.* Www.cincinnatichildrens.org. https://www.cincinnatichildrens.org/health/m/myocarditis

Cohen, Adam MD. (2017). Pink Eye: What To Do. Centers for Disease Control and Prevention. *Public Health Media Library.* Retrieved from https://tools.cdc.gov/medialibrary/index.aspx#/media/id/303014

Collier, R. (2023). Escherichia coli (E coli) Infections: Background,

BIBLIOGRAPHY

Pathophysiology, Epidemiology. *EMedicine.* https://emedicine.medscape.com/article/217485-overview?form=fpf

Conners, E. E., Panagiotakopoulos, L., Hofmeister, M. G., Spradling, P. R., Hagan, L. M., Harris, A. M., Rogers-Brown, J. S., Wester, C., Nelson, N. P., Rapposelli, K., Sandul, A. L., Choi, E., Coffin, C., Marks, K., Thomas, D. L., & Wang, S. H. (2023). Screening and Testing for Hepatitis B Virus Infection: CDC Recommendations — United States, 2023. *MMWR. Recommendations and Reports, 72*(1), 1–25. https://doi.org/10.15585/mmwr.rr7201a1

Coughs and Colds: Medicines or Home Remedies? (n.d.). HealthyChildren.org. https://www.healthychildren.org/English/health-issues/conditions/chest-lungs/Pages/Coughs-and-Colds-Medicines-or-Home-Remedies.aspx?_gl=1

Could My Child Have Acid Reflux? (n.d.). Www.nationwidechildrens.org. Retrieved February 27, 2024, from https://www.nationwidechildrens.org/family-resources-education/700childrens/2020/10/could-my-child-have-acid-reflux

CPR for Infants. (2019). Cincinnatichildrens.org. https://www.cincinnatichildrens.org/health/c/infant-cpr

Cremon, C., Stanghellini, V., Pallotti, F., Fogacci, E., Bellacosa, L., Morselli-Labate, A. M., Paccapelo, A., Nardo, G. D., Cogliandro, R. F., Giorgio, R. D., Corinaldesi, R., & Barbara, G. (2014). Salmonella Gastroenteritis During Childhood Is a Risk Factor for Irritable Bowel Syndrome in Adulthood. *Gastroenterology, 147*(1), 69–77. https://doi.org/10.1053/j.gastro.2014.03.013

Definition & Facts for GER & GERD - NIDDK. (n.d.). National Institute of Diabetes and Digestive and Kidney Diseases. Retrieved February 27, 2024, from https://www.niddk.nih.gov/health-information/digestive-diseases/acid-reflux-ger-gerd-adults/definition-facts#whatis

Durani, Y. (2023). *Shigella Infections (Shigellosis) (for Parents) - Nemours KidsHealth.* (n.d.). Kidshealth.org. https://kidshealth.org/en/parents/shigella.html#:~:text=Call%20the%20doctor%20if%20your

Ellis, Becky (2024). *Omalizumab for Food Allergies: What PCPs Should Know.* Medscape. Retrieved March 20, 2024, from https://www.medscape.com/viewarticle/omalizumab-food-allergies-what-pcps-should-know-2024a10003yu

El-Serag, H. B., Sweet, S., Winchester, C. C., & Dent, J. (2014). Update on the epidemiology of gastro-oesophageal reflux disease: a systematic review. *Gut, 63*(6), 871–880. https://doi.org/10.1136/gutjnl-2012-304269

Flu Information *Flu: A Guide for Parents.* (n.d.). Retrieved February 9, 2024, from https://www.cdc.gov/flu/pdf/treatment/flu-guide-for-parents.pdf

Frenck, R. W. (2023, updated 2024). *Salmonella Infections in Children.* American Academy of Pediatrics: HealthyChildren.org. Retrieved February 29, 2024, from https://www.healthychildren.org/English/health-issues/conditions/

infections/Pages/Salmonella-Infections.aspx?_gl=1

Greenwood, B. (2014). The contribution of vaccination to global health: past, present and future. *Philosophical Transactions of the Royal Society B: Biological Sciences, 369*(1645), 20130433–20130433. https://doi.org/10.1098/rstb.2013.0433

Hauk, L. (2014). AAP Releases Guideline on Diagnosis and Management of Acute Bacterial Sinusitis in Children One to 18 Years of Age. *American Family Physician, 89*(8), 676–681. https://www.aafp.org/pubs/afp/issues/2014/0415/p676.html

Healthy Children (2018). *Food Allergies in Children.* HealthyChildren.org. Retrieved March 20, 2024, from https://www.healthychildren.org/English/healthy-living/nutrition/Pages/Food-Allergies-in-Children.aspx?_gl=1

Healthy Children (2021). *Fever and Your Baby.* HealthyChildren.org. Retrieved March 20, 2024, from https://www.healthychildren.org/English/health-issues/conditions/fever/Pages/Fever-and-Your-Baby.aspx?_gl=1

Healthy Children (2021, April 9). *Polio Vaccine: What You Need to Know.* HealthyChildren.org. Retrieved March 21, 2024, from https://www.healthychildren.org/English/safety-prevention/immunizations/Pages/Polio-Vaccine-What-You-Need-to-Know.aspx?_gl=1

Healthy Children (2024). *Kawasaki Disease in Infants & Young Children.* HealthyChildren.org. Retrieved from https://www.healthychildren.org/English/health-issues/conditions/heart/Pages/Kawasaki-Disease.aspx?_gl=1

Healthy Children (n.d.). *Infant Constipation.* HealthyChildren.org. https://www.healthychildren.org/English/ages-stages/baby/diapers-clothing/Pages/Infant-Constipation.aspx

Hitchcock, Kathryn, and Romantic Emily (2023). "Gastroesophageal Reflux in Infants | Symptoms, Diagnosis & Treatment." *Www.cincinnatichildrens.org,* June 2023, www.cincinnatichildrens.org/health/g/ger-infants. Accessed 15 Mar. 2024.

Hoerst, Amanda (2023). *Kawasaki Disease | Symptoms, Diagnosis, Treatment & Long-Term Effects.* Www.cincinnatichildrens.org. https://www.cincinnatichildrens.org/health/k/kawasaki

How to Stop a Nosebleed. (2019). HealthyChildren.org. Retrieved February 12, 2024, from https://www.healthychildren.org/English/health-issues/injuries-emergencies/Pages/How-to-Stop-a-Nosebleed.aspx

Institut Pasteur. (2021, April 28). *Group A and B Streptococcus.* Retrieved from https://www.pasteur.fr/en/medical-center/disease-sheets/group-and-b-streptococcus?language=fr

John Hopkins Medicine. (2019, November 19). *Pyloric Stenosis.* Www.hopkinsmedicine.org. Retrieved from https://www.hopkinsmedicine.org/health/conditions-and-diseases/pyloric-stenosis#:~:text=Normally%2C%20-

BIBLIOGRAPHY

food%20passes%20easily%20from

Kanegaye, J. T., Jones, J. M., Burns, J. C., Jain, S., Sun, X., Jimenez-Fernandez, S., Berry, E., Pancheri, J. M., Jaggi, P., Ramilo, O., & Tremoulet, A. H. (2016). Axillary, Oral and Rectal Routes of Temperature Measurement During Treatment of Acute Kawasaki Disease. *Pediatric Infectious Disease Journal*, *35*(1), 50–53. https://doi.org/10.1097/inf.0000000000000923

Kasikis, S., Hayfron, M., Galetaki, D. & Bochner, R. (2023). Case 1: Fever in a 40-day-old Infant. Pediatrics in Review, 44(12), 692–693. https://doi.org/10.1542/pir.2021-005397

Kawasaki Kids Foundation (n.d.). *Kawasaki Disease Symptoms*. Retrieved from https://www.kawasakikidsfoundation.org/kawasaki-disease-symptoms/

Klatte, Michel J. (2024). *Coxsackievirus Infections in Children*. HealthyChildren.org. Retrieved February 29, 2024, from https://www.healthychildren.org/English/health-issues/conditions/infections/Pages/Coxsackieviruses-and-Other-Enterovirus-Infections.aspx?_gl=1

LeClair C. E. & McConnell K.A. Rotavirus. [Updated 2023 Jan 2]. In: StatPearls [Internet]. Treasure Island (FL): StatPearls Publishing; 2024 Jan-. Available from: https://www.ncbi.nlm.nih.gov/books/NBK558951/

Lee, & Bowden, D. W. (2000). *Rubella Virus Replication and Links to Teratogenicity*. *13*(4), 571–587. https://doi.org/10.1128/cmr.13.4.571-587.2000

Libby, T. E., Miranda L.M. Delawalla, Al-Shimari, F., MacLennan, C. A., Vannice, K. S., & Pavlinac, P. B. (2023). *Consequences of Shigella infection in young children: a systematic review*. *129*, 78–95. https://doi.org/10.1016/j.ijid.2023.01.034

Maldonado, Yvonne MD (2022). *Polio & Vaccines to Prevent Paralytic Polio*. HealthyChildren.org. Retrieved March 21, 2024, from https://www.healthychildren.org/English/health-issues/vaccine-preventable-diseases/Pages/Polio.aspx?_gl=1

Martin, J., Townshend, J., & Brodlie, M. (2022). Diagnosis and management of asthma in children. *BMJ Paediatrics Open*, *6*(1), e001277. https://doi.org/10.1136/bmjpo-2021-001277

Mattila, J., Vuorinen, T., Waris, M., Antikainen, P., & Heikkinen, T. (2021). Oseltamivir treatment of influenza A and B infections in infants. *Influenza and Other Respiratory Viruses*, *15*(5), 618–624. https://doi.org/10.1111/irv.12862

Mayo Clinic. (2018). *Parvovirus infection - Symptoms and causes*. Mayo Clinic. https://www.mayoclinic.org/diseases-conditions/parvovirus-infection/symptoms-causes/syc-20376085

Mayo Clinic (2022). *E. coli - Symptoms and causes*. Retrieved March 5, 2024, from https://www.mayoclinic.org/diseases-conditions/e-coli/symptoms-causes/

BIBLIOGRAPHY

syc-20372058#:~:text=To%20reduce%20your%20chance%20of

Miyake, Christina & Patnana, Syamasundar Rao (2020). *Pediatric Hypertrophic Cardiomyopathy: Background, Pathophysiology, Etiology*. EMedicine. https://emedicine.medscape.com/article/890068-overview?form=fpf

Murkoff, H. E. & Widome, M. D. (2018). *What to expect the first year*. Simon & Schuster.

National Institute of Diabetes and Digestive and Kidney Diseases (2017). *Treatment for Bladder Infection in Children | NIDDK*. https://www.niddk.nih.gov/health-information/urologic-diseases/urinary-tract-infections-in-children/treatment

National Institute of Diabetes and Digestive and Kidney Diseases (2018). *Vesicoureteral reflux (VUR) | NIDDK*. Retrieved from https://www.niddk.nih.gov/health-information/urologic-diseases/hydronephrosis-newborns/vesicoureteral-reflux

National Institute of Diabetes and Digestive and Kidney Diseases. (2019, October 23). *Definition & Facts for Diarrhea | NIDDK*. National Institute of Diabetes and Digestive and Kidney Diseases. https://www.niddk.nih.gov/health-information/digestive-diseases/diarrhea/definition-facts

National Institute of Diabetes and Digestive and Kidney Diseases, NIDDKD (2020, February 6). *Definition & Facts for Constipation in Children | NIDDK*. National Institute of Diabetes and Digestive and Kidney Diseases. https://www.niddk.nih.gov/health-information/digestive-diseases/constipation-children/definition-facts

Nationwide Childrens (2019). *Constipation in Infants: Symptoms, Treatment and When to Call a Doctor*. Nationwidechildrens.org. https://www.nationwidechildrens.org/conditions/constipation-infant

Nationwide Childrens (2024). *Asthma and Reactive Airway Disease (RAD) (Wheezing)*. Retrieved from www.nationwidechildrens.org. https://www.nationwidechildrens.org/conditions/asthma-and-reactive-airway-disease-rad-wheezing

Nationwide Childrens (2024). *Could My Child Have Acid Reflux?* (n.d.). Www.nationwidechildrens.org. Retrieved from https://www.nationwidechildrens.org/family-resources-education/700childrens/2020/10/could-my-child-have-acid-reflux

NHS. (2017, October 19). *Slapped Cheek Syndrome*. Nhs.uk. https://www.nhs.uk/conditions/slapped-cheek-syndrome/

NHS. (2020, December 3). *Infections in pregnancy that may affect your baby*. Nhs.uk. https://www.nhs.uk/pregnancy/keeping-well/infections-that-may-affect-your-baby/

NHS Choices. (2020). *Rubella (german measles)*. NHS. https://www.nhs.uk/conditions/rubella/

NINDS. (n.d.). *Reye's Syndrome*. National Institute of Neurological Disorders and

BIBLIOGRAPHY

Stroke. Retrieved from: www.ninds.nih.gov. https://www.ninds.nih.gov/health-information/disorders/reyes-syndrome#:~:text=Reye

Olarte, L., & Jackson, M. A. (2021). Streptococcus pneumoniae. *Pediatrics in Review, 42*(7), 349–359. https://doi.org/10.1542/pir.2020-0062

Owusu-Ansah, Sylvia MD (2017). *Sepsis in Infants & Children*. HealthyChildren.org. Retrieved March 20, 2024, from https://www.healthychildren.org/English/health-issues/conditions/infections/Pages/Sepsis-in-Infants-Children.aspx?_gl=1

Nosebleed (Epistaxis) in Children. (2023, November 6). Www.hopkinsmedicine.org. https://www.hopkinsmedicine.org/health/conditions-and-diseases/nosebleeds#:~:text=Tell%20your%20child%20to%20breathe

Raffatellu, M., Chessa, D., Wilson, R. J., Çagla Tükel, Mustafa Akçelik, & Bäumler, A. J. (2006). Capsule-Mediated Immune Evasion: A New Hypothesis Explaining Aspects of Typhoid Fever Pathogenesis. *Infection and Immunity, 74*(1), 19–27. https://doi.org/10.1128/iai.74.1.19-27.2006

Rodgers, D. (2023). *Preventing Urinary Tract Infections in Children – NIDDK Healthy Moments Episode June 12, 2023*. National Institute of Diabetes and Digestive and Kidney Diseases. https://www.niddk.nih.gov/health-information/healthy-moments/episodes/preventing-urinary-tract-infections-children

Rotavirus | Vaccination | CDC. (2019, December 9). Www.cdc.gov. https://www.cdc.gov/rotavirus/vaccination.html

Rotavirus Workup: Laboratory Studies. (n.d.). Emedicine.medscape.com. Retrieved February 5, 2024, from https://emedicine.medscape.com/article/803885-workup?form=fpf

RSV: When It's More Than Just a Cold. (n.d.). HealthyChildren.org. https://www.healthychildren.org/English/health-issues/conditions/chest-lungs/Pages/RSV-When-Its-More-Than-Just-a-Cold.aspx?_gl=1

Ruan, F., Yang, T., Ma, H., Jin, Y., Song, S., Fontaine, R., & Zhu, B. (2011). Risk Factors for Hand, Foot, and Mouth Disease and Herpangina and the Preventive Effect of Hand-washing. *Pediatrics* 127 (4): e898–e904. https://doi.org/10.1542/peds.2010-1497

Schillie, S., Vellozzi, C., Reingold, A., Harris, A., Haber, P., Ward, J. W., & Nelson, N. P. (2018). Prevention of Hepatitis B Virus Infection in the United States: Recommendations of the Advisory Committee on Immunization Practices. *MMWR. Recommendations and Reports, 67*(1), 1–31.

Sicherer, Scott H. (2021). Food Allergies: Practice Essentials, Background, Pathophysiology, revised 2024. *EMedicine*. https://emedicine.medscape.com/article/135959-overview

Sosa, T. (2022). Kawasaki Disease: Practice Essentials, Background, Pathophysiology. (2022). *EMedicine*. https://emedicine.medscape.com/article/965367-overview?lang=en&regEmail=guzziaglobal%40yahoo.com&icd=

BIBLIOGRAPHY

login_success_email_match_fpf

Stein, Sarah (2023). *Eczema in Babies and Children*. HealthyChildren.org. https://www.healthychildren.org/English/health-issues/conditions/skin/Pages/Eczema.aspx?_gl=1

Surgeon General's Advisory on the Use of Salicylates and Reye Syndrome. (n.d.). Www.cdc.gov. Retrieved February 20, 2024, from https://www.cdc.gov/mmwr/preview/mmwrhtml/00001108.htm

Taillefer, C., Boucher, M., Laferrière, C., & Morin, L. (2010). Perinatal Listeriosis: Canada's 2008 Outbreaks. *Journal of Obstetrics and Gynaecology Canada*, *32*(1), 45–48. https://doi.org/10.1016/S1701-2163(16)34403-6

Tejani, Nooruddin (2023). Febrile Seizures: Background, Pathophysiology, Epidemiology. EMedicine. https://emedicine.medscape.com/article/801500-overview

Tesse, R., Borrelli, G., Mongelli, G., Mastrorilli, V., & Cardinale, F. (2018). Treating pediatric asthma according guidelines. *Frontiers in Pediatrics*, *6*(234). https://doi.org/10.3389/fped.2018.00234

Tickell, K. D., Brander, R. L., Atlas, H. E., Pernica, J. M., Walson, J. L., & Pavlinac, P. B. (2017). Identification and management of Shigella infection in children with diarrhea: a systematic review and meta-analysis. *The Lancet Global Health*, *5*(12), e1235–e1248. https://doi.org/10.1016/s2214-109x(17)30392-3

Vaccine Information Statement: Facts About VISs | CDC. (2023, April 27). Www.cdc.gov. https://www.cdc.gov/vaccines/hcp/vis/about/facts-vis.html#law

Vaccine Information Statement. (2019). https://www.cdc.gov/vaccines/hcp/vis/index.html

Vaccine Recommendations for Infants & Children | CDC Yellow Book 2024. (n.d.). Wwwnc.cdc.gov. Retrieved January 30, 2024, from https://wwwnc.cdc.gov/travel/yellowbook/2024/family/vaccine-recommendations-for-infants-and-children#:~:text=Routine%20Infant%20%26%20Childhood%20Vaccines https://doi.org/10.15585/mmwr.rr6701a1

Ventarola, D., Bordone, L., & Silverberg, N. (2015). Update on hand-foot-and-mouth disease. *Clinics in Dermatology*, *33*(3), 340–346. https://doi.org/10.1016/j.clindermatol.2014.12.011

Wald, E. R., Applegate, K. E., Bordley, C., Darrow, D. H., Glode, M. P., Marcy, S. M., Nelson, C. E., Rosenfeld, R. M., Shaikh, N., Smith, M. J., Williams, P. V., & Weinberg, S. T. (2013). Clinical Practice Guideline for the Diagnosis and Management of Acute Bacterial Sinusitis in Children Aged 1 to 18 Years. *PEDIATRICS*, *132*(1), e262–e280. https://doi.org/10.1542/peds.2013-1071

WHO. (2010). *Types of seasonal influenza vaccine*. World Health Organization. https://www.who.int/europe/news-room/fact-sheets/item/types-of-

BIBLIOGRAPHY

seasonal-influenza-vaccine

WHO. (2019, July 8). *Hepatitis E*. Who.int; World Health Organization: WHO. https://www.who.int/news-room/fact-sheets/detail/hepatitis-e

WHO. (2019, December 5). *Immunization*. Who.int; World Health Organization: WHO. https://www.who.int/news-room/facts-in-pictures/detail/immunization

WHO. (2023, July 18). *Hepatitis C*. Who.int; World Health Organization: WHO. https://www.who.int/news-room/fact-sheets/detail/hepatitis-c

Wong, S.-S. ., & Webby, R. J. (2013). Traditional and New Influenza Vaccines. *Clinical Microbiology Reviews*, *26*(3), 476–492. https://doi.org/10.1128/cmr.00097-12

ABOUT THE AUTHOR

JK KARLIESE

JK Karliese is an independent author and book publisher. She is co-owner of the publishing company JKK Books & Media. JK is an advanced practice healthcare professional with over ten years of combined direct care and advanced clinical experience. She has certifications in pediatrics, cardiology, and family practice. JK publishes in the following health-related niches: maternal health, well-child, parenting, family relationships, and self-help/motivational. Occasionally, she publishes on hot-button medical topics that affect women and children. Publishing is one of her ways of reaching out and helping a wider audience outside of her local community. She is known for using unconventional but relatable means and methods of teaching. JK is married with two surviving children and enjoys music, fashion, and traveling.

www.ingramcontent.com/pod-product-compliance
Lightning Source LLC
LaVergne TN
LVHW041752060526
838201LV00046B/979